Biblical Resources for Suffering People

JOY
Through the
NIGHT

Aída Besançon Spencer
& William David Spencer

Wipf & Stock
PUBLISHERS
Eugene, Oregon

Dedicated to the memory of
William Day Spencer,
artist, hunter, mineralogist,
poet, father, and more:
a Renaissance Christian man.
This book is not all flattering,
but you despised anything
less than the truth.

Wipf and Stock Publishers
199 W 8th Ave, Suite 3
Eugene, OR 97401

Joy Through the Night
Biblical Resources on Suffering
By Spencer, Aída Besançon and Spencer, William David
Copyright©1994 by Spencer, Aída Besançon and Spencer, William David
ISBN 13: 978-1-55635-502-8
ISBN 10: 1-55635-502-5
Publication date 5/25/2007
Previously published by Intervarsity Press, 1994

The House of Prisca and Aquila

Our mission at the House of Prisca and Aquila is to produce books that expound accurately the Word of God to empower women and men to minister together in a multicultural church. Our writers have a positive view of the Bible as God's revelation that affects both thoughts and words, so it is plenary, historically accurate, and consistent in itself, fully reliable, and authoritative as God's revelation. Because God is true, God's revelation is true, inclusive to men and women and speaking to a multicultural church, wherein all the diversity of the church is represented within the parameters of egalitarianism and inerrancy.

The Word of God is what we are expounding, thereby empowering women and men to minister together in all levels of the Church and home. The reason we say women and men together is because that is the model of Prisca and Aquila, ministering together to another member of the church—Apollos: "Having heard Apollos, Priscilla and Aquila took him aside and more accurately expounded to him the Way of God" (Acts 18:26). True exposition, like true religion, is by no means boring—it is fascinating. Books that reveal and expound God's true nature "burn within us" as they elucidate the Scripture and apply it to our lives.

This was the experience of the disciples who heard Jesus on the road to Emmaus: "Were not our hearts burning while Jesus was talking to us on the road, while he was opening the scriptures to us?" (Luke 24:32). We are hoping
to create the classics of tomorrow,
significant and accessible
trade and academic books
that "burn within us."

Our "house" is like the home to which Prisca and Aquila no doubt brought Apollos as they took him aside. It is like the home in Emmaus where Jesus stopped to break bread and reveal his presence. It is like the house built on the rock of obedience to Jesus (Matt 7:24). Our "house," as a euphemism for our publishing team, is a home where truth is shared and Jesus' Spirit breaks bread with us, nourishing all of us with his bounty of truth.

We are delighted to work together with Wipf and Stock in this series and welcome submissions on a wide variety of topics from an egalitarian inerrantist global perspective. The House of Prisca and Aquila is also a ministry center affiliated with the International Council of Community Churches.

For more information contact housepriscaaquila@comcast.net.

To Limp Is to Show Forth the Glory of God

To limp is to show forth the glory of God,
To be blind is to praise all of God's handiwork.
"Lord, on whose account was this man blind?"
The puzzled disciples like schoolchildren pointing,
"Look at the blind man! Look at the blind man!"
The law was a teacher, just, stern,
But Jesus the proctor.

A chronic disease in the faithful is odd,
An anomalous record of some duty shirk?
"Lord, on whose account are you unkind?"
The puzzled believers like startled sheep whining,
"Look at the blind man! Look at the blind man!"
Beneath the drawn sheet of heaven
Works Jesus the doctor.

The shepherd protects with a staff and a rod.
Held at bay in the shadows, the predators lurk.
"Lord, please give account, is this the time?"
Proleptic pleading forever's anointing.
Look at the blind man! Look at the blind man!
Veiled wounds in daily battle gained,
But Jesus the healer.

Read Christ's remedy on heaven's blue notepad,
Cramped figures stark on raised paragraphai,
"My heel is stung, but its head is crushed.
Take once for eternity,
Daily for pain."

WILLIAM DAVID SPENCER, 1991

Preface

My heel is stung, but its head is crushed.
Take once for eternity,
Daily for pain.

When God was cursing the serpent in Genesis 3:15 for bringing calamity upon humanity, God promised to put hatred between the woman's descendant and the serpent's, such that each would *shup* (bruise, crush, pierce, bite) the other.

Christians follow this descendant whose heel is bruised, the Jesus who asked his disciples to pick up their cross daily and follow him. As a result, none of us who seek to minister can expect to emerge unscathed. A former missionary once sued the Southern Baptist Convention when he was "set upon" and "beaten into unconsciousness" by the Turkish immigrants to whom he was sent to minister in Augsburg, Germany. He claimed the Southern Baptist Convention had not revealed that missionary work "could be hazardous to the plaintiff's personal safety."[1] Serving Jesus certainly is hazardous to one's health and safety. Perhaps every church should be mandated to plaster a

Surgeon General's warning on the corner of its bulletin board. God warned us back in Genesis 3:15. Like our deliverer, Jesus, in the thick of ministry our heels are bruised by persecution, illness, disappointment and natural disaster as evil works to weaken and impede our ministry and Christ's work. But with the strength of Jesus Christ we work to crush evil's head, and through the power of God's Holy Spirit we benefit not only ourselves but also those around us.

However, whether we choose to serve God or not, whether wounded fighting for a noble cause or brought down while trying to escape combat, none of us will emerge from life unscathed. Suffering, the "bite" of the serpent, is the universal human experience.

In the light of this reality we wrote *Joy Through the Night*. And we wrote it out of our own lives, intending it for every thinking Christian individual, every intelligent woman and man in the pew, for doctors, nurses, police, laborers, counselors, social workers, pastors, parents, Sunday-school teachers, college and seminary students and their professors, for every individual who has suffered and who has ministered to those who suffer, and particularly for church lay study groups (following in the manner of our preceding books, all of which are being employed in this fashion on campuses and in churches). We write again as an exegete and a theologian who teach, pastor and parent. And we write from both a female and a male perspective.

We built into *Joy Through the Night* a strong emphasis on joy, for our Deliverer enjoyed life thoroughly within and above its suffering. No theoretical examples are included. All explanations and illustrations are drawn from our own study, personal experience and twenty-five-year ministry.

In trying to find books for our courses we noticed that most books available on suffering offered us one or two of these perspectives. We wrote this book to offer all of them. We not only study the biblical reasons for suffering; we also suggest ways to respond to the varieties of suffering. Each chapter shows how to use the principles derived as a diagnostic tool for ministry, to see how these questions come alive in people's lives. As well, we have included two appendices: group and individual study questions (set up for optional use as an eight- to ten-session curriculum) and lists of biblical passages supporting each of the reasons for suffering.

The theories people formulate about suffering are intimately related to their understandings of God and God's actions, and these theories affect the way they live. When we study suffering, our goal ought to be to think about suffering in such a way as to increase our love and awe of God, our empathy toward others' suffering and our potential to make suffering and pain an opportunity for advancing God's reign. Toward this end, we present an exegetical study of the biblical material in order to derive scriptural reasons for and responses to suffering and pain in the light of God's nature.

As in all experience and reflection, many people have had an impact on us. In fact, the people we want to thank are so numerous we despair of listing them all. The incomparable Heidi Hudson typed the manuscript. The trustees, faculty, staff, and our students, especially Deborah Milhous, Rosalie Norman-McNaney and Ernesto Alers-Martir, at Gordon-Conwell Theological Seminary in South Hamilton, Massachusetts, all enriched this work. Bill wishes particularly to thank his doctor, Madhukar N. Shah, for many delightful talks and for perceptive care. Our dear friend the Reverend Paul Bricker contributed wise insights supplemented by countless nurses, doctors, colleagues across the years, especially Herb Greenspan. We deeply appreciate Rodney Clapp, editor at InterVarsity Press, and his helpful style and flow suggestions, as well as the other staff at InterVarsity Press. R. Rice Nutting, formerly director of Gordon-Conwell's and Gordon College's Master in Church Music program, was kind enough to typeset "Hymn of the Comforted."

Introduction

A certain man in a thriving church had everything to live for and every reason to be grateful to God. Five years after he converted to Christ, his house-painting business was booming. His wife loved him and he had two children: a beautiful, brilliant, lively daughter and her devoted shadow, an affectionate if sickly little son. The church people were giving him so much business he could not take a vacation. He was made advisor of the adolescent and young adult group. He was living proof that God truly blesses those who love Jesus. Every year was a year of plenty. He loved life and he worked hard for his family and for his God.

Every month he went to the McAuley Cremorne Mission on New York's 42nd Street and preached to the men. He himself was a living sermon of God's grace. He sometimes took with him his daughter, his constant companion, and once his little son.

He took a hobby and created out of it evangelistic sermons so effective that he was invited everywhere to speak. "Take this stone," he would say to a volunteer, handing him a phosphorescent stone. "This represents sin. Go ahead, handle it. Now, put away that sin."

He would hand the volunteer a towel. "Get rid of that sin! Right! Wipe it off. Sure, wipe it on your pants. Good. All gone? Fine. Somebody turn out the lights." Then he would switch on a black light and the volunteer would glow like a firefly. "That's what God sees," he would say. "You can't wash sin off! You've got to be washed in the blood of Jesus."

Here was a man who used his plenty to serve God and his family with every ounce of strength. He attended church almost every night of the week, faithfully, for midweek service, trustees' meetings, Sunday-school teaching, Bible study, lay preaching. He was a living testimony, a walking argument that the haves are haves because God gives it to them and they work hard. And the have-nots do not work hard to gain the good things life has to offer, so they do not receive God's blessings.

Yet he was never cruel or haughty. He did not gloat before the less fortunate; instead, he was always kind and encouraging. His home was an open house: many people too poor to afford homes, visiting missionaries, indigent college students stayed one after another on his third floor.

One sunny summer day in the sixth year of his prosperity as a Christian, he told his wife he was too busy to go on vacation in Canada with his family. The church people had all been pressuring him to get various jobs done for them and, since summer was the peak house-painting time, he simply could not break away. Business was like a bucking bronco. If you loosened your hold, off you went.

Mother had to explain to the children that the trip had to be postponed. They would have to stay home this year, because Dad could not fail to keep his commitments.

"Mom, can I go on the playground swim trip to Mount Kimble Pool?" asked the eleven-year-old daughter.

The mother was preoccupied. The night before, she had awakened, troubled with a sense of foreboding. She had not been able to go back to sleep and had gone out in the still hours of the lovely summer morning to sit on her porch rocking and wondering. Now she looked at her daughter, full of energy with a long and boring summer stretching endlessly ahead of her.

"I guess you can go," said the mother, pitying her. She packed her a lunch and called, "Don't forget a towel." Grandmother came limping down the stairs, asking for some help. Distracted, the mother took up her new service project and the daughter dashed out the door. "Bye, Mom!"

"Bye," called the mother. She did not even have time to kiss her daughter goodby. The little boy played on the floor.

Later that afternoon they heard a banging on the door. Two police officers stood outside. They handed the mother a bag of clothes. "These are all her effects, ma'am. Where did you want her body sent?"

The little son peered baffled from behind the skirts of his mother.

The mother did not speak for a while, simply staring at the police officers. Then she said in a low, severe voice, "You haven't even told me my daughter is dead."

"Didn't they call you?" exclaimed the policeman, and muttered, "They leave all the dirty work to us." His partner looked away.

When the father returned home, he was crushed at this totally unexpected news. For his daughter had been his favorite. And he was full of self-incrimination. If he had only put his family rather than his business first and gone on that trip, then his little girl would not have drowned.

The church offered inadequate condolences. Death in such a fashion, after all, really did not work into its theology. "They must have all done something wrong," the church people whispered, "or maybe they *would* have done something wrong . . ."

"Maybe it's all for the best," offered one well-intentioned matron. "After all, we don't know what would have happened when she grew up. Maybe she would have wandered away from the faith. This way you know she went to heaven."

"My daughter would not have wandered away!" cried the mother, stung.

The little boy, standing by a table, slowly breaking a toy car he had been offered in condolence, gathered up all that he heard and saw in his heart.

Life While Suffering

That horrible year dragged through a bleak winter. The little boy, whose job was to set the table, kept putting out four place settings and having to put one back. He could not understand that his sister was not coming home. He turned six, still puzzled.

Spring came and the man worked, for he still had a business to run and a family to support. The church members, now in pity as well as for sound business reasons, kept giving work to the man, for he was the best at his business.

The second summer following the loss of the daughter, on another beautiful evening, the mother again had a troubled night. In the morning she begged her husband to take that belated vacation. But he was being pressured to take one more job from a powerful parishioner— and so he kissed her and promised he would, he would, and on a Friday he took his equipment to the house. What the man did not know was that one of the parishioner's grandsons, a heavy-set teenager, had played on the extension ladder and, jumping up and down on it as it lay on its rest, had broken a rung. Frightened, he had arranged the ladder, covered it with its tarpaulin and told no one.

The next day was like a bad scenario in a predictable television tragedy. The unsuspecting man, at the top of the ladder, grasped the rung above him with his hand, and it snapped beneath his weight. Over backward he went, still clutching the rung, plummeting head-first toward the macadam driveway three stories below. He managed two things as he fell. He whistled to the men on ladders below to hug close to the house so he would not dislodge them. And just before he struck the driveway he twisted up his head, taking the fall along his left side. Ribs snapped, his skull caved in, his hand was smashed to bits.

Rushed to emergency, he nearly died several times on the operating table. So demolished was his left hand that the doctors, though they called in the most skilled specialist to take charge, were unable to put the pieces back together correctly. When he finally regained consciousness, the man was assured he would never walk again.

Bitterly he watched his wife go to work, in the days when a man's wife working was a sign of his failure and women in the work force were paid significantly less and promoted significantly less than were men.

He was months in the hospital, struggling to walk and regain use of his hand. At last, one day, supported by a cane, he was released. He had fought to use his hand; he had struggled and struggled to learn to walk again; he had achieved the day he had been told would never come. Awkwardly, he limped out of the hospital. But he was a different man.

His seven-year-old son, gamboling by his mother's side, so happy to have his daddy back out of the hospital, whispered happily to his mother, "It's great to have Daddy walking with us."

Like a whip the cane shot out and struck the boy across the legs. The man snarled, "Stop talking about me."

The boy's legs stung and something like a fist clenched in his throat, while something else fell away inside him. He felt a great gap open up. They walked on in silence.

For two years the father could not work; he watched his business disintegrate. His crew went to work for others. He lost his truck because he could not keep up the payments. He learned about the ladder and brought the incident before the church. But he was only a new trustee. The adolescent who had broken the ladder and silently put it back was the grandson of a powerful founding member of the church. The church members, embarrassed by the complaint, preferred to shove checks and bills in his pocket on Sundays. Humiliated and feeling betrayed, the man gradually ceased going to the church and turned more and more bitter. He tried other churches; for eleven more years he gave his evangelistic talks. Then he slowly stopped doing everything and sank into an old age of regret, silently bemoaning his lost daughter and his lost life, as the pain in his hand, his arm, his leg troubled him more and more. So much pain did he experience that he did not notice the tumor that slowly grew in his stomach and finally took his life—thirty years after he lost his daughter, his health, his dignity, his sense of worth and much of his faith.

"What have I done?" the man must have wondered again and again. "Why am I being punished so utterly and bitterly?"

Salvaging Life from Suffering

This book is not a theoretical exercise, and this story is not a preaching parable conveniently constructed to illustrate a point. The little boy who watched his sister drown in reality and his father in regret is now a father himself and is coauthor of this book. The questions his father asked were the same ones that the great Job asked when he knew he was righteous and yet catastrophe followed catastrophe. Job's story had a happy ending. New children were restored to him and his business prospered again. The young boy's father did not see a happy ending. Each child after the sickly little boy came stillborn or naturally aborted since the mother had a tilted womb. His business never flourished as it had before, since he could only work slowly and with great pain. Instead, he bought a succession of old station wagons and strapped his ladders on them, working with his growing son on what jobs the two could handle. When the boy graduated from college, the father gave up and tried several other lines of work.

Why do the righteous suffer?

If all suffering were caused by personal sin, how easy life would be. All we would need to do would be repent of our sins, and we would prosper. People would know we were Christians by our money rather than our love. Instead, Scripture assures us specifically, in Psalm

34:19, "Many are the afflictions of the righteous."

Jesus said, "If any one would come after me, let that one deny himself, take up his cross daily and follow me" (Lk 9:23; cf. Mk 8:34; Mt 16:24).

Yet the church is neither prepared nor preparing itself to take up its cross. Disease, persecution, loss—all sorts of tragedy come upon us as shocks. We step out one day from the safety of our theology and cancer mugs us. Evil is an armed marauder lying in wait to seize us when we least suspect its presence. And few of us are prepared emotionally or spiritually for its onslaught. Instead of bearing one another's burdens (Gal 6:2) or suffering with those who suffer (1 Cor 12:26), we often find ourselves withdrawing or being withdrawn from—as if catastrophe were something that was catching.

We need to work out our view of suffering *before* we meet catastrophe so that we will be prepared for it. That is the point of this book.

We are not writing it because we enjoy suffering. One of our mothers recalls her revulsion at the professional mourners who used to attend her newly-arrived-from-Europe family's funerals. "Why did she die? Oh, why did she have to die?" they would wail—when they did not even know the deceased. Each one was trying to outdo the other. One mourner even threw herself indecorously on the coffin. All of them took pride in their work, their funereal art form, a performance in lamentation which each actor thoroughly enjoyed. Such a warped view is far from ours.

Nor do we take a perverted interest in pain. When we were college chaplains, Bill at Rider College and Aída at Trenton State, we attended a conference on sexual counseling held at the medical school of Rutgers University, our alma mater. Among the fetishes and perversions we were burdened with was exposure to a woman with a sick desire to be crippled. Perhaps hers was a pathetic cry for sympathy, when really, physically, she evoked none. The doctor showed us several pictures of her smiling with her uninjured legs in various casts. "Finally," he said, "triumph." She had gone somewhere, found an unscrupulous surgeon, and there she stood, beaming, on crutches, her perfectly sound leg amputated.

"Choose life," God warned Israel when setting the covenant before them in Deuteronomy 30:19, but many seem to find calamity and death fascinating. Whenever people learn that Aída is teaching a course on suffering, someone stops her and tells her about the catastrophe that has befallen some poor soul. They do it with the same relish with which they inflict upon some bewildered first-time mother-to-be all the horrible pregnancy stories they have gathered.

Our interest in writing this book is different. We realize that suffering is inevitable. Neither we, nor our families, nor anyone else we know has escaped it. Everywhere around us are suffering people with whom the church has been unable to cope. Instead, the church has taught them false theories about suffering that have destroyed them once they were forced to suffer. As a result, like Bill's father, they could not cope with their illness or difficulty. They were not supported effectively. Some have even begun to hate God. Their view of God as loving parent has turned to God as cruel and arbitrary despot, a Cosmic Caligula, gloating in the skies: "Let's see if they can handle *this* one!"

Well-meaning Christians, like that long-ago matron at Bill's sister's funeral, counsel and make life more miserable for the person with difficulties. When Bill first came down with his chronic illness, Crohn's Disease, a fellow chaplain offered to pray for him. "Fine," said Bill.

They bowed their heads and the chaplain began thanking God profusely for the illness and all the benefit of learning that was going to come from this incurable disease. Bill's head popped up in the middle of the prayer and he exclaimed, "Hey! Whose side are you on? If you think this disease is so great, why don't we pray *you* get it!"

Simon, the son of Paul's teacher Rabbi Gamaliel, once said, "All my days I have grown up among the Sages and I have found naught better for a man than silence; and not the expounding [of Law] is the chief thing but the doing [of it]; and he that multiplies words occasions sin" (*m. Aboth* 1:17). And yet, thousands of years after this sage advice was given, we still bring about sin often—in our best efforts yet un-prepared, fumbling—by the fatuous things we say when trying to comfort others. We need to appreciate the real biblical reasons for human suffering. And we need to understand and appreciate at an emotional and at a spiritual level the suffering that we ourselves and others face. To many Christians—no, after twenty-five years of ministering in many places from the colleges to the churches to the prisons to the streets, we believe to *most* Christians—suffering is baffling.

One neighbor explained to Aída that one night when her child became ill he asked, "Why does God let little children like me get so sick?"

The mother answered, "Honey, God does not make people sick, but God heals the sickest person first and then moves to the less sick."

The little boy queried, "So when is my number coming up?"

Children make our abstract language concrete. They are not interested in speculations about the theodicy question; they want to stop vomiting, get the cast off, have sister come home. Peter counsels us to have defensible reasons for the faith that is in us (1 Pet 3:15). We need concrete explanations for suffering, explanations that will become strong working principles to help us endure suffering and be a true comfort to others.

Every theory about suffering is intimately related to one's understanding of who God is. And each operating theory affects the way we live. What we hope to do in this book is to help readers develop an understanding of suffering that is biblically sound and can help each reader live more joyfully and learn more fully about the true nature of God, the world, and God's work in the world. Our intention is to help each reader increase in love and in awe of God, to increase in empathy toward others' suffering, and to increase in the potential for making suffering and pain our servants, authentic opportunities for advancing God's reign.

Why We Suffer
All reasoning about the source and reason for suffering begins and

ends at one problematic question: Who is God?

Our answers for suffering initially appear enigmatic. Why do we suffer? Because God is *just*. Why has God allowed the possibility of suffering? Because God is *love*. Such answers take a book to explain them. (This is the book.) Of course they look like nonsense at first glance. Paul tells us in 1 Corinthians 1:25 that the "foolishness" of God is wiser than human wisdom and the wisdom of sacrifice (the cross) is folly to those who are dying in selfish sin (1 Cor 1:18). But God tells us God's heavenly truths that our minds might open to things hidden from us by the limitations of human reason. "The secret things belong to the Lord our God; but the things that are revealed belong to us and to our children for ever, that we may do all the words of this law," reads Deuteronomy 29:29. Any exercise like this will teach us more about God because we are examining what God has revealed.

How will our study proceed? Four foundational biblical categories that explain suffering underlie the biblical text: *a world of pain, punishment for sin, advancing God's reign, mystery.*

The first, a world of pain, observes that evil and its accompanying suffering destroy innocent people and the animals and plants who share this world with us, because our world has fallen under the power of death and the prince of lies. Suffering in this sense is inevitable; it happens to all. Even God's child suffered when entering this world, and, not greater than our master, we are powerless to escape it completely.

The second category, punishment for sin, notes that God's response of punishing those who sin means for us that a person or a nation is culpable for the suffering and pain received when that suffering comes in judgment for past wrong choices.

The third, advancement of God's reign, reveals that suffering may come because we choose to work to further God's rule over this wicked and rebellious world. Suffering can be a blessing and a privilege because we become like our Savior. And as Jesus was persecuted and suffered for us, so reciprocally in gratitude are we persecuted, accepting suffering for him. Our suffering when standing up for Christ and living out Christ's ideals can be vicarious (as his was). We can suffer for new believers we have helped into Christ's rule or for the benefit of others in or outside the church. On a personal as well as a corporate level, growth can also be painful. Like babies teething, we are growing up, and we can suffer in the process of growth to spiritual maturity. The deliverance or healing from suffering can result in the manifestation of God's works for God's glory.

The fourth category is mystery. This, we will see, is the question posed by the book of Job and echoed throughout history. Why does a specific righteous person suffer? We will unearth these four explanations, analyze them and suggest some appropriate responses. Then we will draw out principles for coping with suffering and wresting a joyful life from our suffering despite what misery befalls us.

Our ultimate goal is to learn more about the true nature of our Creator and therefore about ourselves as this Creator's creations. And though we may still suffer, we may give to and find in one another and in our heavenly Parent true comfort, exclaiming with the psalmist and with assurance: "O give thanks to the Lord, for the Lord is good; for his steadfast love endures for ever!" (Ps 107:1).

When Death Comes to Me

When death comes to me, how will it come?
Will it be in the flash of brakes and tires
Of one great crash,
Or reflected in the quiet of a hospital glass,
Creeping slowly as a nursing nun—
When death comes to me, how will it come?
Will it be kind or cruel,
Silent or loud?
Will it take me brave or frightened,
Humbled or proud?
When death calls to me, how will I come?

WILLIAM DAVID SPENCER, 1989

1

WORLD OF
PAIN

*I*t was a terse little news item in the local paper, New Jersey's former *Plainfield Courier-News,* the kind of thing our eyes glance over every day, but a life-changing announcement for the one who has fallen and for his family. The date: Monday, August 27, 1956.

Borough Man Hurt in Fall from Ladder
A ladder rung snapped under William Spencer, 46, of 114 Grove Street Saturday and he fell 30 feet to the ground suffering a broken left arm and leg and head injuries. He is reported in fair condition today at Muhlenberg Hospital where he was taken by the Plainfield Rescue Squad.

Today we are looking at this nearly forty-year-old, yellowed, tattered shred of a newspaper front page. For the first time we are looking at it and thinking about more than this one paragraph. How many eyes slid over it nearly forty years ago? But then, in the same way, what did *our* eyes slide over?

For us the world began and ended with this report about the one we loved, who was hospitalized for months and subjected to physical difficulties for the rest of his life. But three columns over to the right, an article just as brief announced, "Hospital Treats Women After Car Accident." Two columns to the left: "Four Injured by Landslide" in Santa Monica, California. In the column directly beside it: "Police to Resume Grilling LaMarca."

"Authorities," we read, "say LaMarca has confessed kidnapping the 32-day-old baby from his Westbury, N.Y., home last July 4 and abandoning him in a roadside honeysuckle patch. LaMarca, a swarthy 31-year-old cab driver, was arrested Thursday. The infant's decomposed body was found the next day. LaMarca's wife, Donna, was allowed to visit him for a short while Saturday."

In the column next to that, a teenager steals a car and knocks down a police officer who is already investigating a car which has crashed into an ambulance which was "rushing to treat a heart patient." In the column next to that, a cabin cruiser explodes, burning five Margate, New Jersey, men on board. Two columns to the left and above, an ex-inmate is arrested again for burglary. And beside that, the lead article announces that Russia has resumed "nuclear weapons tests"—tests, we are told in another article below, that the Japanese could not detect, though their instruments did catch the "shock" of "U.S. nuclear explosions at Bikini this year."

On this page we find illness, accident, murder, violence and natural disaster happening to people. And persecution is here too. In the center of the reverse page, Tallahassee, Florida, reports, "Minister Held in Bus Boycott." The charge was "operating a Negro car pool automobile without a 'for hire' tag. The Inter Civic Council is sponsoring the boycott of Tallahassee buses by Negro riders in protest against segregated seating. Attorney General Richard Ervin recently ruled that the boycotters' car pool vehicles must carry 'for hire' tags which cost an average of $15 more than private license plates."[1]

And all of this on one single, yellowed page, recorded on one routine summer day in a small town in central New Jersey, one August some forty years ago.

All our family's eyes could see was our father's misery, but his catastrophe occurred in a larger context of disaster, illness, accident, suffering, persecution. Dip into any newspaper on any day in any place and you will see the same.

Why does such evil exist—so destructive of innocent people, plants, animals?

To understand why today's innocent suffer, we must begin by going to the root cause of suffering. And to do this we are driven back to examining Genesis 1—3. All good theology, we are often told, goes back to the creation account, and this is certainly true in this case.

Evil Was in Eden

"And God looked at all which God made and, look, all was exceedingly good" (Gen 1:31). When we examine the record of God's creation, we can see clearly that everything God created was good. God provided the first human with many things good and pleasant to enjoy, including many things pleasant to eat. "From every tree of the garden you may surely eat," recounts Genesis 2:16. God treated our first parents as fully responsible and thus able to follow God's one prohibition:

> But from the tree of the knowledge of good and evil do not eat from it because in the day you eat from it you will surely [begin to] die.
> (Gen 2:17)

"In the *day*" signifies a time period in the Hebrew of Genesis such as we see in the phrasing of Genesis 2:4, "In the day that the Lord God has made the earth and the heavens." Thus, when humans violated this decree of God's, they (and with them their unborn descendants) began to die.

Were the first humans too immature to obey God's prohibition? Or, as some (from the old Roman Missal to today's John Hick[2]) suggest, did God, when prohibiting their eating, actually *want* the fruit eaten so that humans might pass from the innocence of childhood to the maturity of choosing between good and evil, in this rite-of-passage saga?

God, we are assured in Exodus 34:6, is truth. When God became flesh and lived among us, humans perceived that God-among-us was full of *grace* and *truth* (Jn 1:14). God, by God's nature, could not command humanity and then punish humans for breaking God's command, if the command were in reality a lie. God clearly did not consider our first parents too immature to obey. And further, far from pleased, God was angry that they had violated the command. "What is this that you have done?" God demands, and "Have you eaten from the tree from which I commanded you not to eat?" (Gen 3:13, 11).

Since Eden was paradise and full of beautiful, savory fruits, God had not placed Adam and Eve in an impossible situation. They were not in a desert where God had commanded them, "Don't drink this sweet, luscious water," as the sun beat mercilessly down and their tongues turned black and swelled up beneath their fevered eyes. Attractive things to eat were all around. Yet, what reasons did Eve give for eating of this specific fruit and disobeying God's commandment?

> And the woman saw that the tree [was] good for food and that it
> [was] a delight to the eyes and the tree was desirable to be wise and
> she took from its fruit and she ate and she gave also to her husband
> with her and he ate. (Gen 3:6)

Before Eve ate the fruit she saw that it was nutritious, aesthetically pleasing and educationally valuable. However, she used those nutritional, aesthetic and educational values of the fruit as excuses, rationalizations to disguise her real desire—to be as God, knowing good and evil. Only *after* the serpent suggested that "you both will be as God knowing good and evil" (v. 5) did Eve think of other benefits of the tree: it was good for eating, pleasant to the eyes, desirable for wisdom. But all of Eden's fruits were aesthetic, nutritious, pleasing.

Even further, Eve's and the tempter's attitudes toward God are reflected in the language they use. The serpent and Eve always call God *Elohim* ("God"), whereas the narrator identifies God as *Adonai Elohim* ("Lord God"). By the language we see that Eve and the serpent know God to be God, but they were not affirming that God also is Lord over every area of their lives.

What did Eve and then Adam in his turn do wrong? What Eve desired—her goal—was not wrong, but the way she went about achieving that goal—her means—was wrong.

God was ready and willing to give her good food and aesthetic enjoyment. God was the fount of wisdom too. But rather than receiving these things and this wisdom from God, she seized them. Her desire and her husband's after her was to be like God, perhaps *to be God*. She *had* been created in God's image. As such she had known good. Now, ironically, instead of achieving her goal, she took on the serpent's likeness. Eve and Adam, instead of knowing good and evil, now learned only evil. The image of God within them was shattered and from its sherds leered the reflection of the snake.

Immediately they began to experience the consequences: on that day, just as God had promised, they began to die. First, they learned shame. "I was afraid because I was naked, so I hid myself," muttered Adam, skulking in his fig-leaf covering.

Then they became estranged. Before the Fall Eve talked about *we*— "we may eat," she said. Now Adam and Eve use only the singular, "I heard, I feared, I was naked, I hid."

Further, they became irresponsible. They no longer took responsibility for their actions. God asks Adam, "Have you eaten from the tree from which I commanded you not to eat?" Adam blames Eve. "The woman whom you gave to be with me," he pleads, it's *her* fault. Eve in turn blames the serpent, "The serpent beguiled me." It's *its* fault. In effect, instead of becoming like God, Eve and Adam became like the serpent, crafty, cunning, knowing and doing evil. In Hebrew the

serpent is called *'ārōm:* cunning, sly, crafty. Adam and Eve, the Hebrew tells us, had become *'ērōm:* half-dressed, naked. The word play
tells us that the serpent's slyness was really akin to shame.

What we see here is that the serpent, the one opposed to God and
to goodness, has begun its own dominion with its own creation in its
own likeness. God says to the snake, literally, "because you created
this" you are cursed (Gen 3:14).

This new creation, which has departed so dramatically from God's
blessing, falls under God's cursing. The evil tempter is cursed and
estrangement is decreed between his and the humans' descendants.
The relation between Eve and her source (Adam) is cursed: childbear-
ing, her response, will no longer be pleasurable to her but will be hard
and painful work. The relation between Adam and his source (the
ground) is cursed: "In toil you will eat from it" (literally, "in the sweat
of your nose").

To God, Eve and Adam were fully responsible for their disobedience. And from this disobedience issued real consequences for themselves and for their world. Although each human and the tempter had
individual punishments, because each was culpable before God, their
punishments were also collective, affecting their relationships with one
another, taking in the ground, its animal inhabitants, and the descendants of each of them. Like the effect of a pebble in a pool, shock waves
shot out across the cosmos, across the ages. God's creations are both
individual and corporate in identity. One day God will argue with
Jonah for mercy both for the people of Nineveh and for the livestock
as well (Jon 4:11).

Eden's Evil Echoes
In this light, what is the meaning of a world of pain today? We live
in the ruins of the fall of Eden. The tempter is the ruler now over this
world. It clings to its dominion by any means possible, a grasping
dictator, at war with its subjects, holding them in subjection by terror
and by might. The Bible is very clear on this point. First John 5:19

notes, "the whole world lies within the power of the evil one," whom
Ephesians 2:2 identifies as the "ruler of the power of the air," and 6:11-
12 as the "world rulers." Humans are fallen; nature has fallen; all now
labor within the consequences of the curse. So we have death and
natural disasters, accidents and human cruelty.

Romans 5:12 points out to us that this condition is handed on. A
literal reading shows what is emphasized, "Therefore, just as through
one human *[anthrōpos]*, the sin into the world entered, and through
the sin the death also in the same way *[outōs]* into every human the
death spread, because of which all sinned." Verse 14 continues, "but
death reigned *[basileuō]* from Adam." Here "Adam" stands both for
our first parents and for every human descendant who has followed
throughout the ages. Sin entered the world, followed by death, and it
has affected the whole state of the earth, spreading death to every
human being and to nature as well, whose "eager longing," Romans
8:19-20 tells us, "awaits expectantly its deliverance from the curse,
having become subjected to frustration *[mataiotēs]*," that is, "emptiness, futility, purposelessness, transitoriness," "not of its own free
will." Romans 8:22 testifies, "For we know that all the creation groans
together and suffers agony together [that is, "be in travail until the
present"]," languishing like a prisoner of war, yearning to be freed by
God's liberation and restoration.

Evil holds onto its dominion. Evil assaults goodness in a war going
on around us that makes recent world conflicts look like a game
played by little boys in a back yard. The news articles we reviewed at
the outset of this chapter are a minute portion of the front-line reports
of this conflict, for it is global, encompassing every human being and
all of nature. The enemy is entrenched and malignant, using degrada-
tion, torture, rape, disaster and murder as its weapons.

The war is fought on many fronts—individually, socially, econom-
ically, musically, spiritually: through slavery, prostitution, pornogra-
phy, child and spouse abuse, abortion as a prophylactic, war, exploitation of others; when a Third World country is colonized and

exploited; when a cross is burned in hatred on a lawn; through black-listing, apartheid, class systems, immutable hierarchy; when a business pollutes a river, industrialization rips out a rain forest, styrofoam is fed into a landfill; when a woman is depicted tortured, raped and killed in a two-chord heavy metal chant, appended as a sex object on a pop video, caricatured as a seductress or brutally butchered in a classic opera; when a cult woos children into religious slavery, a television evangelist urges money from the poor and aged to pay for a Lear jet, when a satanic cult sacrifices a child. The list is endless and could literally comprise the remainder of this book. What we see most graphically is the conflict's physical level on the grand scale in invasion and warfare, in earthquake and famine, and on the small scale in abuse, assault, illness and accident.

All of this is as intensely personal to each of us as it was personal to our first parents. No observers exist in the human plight of suffering. We all suffer the consequences of evil's entry into our world. All of us get slugged by it, many of us repeatedly.

Paul the apostle wanted to convey the personal dimension of evil's onslaught against humanity and nature when he employed prolonged personification to depict the concept that "death reigns." In describing the plight of nature he used verbs usually associated with human activity *(wills, enslaved, hopes, is free, expects, awaits, groans, suffers)*, a technique which throws grappling hooks between human suffering and the agony of the natural world. Unlike humans, nature was not responsible, yet it receives repercussions from a world now dominated by death.

As the ground and the man are inextricably tied up in the curse, so will nature benefit when humans are ultimately rescued from death. As Ephesians 1:10 reveals, the mystery of God's will is to unite all things in heaven and in earth. Nature is undergoing a torturous experience of labor, like the woman, looking forward to a new birth. The human and natural consequences of evil exist together. God will end them together.

Why God Has Allowed Evil

The answer to this question, what in theological thinking traditionally has been called the theodicy question (from *theos,* "God," and *dikaiosynē,* "justice"), seems at first to be a contradiction. Why has God allowed the possibility of evil? Because God is love. Why is there suffering? Because God is just. What can such answers mean?

Free will is real. True love must therefore be voluntary. God wanted Adam and Eve's true obedience in a mutually honored covenant of love. Any voluntary covenant allows its inverse. When humans chose to challenge God, choosing personal power over deference to God, disregarding God's part of the covenant, they chose against goodness and life, thereby choosing evil and death. Everyone who follows enters the repercussions of this choice, existence in a world where pain and death have been set free to molest.

God's love does not nullify God's justice. If that were the case, after Jesus' triumphant crucifixion, resurrection and ascension, all suffering (at least for believers) would have ended.

But God is love *and* justice. When Moses begged to know God, in Exodus 34:6-7, God passed before him proclaiming:

The Lord, the Lord God, merciful and gracious,
patient [or longsuffering] and abounding in steadfast love
    and truth,
keeping steadfast love for thousands,
forgiving crime and sin,
by no means clearing the guilty,
visiting the suffering [or punishment, or guilt, or perverseness,
or sin] of the parents upon the children and upon the
children's children to the third and fourth generation
[to the great-grandchildren and to the great-great-grandchildren].
God, we see, is "longsuffering," patiently putting up with disappointment in God's creation, yet allowing the consequences of sin to remain with people and with their descendants.

Thus, God's mercy allows people to depart, rather than forcing them to love. As J. B. Phillips observed in *God Our Contemporary,* "The whole point of real Christianity lies not in interference with the human power to choose but in producing a willing consent to choose good rather than evil."[3] Aquinas's concept of habit is built on this premise. Every good choice makes the good easier to choose.

Normally, we read such a passage and then emphasize to one another the need to choose good, to give that willing consent. But we may infer that the opposite is also true, that the possibility exists to choose evil and this is what in fact is done again and again and again with the result that misery has invaded the world. Evil is endemic now, permeating the fabric of things, and it is inflicted again and again by nature on us and by us on ourselves.

What makes horror movies so terrifying, from *Nosferatu* through *Dr. Jekyll and Mr. Hyde* through *The Terminator* through *Fatal Attraction,* is visualizing the inability to rid oneself of evil. Evil is a vampire that sucks our life from us; evil is a lurking monster within us that seizes us at will; evil is an inhuman force that pursues us relentlessly; evil is a past sin that inexorably finds us out. We struggle desperately, yet we cannot rid ourselves of evil. Someone ultimately must do it for us or, as with Dr. Jekyll, the Mr. Hyde engulfs us and we die.

Summary
This is a world of pain. The sin of our first parents is visited upon all their children throughout the ages. Like the rain and like God's mercy, disaster and trouble fall upon all. The newly committed house painter, the innocent baby, the black minister, the victims of fire in our opening articles, all experience evil, accident, illness, loss, calamity, financial reversal and death as surely as the powerful dictator who has given way to evil, challenging God and holding his people in thrall, or the powerless alcoholic wanderer.

"Many are the afflictions of the righteous," the psalmist assures us in Psalm 34:19, "but the Lord delivers that one out of them all." We took great comfort in this verse until we realized the "deliverance" here in context may mean salvation *after* death. This is no promise that the God whose own Child was tortured and died will rescue us from all the consequences of this world of sin. But it does mean that God did not abandon us. God came in Jesus to suffer what we suffer along with us—and then to do for us what we could not do for ourselves: provide an ultimate rescue from this world of pain so that this world's pain would not be our eternal lot.

But what we want and need to know is: What can we do about evil and the suffering it causes, in order to help others and to be helped ourselves? The next chapter will begin to address this question.

Cloud

Why do I do this?
Why am I here?
Step by step
I have found myself here.
It is as if I took
one step after another
in a deep fog
where I could only
see one step at a time.
At times
as I stand dripping in the fog
apparently
in the middle of nowhere,
I look around me
and say,
"What on earth am I doing here?"
But at other times
I look around
and I say,
"Yes, it is God
who has gently
held my hand
and led me to where I now am."

Why do I do this?
Why am I here?
Step by step
I have found myself here.
It is as if I took
one step after another
in a deep fog
where I could only
see one step at a time.
At times
I look around
and I say,
"Yes, it is God
who has gently
held my hand
and led me to where I now am."
But at other times
as I stand dripping in the fog
apparently
in the middle of nowhere
I look around me
and say,
"What on earth am I doing here?"

"I believe; help my unbelief."

AÍDA BESANÇON SPENCER, 1977
QUO VADIS *15 (FEBRUARY 1992), 3*

2

RESPONSE TO
A WORLD OF PAIN

*A*ll of us are on a chain gang in the prison of pain. But through Jesus' death our bonds to our sinful fallen world can be broken. By begging God for Jesus' death to be the state's pardon for our sin, we are paroled to an eternity of freedom where tears will be wiped away and (as we shall see in the latter sections of this book) where joyful hope is not simply a TV promotional promise.

Further, we can begin enjoying this freedom *now* by doing certain things for others and for ourselves.

What We Can Do for Others
How can we help others when evil attacks them and they are suffering?

1. We can free people from shame.

In the movie *Fatal Attraction* a husband is pursued by an increasingly psychotic paramour whom he cannot evade. Because of shame, he can bring himself to tell anyone of his sin and its repercussion only when the lives of the ones he loves most are in mortal danger. Inextricably entrapped in evil, he can escape only with his wife's aid.

When, with the inverse effect of a spouse, our first parents were plunged into evil, God was the first to alleviate their shame and help them to accommodate to the altered state of the universe: "And the Lord God made for Adam and for his wife garments [tunics] of skin and clothed them" (Gen 3:21). We too need to continue what God commenced, helping people go beyond the sins of their past, beyond the curse that now hobbles them.[1] Shame is terminated by true repentance. We need to help humans humble themselves before God, beg forgiveness, then rise and live assured of a new start in God's grace, avoiding a repetition of their sin and living free of the shame and guilt with which it struck their conscience.

2. We can try to stop or lessen others' pain.

Aída recalls staying once, as a child, in the home of a woman who dressed perpetually in mourning clothes for different remote family members and friends. One day while they were sewing, this woman suddenly stuck a pin in Aída's leg to teach her to understand pain. Aída must have had the concept of this book already germinating in her mind, because she shrieked and dashed away.

Ascetics like this woman consider enduring suffering worthwhile in itself. While enduring suffering may teach someone to be longsuffering and may even have other edifying dimensions, we do not see Jesus lecturing the man born blind, the woman with the issue of blood or the grieving Jairus about the purgative qualities of suffering. Jesus acts to *alleviate* human misery.

Further, no one need seek out opportunities to suffer to prove one's mettle or manufacture problems to overcome. Act for Christ, serve others—for that matter, simply wait around—and plenty of suffering will assail you. Why should anyone suffer if she or he can avoid it? And when suffering is unavoidable, we should work to lessen pain whenever possible.

The Bible reiterates what many have noted in medicine, that when one is happy, one is less susceptible to germs. When one is less happy, one's immune system does not perform at peak effectiveness. Proverbs captured this ages ago: "A cheerful heart makes a good medicine [or healing], but a downcast [troubled, saddened] spirit withers the body" (Prov 17:22); and "a cheerful heart makes a cheerful face, but by sorrow [pain, grievance, affliction] of heart the spirit is downcast" (Prov 15:13).

Inversely, how much evil exists because God's people do not let God's Spirit work within them to fight injustice? Rather than being like the Lord who "works justice and judgment for all who are oppressed" (Ps 103:6), we often *add* pain by increasing people's burdens (burdening our leaders, for example, so that they lead "sighing" or "groaning" and not "joyfully," in our disregard of Heb 13:17)—or by increasing injustice as we countenance prejudice and exploitation. Sociology teaches us that the most as well as the least prejudiced people attend church. When Jesus returns, will he find a faith on earth, a Christianity practiced in our daily lives that is recognizable to him (Lk 18:8)? We need to watch out that we do not make people anxious, oppress them, place heavy burdens upon them, or actually be the cause of their troubles and even indirectly of their illnesses!

3. We can be present with people in pain.

Methodist Minister Charles Merrill Smith's *Reverend Randollph and the Avenging Angel* contains a marvelous scene of true ministering.[2] Called to comfort a family suffering from an unexpected death, the bishop takes the fledgling pastor Randollph in tow. Entering the grieving room, the bishop merely sits down in silence. After a long while he offers a quiet prayer, the family thanks him and he and Randollph leave. Silence, in caring presence, he informs Randollph, is often the best counseling one can offer.[3]

The "ministry of presence" is a potent weapon with which to combat pain. Simply being there in a time of trouble is often enough. As a new minister learns not to sit on the bed or talk loudly or invade a patient's privacy, so does the new minister discover that one does not always have to have something to say. "Why has this happened to me?" is often an exclamation, not a question, as anyone who has sought to answer that complaint has often curtly and abruptly been taught. Simply listening and loving is what is needed as sufferers seek to work out their own understanding of their pain. Proverbs 10:19 warns, "When words are many, transgression is not lacking, but the one who restrains his lips is prudent."

When death occurs, the moment of silence is more than just a tribute, it is a good rule to guard us from some of the fatuous things we might babble in our nervousness in the presence of death. For forty years, since the age of five and a half, Bill can remember vividly the useless and even hurtful things said in the name of comfort at the death of his sister. Start with loving silence and speak only when impelled. Job's friends began correctly. After a week they should have remained silent; they would have fared better than they did.

Death is inevitable. The Enochs and Elijahs in human history are countable on one hand—the rest of us die. Psalm 90 notes that our lives are over in a breath. We live for seventy years, eighty with good health; few of us reach one hundred. The psalmist begs, *Teach us to count how few days we have and so gain wisdom of heart. Let us wake in the morning filled with God's love and sing and be happy all our days.*

At the same time, we should try to treat people with the tolerance that comes from the knowledge that they may die tomorrow, or that *we* may. When you feel you should visit someone, do it. If you feel you should take time with your friend, your spouse, your parents, your child—do it. Time cannot be recaptured, and little of what we did instead looks worth doing from our deathbed.

Bill has been hospitalized six times so far, in 1965, 1972, 1974, 1976,

1985 and 1989, the last time for two and a half months. The cause is his Crohn's Disease, an unexplained, recurring inflammation of the intestines that causes fever, weakness, weight loss, pain and life-threatening blockages through the accumulation of residual scar tissue. Each time, he pauses and reflects on what he has done in the period between hospitalizations, how he has invested his time. One time he regretted not having spent enough time with Steve, our son. Another time he felt that his career was a hiatus from what he really wanted to be doing. Another time he felt the need to work on his life of prayer. Each time he used the next section of his life to work on improving that particular lack. Not all of us have these enforced periods of reflection when we can reorder our lives. But all of us should stop and take stock.

James Johnson, one of Bill's favorite authors in the clerical crime novel, wrote his own obituary to be read at his funeral, which followed shortly thereafter, upon his death from heart disease. In it this man, who had written wonderful, edifying books, who had established a learning program of higher education and pioneered missionary work, found himself regretting that he did not stop to sniff flowers, bask in the starry summer night, stroll through the majestic autumn—all moments never to be recaptured.[4]

Why lie in a bed of regret? Order your life now as if this were your last day, and live in God's presence and in love with others. Prepare your family for life without you. Get life insurance, at least enough to cover your funeral expenses. And when you think or speak about death, center on the resurrection of the dead, for comfort and joy are available to us through our Christian assurance that a full, pain-free life exists beyond this painful one.

4. We can allow people to express their pain.

Do not feel guilty because someone else is in pain (unless, of course, you deliberately caused it). Do not counter their agony by telling them about your lumbago, a cousin who died, suffering people in Maui. They are currently in pain, not you. Sometimes prohibiting someone else from expressing pain is a way to keep ourselves from noticing that we live in a fallen world where we too will die. Or we may think that somehow our faith will prove untrue if we admit that Christians suffer, have troubles, go insane, weaken, die.

One example of religious faith that does not help people confront the reality of death is the West Indian Rastafarian theology. The Rastas believe death is a direct result of sin. Only sinners die. So Rastas traditionally have avoided corpses, leaving their dead to be buried by others.[5] Peter Tosh of the original Wailers, the legendary reggae band that promoted reggae music and the Rastafarian faith worldwide, refused to attend the funeral of his comrade Bob Marley, complaining he had no time for "generals and funerals."[6]

But death has plundered Rastafarian theology, for Peter Tosh himself died along with Marley and with the Rastas' god-on-earth, Haile Selassie. A theology without a place for death is a deeply troubled theology. One young former Rasta, now a Christian, told Bill he gave his life to Jesus Christ when he saw a young man stabbed to death at a dance before his eyes. His theology had no place for a confrontation with death. Christianity is built on the basis of confronting death. With sin, death entered. Jesus came to die and so defeat death. No Christian should shun the presence of death, acting as if death were unreal. By that we are traitors to the full good news of what alliance with Christ is all about: overcoming death eternally.

Let people confront their own pain and, if need be, their own deaths. Each person knows best his or her own pain: "A heart knows its own bitterness [literally: bitter life or self], and no stranger shares its joy" (Prov 14:10).

5. We can treat a person in pain as a full person.

We should treat a person in calamity as a normal person—in other words, as we ourselves would want to be treated. After Bill's sister died he went walking with his mother on the street where they lived. They met one of his sister's friends who was walking with another girl. At the sight of her dead friend's mother, she began whispering, obviously about Carol's death. Bill's mother greeted her but the girls acted aloof. After Bill and his mother passed, the little boy looked back and caught sight of the two girls still standing on the sidewalk staring after them. "In all times the friend loves, and a brother is born for adversity [or distress or anguish]," lectures Proverbs 17:17. A true friend is not aloof.

No matter what our condition, we are still under the lordship of Christ and engaged in the battle with evil. In one of Bill's early hospitalizations, he received a letter purporting to be one of comfort from a fellow minister, hoping he would soon be back in the "race of faith." "I'm more involved in the struggle for faith lying here," he snarled, "than when I was running around doing all that piddly-crap I was forced to do that passes for ministry!"

Someone once pointed out that if the church ceased holding meetings it would dissolve. "Attending meetings," one of our Doctor of Ministry students pointed out to us, "is not ministry but preparation for ministry." The front-line war against evil takes place in counseling sessions, in hospital rooms, at accident sites, in street encounters, in family interventions, in prison and college counseling, at food and clothing distribution sites, at homeless and literacy centers, in substance-abuse sessions, in combat zones, as well as in the myriad of duties that religious institutions require.

We do not want to deprecate any necessary facet of running a church building and program. Without each crucial activity we would all be impoverished. But often the ministry that happens or should happen outside dwarfs some of what goes on within. When people are suffering, what we need are Christians with longsuffering (patience) who meet sufferers with "kind words . . . like dripping honey, sweetness to the self and health for the body" (Prov 16:24) that minister to them, worrying less about the carpet in the fellowship hall and more about pointing sufferers from the fragmenting consequences of sin to the wholeness which is in Christ.

What We Can Do for Ourselves

Now that we have looked at how we might help ease the suffering of others, we need to ask, How can we expand the list we are making to help ourselves as well?

1. Draw on your spiritual resources.

Other Christians are a major resource given us by God. In fact, communion with God and communion with God's people, set in nature's healing context, *are* the spiritual resources God provides. Why then do so many people feel alone today?

George Gallup Jr. has made a career out of polling people to find out current opinions on major issues. Recently, speaking at Gordon-Conwell Theological Seminary where we teach, he asked the professors and staff assembled what they thought his polls had discovered to be the two major issues facing our world as we enter the close of one century and the beginning of the next. What is the major issue facing the entire globe? he asked. We learned it was the environmental issue: how we can keep from polluting ourselves into oblivion. And what is the major issue facing those of us living in the West? Loneliness. With all our Western affluence and mobility, we are starved for true companionship. We have identified ourselves as being in the "free" world, but what a terrible freedom it has become.

God never intended us to be lonely. From the start God recognized our parents needed one another. God even walked in the cool of the evening with God's creatures. When sin drove a wedge between the communion of humans with God and with one another, estrangement began. Therefore, God reached out over the abyss of sin and came in Jesus to walk again with God's beloved creatures.

Christmas is the time when we celebrate that advent of God among us, God's arrival. This is the time, the apostle John tells us in his Gospel, that Jesus pitched his tent among us (Jn 1:14), which is the literal meaning of the Greek word employed. Why then do so many people die from loneliness at Christmas?

We live directly across the street from the police chief of our town, and we know the police hate to work at Christmas because of all the suicides and suicide attempts. Any caretaker of the elderly will tell you that at Christmas and at other holidays—but particularly at Christmas—many of our senior citizens give up and die. Loneliness can be fatal. People simply give up living. Why cook for one? For whom am I dressing up? Why do I bother to work? Who really cares about me? Who indeed?

The Scripture gives us a different picture of the attitude of Jesus. Mark 1:35 tells us, "Very early in the morning, long before daylight, Jesus got up, left the house and went off to a solitary place, where he prayed." Matthew gives us a similar report of Jesus seeking solitude for prayer in 14:23, "After Jesus had dismissed the crowds, he went up into the mountain by himself to pray." Again in 14:13, "Now when Jesus heard [of John the Baptist's death] he withdrew from these in a boat into a solitary place by himself." Jesus handles the catastrophic news of his cousin's execution by withdrawing alone. Luke completes this picture in 4:42, "At daybreak Jesus went out to a solitary place," explaining in 5:16, "And Jesus himself was withdrawing in the solitary [uninhabited] regions and praying."

Jesus had no fear of being by himself. In fact, Jesus would bring his disciples to a lonely place and then withdraw from them in order to pray. Luke 9:18 observes, "Now it happened that as he was praying alone, the disciples were with him." At Gethsemane, after charging his disciples to "pray that you may not enter into temptation," Jesus, we are told in 22:41, "withdrew from them about a stone's throw, and knelt down and prayed."

Why did Jesus welcome being alone, and why do so many people living in our world today fear it? The reason is that *there is a difference between being lonely and being alone.* They are not the same thing. When Jesus was alone he was not lonely, because he was not really alone. He had moved from the presence of people into an awareness of the presence of God.

In 2 Kings 6:8-17 we are told of the terror of Elisha's servant when the enraged king of Aram, furious at the realization that the prophet could tell the king of Israel "the very words you speak in your bed," besieges Dothan in order to capture Elisha. Waking in the morning and seeing the city surrounded, the servant is beside himself, pleading, "Oh, my lord, what shall we do?" (v. 15).

"Don't be afraid," answers Elisha. "Those who are with us are more than those who are with them!" (v. 16).

The servant must have been dumbfounded. Here we are trapped like rats and my master's gone berserk! Great working conditions . . .

But Elisha prays, "Lord, now open his eyes so he may see!" (v. 17).

What he saw is what Jesus knew and what we need to realize. The hills are full of horses and chariots surrounding the evil that besieges us. The One who is with us is much greater than the one who opposes us (1 Jn 4:4).

That is why Jesus was not afraid to be alone. He was in the presence of his heavenly Father. And, as we see in Mark 1:13, these angelic warriors would minister to him. This is why Jesus wisely recommended solitude to his disciples too.

In Mark 6:30-32, after Jesus sent out the Twelve to minister, we are told:

> The apostles gathered with Jesus and told him all they had done and taught. And he said to them, "Come away by yourselves into a solitary place, and relax a little while." For many were coming and going, and they had no convenient time to eat. And they went away in the boat to a solitary place to be by themselves.

This is why Jesus recommends the same practice to us in the Sermon on the Mount, "But when you yourselves pray, go into your inner, secret room and shut your door and pray to your Father who is in secret; and your Father who sees in secret will reward you" (Mt 6:6).

Jesus has just warned his followers not to practice a piety like that of the hypocrites who are rewarded by people's admiration when they display their piety in public. Instead, he begins, literally, "But when you yourself may pray," that is, "When you may happen to be praying." Notice that he assumes we pray.

Today, of course, we cannot make that assumption. An article by Sarah Francis in the April 25, 1991, *Boston Globe* tells us that more than thirty Catholic priests, Protestant ministers and Jewish rabbis, banded together as the Cranston, Rhode Island, Clergy Association, have focused sermons and newspaper ads on Sunday youth sports schedules that have virtually emptied services on Saturday and Sunday of youth.

One minister complains of a fifty percent drop once Little League season alone arrives. And as Greek Orthodox pastor Andrew George observes, "A child today may be in three or four leagues." Children are under severe peer pressure to play. "When kids have to make a choice about going to church," reports the Reverend Clyde Walsh of St. Matthews Roman Catholic Church, "they hear from their teammates: 'It's important you make the team. You're really good; we need you.' " When the head altar boy of the Greek Orthodox Church "bucks practice," he gets picked on and made fun of as a result. Even basketball leagues are scheduled on Sunday mornings, and the pastor of the Faith Lutheran Brethren church speculates that his own son's inability to make those practices damaged his playing ability to make the team.[7]

Charles Spurgeon once remarked that he would rather have his sons learning to pray than to preach, for many a preacher has made shipwreck of his faith, but never one who has learned to pray. Many of us have not learned to pray. When we are alone we are lonely and we suffer from that emptiness. We suffer for no reason because we have drowned out communication with the most important source of comfort of all, our heavenly Parent.[8] We have cut off our own spiritual resources.

Jesus gives us a radically new perspective on the besetting problem of loneliness that is our number one problem and a major cause of suffering. Pray, he counsels us, and when you do "go into your inner or private room."

God, we are told, is waiting in solitary secrecy to hear from us and reward us. But when we are alone—what do we do? We turn on the TV or radio and blast away our awareness of God's presence.

We can become most aware of the presence of God when we are alone, if we develop eyes to look for God and ears to listen for God. God is waiting in secret, calling us to come aside, but the noise of everyday life can block out the voice of God. Only if we take time to get away from the distractions and go where we can be alone, where it is quiet and undisturbed, can we hear God. Rather than fearing solitude, we need to seek it.

We can be alone but not lonely. Prayer is the strong lifeline that connects us to God. It is the essential element that fills up the empty cup of loneliness with the sweet, nourishing nectar of God's presence.

Therefore, how can we break free of the loneliness that curses so many—this major problem of our times—and tap into our spiritual resources?

To begin with, we must recognize that the God we worship is everywhere, as Paul assured the thinkers on Mars Hill (Acts 17:28). And God's spiritual warriors, angelic and human, are everywhere poised to come to our assistance. If we seek out the presence of God, look for an opportunity to withdraw to God each day, find a private place to be alone in God's presence in order to develop our relationship, then when solitude in a hospital or at home or even in prison takes place, it is not a strange condition for us. We are simply freed to be in God's presence.

At the same time we need to recognize that the Christian community is also there and poised to come to our assistance.

God has not ordained us continually to be alone. "It is not good for the man to be alone," we recall God observing in Genesis 2:18. "Do not neglect the gathering together of yourselves," Hebrews 10:25 warns. "Therefore confess to one another sins and pray on behalf of one another in order that you may be healed," James prescribes in James 5:16. "One another," the Christian community, is a spiritual resource given us for our healing. Therefore, we need to draw on these spiritual resources God has given us. We do not want to end up like the dwarfs at the end of C. S. Lewis's *The Last Battle,* hunched in misery when comfort and blessing are all around us. We need to receive and extend comfort when we are in the visible presence of other people (a topic we will develop more fully in our chapter on joy), while when we are alone we need to relax in the unseen presence of God.

   2. Recognize your own and others' mortality.

   God's love salvages many things that the entry of sin destroyed. God reopened the channel of communication through Jesus. God eliminated the need to suffer eternally in estrangement from God through Jesus' sacrificial death for our sins. God gives us love and comfort and peace, as much as can be experienced in a world gone awry. But what God cannot restore to us is immortality in our present state. Sin and with it death has entered our bodies. Yet the memory of Eden still lingers, echoed in our heritage and treasured in our collective consciousness. So humans cannot and do not live satisfied or even in conformity with this new state of affairs. We yearn to rediscover the Edenic state—a quest, often unconscious, to regain immortality. With it comes the essential human frustration of not being able to do so. Why do older men chase younger women? asks the weary wife in the comedy *Moonstruck.* Her answer? Because they fear death. We want to remain young, strong, free of illness, accident, injury and death. We cannot. Many of our contemporary novels and motion pictures are full of this longing. Poignant films like *Cocoon* are built upon it.

   Some of us seek immortality through our children: they will carry on our name, finish what we leave undone, and we will live on in them. Some seek it through science, attempting to freeze their bodies in order to be resurrected in a utopian future where there is no death. Some build buildings named for them or for a loved one. "Books may speak," a Puritan writer once wrote, "when the author cannot and, what is more, when he is not." Some build monuments of wealth, but, as Billy Graham has pointed out, one never sees a hearse with a U-Haul. Some give scholarships in the name of loved ones (a practice the authors as educators, of course, commend) while some simply overwork, crowding out the fear of death. Bill remembers a family friend who constantly had the radio blasting. One day as a child Bill went on a family trip to a swampy area to dig for tiger-eye semi-precious stones. This man drove his car as far as he could into the swamp, then would not leave to look for gems in any area out of earshot of the car radio. Bill's parents told us that this man played the radio all night long as he tried to sleep, because he was afraid of being alone. Not long afterward he died of a heart attack.

Joni Mitchell's flagship song "Woodstock," which popularized the utopian flower movement of the sixties, announces that people have to get "back to the garden."[9] Solomon captured the human dilemma completely in Ecclesiastes 3:11: "God made all beautiful in its time, also everlasting time [eternity] he placed in their heart [or will], yet humanity cannot discover the doings which God does from the beginning to the end."

Humans are in a frustrating position. God did not remove from us that sense of everlasting time which was so appropriate to Eden. If God did, how could we know God who is eternal? So we have the desire for immortality but not the power to achieve it. And this state of affairs is as true for Christians as for anyone else. Are Christians exempt from frustration and a sense of loss? No. Do Christians yearn to regain immortality? Yes. Can we ourselves change our basic condition? No. Can our position be changed? Yes. It has already been changed for us. Christ is the victor over death. A new world is coming where we can approach God—no longer in the midst of our suffering and death, for no suffering and death will be in this new world (Rev 21:4).

Living in Two Worlds

If Jesus is our Lord, we have gained that world already, yet we still live in this transitory age. Such is the significance of the word *hebel,* usually translated "vanity" in Ecclesiastes. The word literally means "to breathe out" in the verb form, or "breath, vapor" in the noun form. This meaning is no doubt what James echoes when he points out that human life is like a vapor (4:14). What Ecclesiastes is saying is not so much that our work is wrong or worthless or in vain, but that it is transitory. While we know our eternity is secure in Christ's love, we must live as mortal ("vapor") beings in a fallen world. Bounded by death, we look forward to the resurrection from the dead, a resurrection Christ has already modeled for us. That is why Paul points out that if Christ is not raised we are most to be pitied because we are fools, so we might as well embrace true vanity, making our lives theaters of the absurd, an adequate match to the universe (1 Cor 15:19, 32). But the good news of the gospel is that Jesus has conquered death and risen again! And that is the rock to which we secure ourselves in this shifting mire of death, accident and catastrophe.

How can we live in the now while we look forward to the not quite yet? Ecclesiastes 3:12-14 has a simple prescription: "I know that there is nothing better for people than to be cheerful and to do good in their life and also that everyone should eat and drink and regard the good in all their labor which God gave to them. I know that all which God does endures forever." Our own family's creed is built on this thought. We try to enjoy life, eat well, do all things in moderation and help as many others as we can to do the same. When miserable circumstances hit us, our extended Christian family helps us in return.

As for what makes us happy, we follow James's advice, which almost seems to be a commentary on Ecclesiastes. We derive our fulfillment from daily life rather than relying totally on long-range fulfillments, understanding that in all things we should say, "If the Lord wills, we shall live and we shall do this or that" (Jas 4:15).

All of us live not knowing the future. But we can know that our eternity is secure in Christ Jesus. Therefore, we can enjoy the good of the present, which God created us to enjoy. This affords us an opportunity to be with one another, to enjoy one another and in that context to serve one another.

We have managed in our church to schedule three out of four Sundays of each month to eat together—the comestible experience. On the first Sunday our small group eats together, on the second the elders eat together and conduct church business over the meal, the third is open for inviting guests home or being invited, the fourth is a church-wide meal after the special service that closes each month. In this way we enjoy one another. For almost two months in his last hospital stay Bill was not permitted to eat or drink. Intensely, personally, he knows the significance of the pleasure that comes from such a simple, such a thoroughly delightful activity as enjoying a meal.

In moderation, we have attempted to limit our schedules to keep us from the deception of immortality through overwork. We are not omnipresent, nor can we be. We order our schedule, and what cannot be done in that time cannot be done by us. We can be available only to our child twenty-four hours a day, and even that is not entirely true, as illness, exhaustion and the vicissitudes of life lecture. We are mortal and limited.

When Bill was first hospitalized with Crohn's he was doing a city ministry in Philadelphia and his calendar was full of crucial events he "had to attend." He was amazed to see how well the Holy Spirit held the world together in his absence. Growing on him was the firm suspicion that if he had died things would still have basically progressed in a similar way. We are mortal and limited. God is not. God is at work even when we cannot be. When we forget this lesson, we relearn it rapidly from illness or exhaustion.

G. K. Chesterton, in his Father Brown tale "The Honour of Israel Gow," has Father Brown ask, "Do you know what sleep is? Do you know that every man who sleeps believes in God? It is a sacrament; for it is an act of faith and it is a food."[10] When we rest we are acknowledging that God is sovereign.

Hebrews 4:9-10 explains, "So then, there remains a Sabbath rest for the people of God; for whoever enters God's rest also ceases from his labors just as God did from God's own." The author tells us we must practice obedience to enter God's rest (4:11). Psalm 127:1-2 summarizes these thoughts:

If the Lord does not build the house,

those who labor building it labor in vain.

If the Lord does not watch over the city,

the watchman stays awake in vain.

It is vain that you rise up early

and go late to rest,

eating the bread of anxious toil;

for God gives to his beloved sleep.

Only a fool would understand all this to mean that we should not bother to rear children, seek cures for illnesses, build buildings, write books, enjoy material comfort, give away money, listen to music, be well known for our good thoughts, seek more information, learn about the future because we live in a world of real pain and we might as well reconcile to it.

We have been commanded by God to work (Gen 1:28; 2:15). Ecclesiastes counsels us to take pleasure in our work (3:13). What we have to guard against is taking the good things in life as means to achieve immortality or as ends in themselves. Children are delightful, but—as Bill's parents learned so catastrophically—they are not a means to continue a family or even a family name. Buildings are helpful to keep us warm and protected from the elements, but they immediately begin to need repair and eventually they will crumble. Churches need to be reminded of this fact continually. The church is the people, not a crumbling building. Being well known puts one's reputation in the power of others' whims, and for many motives they may speak well or ill of us, sometimes furthering their careers on recounting our misfortunes or sins. Education may help us achieve a more powerful place in society because we are more knowledgeable, but it does not justify us before God or make us more lovable to our fellow humans.

"God made all beautiful in its time," explains Ecclesiastes 3:11. All is beautiful in its time, but trying to make immortal what is not destroys that beauty. This is one of the lessons folklore's vampire and zombie myths try to teach. Continuing even human life beyond its time may produce something monstrous.

George MacDonald has written a lovely poem about a girl who lost things: her thimble, her dolly, her heart, her health, her self to God, her mother to death, her sight and finally her own life. But to her delight she discovered God had gathered them up for her in the treasure chest of heaven where thieves cannot break in and steal and moths and rust cannot destroy (Lk 12:33).[11]

Redeeming or making the most of the time is a scriptural concept of how best to use the transitory nature of our time on earth (Eph 5:16). We talk about *spending* time. This is a very good image. We are God's investors. Like the servants in the parable (Lk 19:11-27), we have been given an investment by our master, and Jesus will see what we do with it. What we do with what life we have is what really counts.

As teachers, we are approached by an increasing number of more mature students who lament the fact that the years have passed for them and further study seems out of the question. "It's too late," they mourn. "Look how old I'll be when I finish." We always give the same answer: "The time is going to pass anyway. Look how old you will be without anything! *The time is going to pass.* You might as well have a further degree to show for it." We need to invest our time according to our priorities. Suffering will inevitably come, but God's work will give us something worthwhile to show for our lives, despite our suffering and often over against and above our suffering.

Bill's father fell on a Saturday. Busy house painters take days off only when it rains. On a Saturday, when many families are doing things together, this man was at work trying to provide a better financial life. He had also been at work the day his daughter drowned. When she died, one of his main reasons for working left him. How many times he would wish he had spent his time *with* his daughter and family rather than working *for* them.

Summary

How, in summary, can we begin to enjoy God's freedom now? Look realistically at the human situation. God created us good, able to choose to remain good or to disobey. The sins of our first parents that drove a wedge between God and us now threaten to blight our lives. We inherited death from them in its major and its minor forms: illness, catastrophe, unhappiness. God crossed the gap in Jesus, giving us strong coping resources: freedom from eternal death through Jesus' action; freedom from shame; human love and joy to help lessen pain; silence, sleep, food, drink, work as emotional balm; God and other people to suffer along with us; God and God's hosts to strengthen us; prayer as a lifeline to God; the hope of heaven in our hearts. We can begin enjoying a taste of heaven, that is, a right relationship with God, now. But we enjoy it with our eyes open in a world where we understand that pain and suffering are still inevitable and very, very real.

Therefore, we need to have a right perspective on suffering. We need to keep aware that *suffering is evil.* We should never see the suffering of a fallen world as good. Furthermore, we need to realize that even we Christians cannot escape suffering. But even in a fallen world, God is victorious. Therefore, with confidence and sure hope we can draw on the spiritual resources God has given us.

Parenting

"Daddy, if you really love me,
   why do you punish me?"
What can I answer to this little life,
   trusting my fledgling parental skill?
Am I God that I should sit above him,
   meting out rewards,
As if all the wisdom of his world
   met in my judgment and my will?

"Father, if you really love us,
   why do you punish us?
What can you answer to these fallen lives,
   seeing our chronic unhappiness?
Are you human that you suffer with us,
   looking down from your perfection and your glory,
As if all the sorrow of our world
   met in your heaven and your bliss?"

"Daddy, if you really love me,
   why do you punish me?"
I see myself a child small and supple,
   being bent toward goodness like a young tree.
"I punish you because I love you,
   dear one,
Having lived to see such sin
   cause misery."

"Dear God, if you really love us,
   why do you punish us?"
"I see another child pure but broken,
   and in its mouth a world of children groaning its distress."
"But, were you ever tempted and broken as we are?"
   "Yes, my children, yes."

WILLIAM DAVID SPENCER, 1992

3

PUNISHMENT
FOR SIN

*T*hey must have all done something wrong," the church people whispered, "or maybe they *would* have done something wrong . . ."

"What have I done? Why am I being punished so utterly and bitterly?"

Often our first response when we suffer is to assume that God is punishing us because of our sin.

One day when Steve, our son, was only six, he surprised us by starting on his own to stack a cord and a half of wood that had just been delivered. By the time he alerted his mother quite a while later he already had a big stack going. He explained he wanted to surprise Mom and Dad and insisted on continuing until the whole pile was stacked.

That night he insisted on making the hamburgers for us. But while we were having a fine, joyful time at the meal, he suddenly came down with a stomach virus. One of his friends had brought it to school the day before.

Later on in the evening, forlornly sitting cramped over between vomiting spells, he said suddenly, "Daddy, wasn't I a good boy to-day?"

"Sure, Steve, you were an excellent boy. You stacked all that wood and you fed us . . ."

"And I made the hamburgers and cleaned my fort, right? So then?" and he pointed to his tummy.

Why, after being such a good boy, should he get a stomach virus? Is this fair? Is this the way the world is supposed to work?

All Suffering Is Not Caused by Punishment

A person or nation can be judged by God, directly or indirectly, for wrong choices. Yet people jump to see suffering as caused by sin more frequently than they should.

Ancient Jews were very similar to many twentieth-century people. Rabbi Ammi said, "There is no death without sin, and there is no suffering without iniquity" (b. Shab. 55a). The Babylonian Talmud also records that every measure of punishment or reward taken by God befits the human deed (b. Sanh. 90a). Rabbi Eliezer ben Jacob, who taught in the second century, said: "He that performs one precept gets for himself one advocate; but he that commits one transgression gets for himself one accuser. Repentance and good works are as a shield against retribution" (m. Aboth 4:11).

So fixed was the law of measure for measure that many rabbis taught that certain sins were inevitably followed by certain penalties. The Mishnah, a collection of oral teachings before and up to A.D. 200, records that seven kinds of retribution come upon the world for seven classes of transgression. If the people of a nation did not tithe or give ten percent of their produce to priestly service, then famine would result. If they committed crimes deserving of death and did not bring penalties to the court and did not obey all the laws for produce in the seventh year, pestilence would result. If justice were delayed or perverted, then a conquering army would come. If people profaned God's name, then devouring beasts would come. If the people were idolatrous, committed incest, unfairly shed blood or neglected the seventh-year rest of the land, they would be exiled (*m. Aboth* 5:8-9).

The basis for such belief came from past dealings with God. God *is* a God of justice. When the original inhabitants of Canaan began to kill their own children and worship other gods, God no longer allowed them to live peacefully in Canaan (Deut 9:4-5).[1] In the same way, when the Hebrews continued to oppress foreigners, orphans and widows, to kill innocent people, break the Sabbath rest, enslave their own people and worship other gods, God did exile them (Jer 7:5-7).[2] But can all suffering be reduced to punishment for sin? Most definitely not.

Jesus dealt with this problem when on earth. After he explained that allegiance to his reign would result in division among family members and that effort should be made to be reconciled with those who accuse one (Lk 12:49-59), some of Jesus' listeners reported to him about Galileans who were killed by Pilate's soldiers. Jesus perceived their unstated assumption: "These Galileans must be more sinful than we are because they were killed and we were not." Jesus answered this assumption: "Do you think that these Galileans were worse sinners than all other Galileans since they suffered these things? No indeed, I tell you . . ." (Lk 13:2-3). He gives another example: "Or those eighteen upon whom the tower in Siloam fell and killed them, do you think that they were worse debtors than all the people inhabiting Jerusalem? No indeed, I tell you . . ." (Lk 13:4-5). He concludes each example with almost the identical words: "No indeed, I tell you, but unless you may repent all of you likewise will die."

Jesus accomplishes three goals in this conversation. First, he tells them that the teaching "There is no suffering without iniquity" can *not* be used to explain *all* suffering. The Galileans who were killed and the Jerusalemites who were killed did not die because their personal sin was worse than that of other people. They died because they lived in a fallen world where rulers can misuse their authority and where buildings can be poorly built.

Second, Jesus warns that using such an all-encompassing doctrine (all suffering is to be blamed on the sufferer) is not only untrue (about the sufferers) but also unedifying. Such a doctrine can cause people to believe untruth about themselves and become self-righteous: "If I am not suffering, that must mean that I am a good person."

Third, Jesus made them focus on their own response to God, not their evaluation of others. (Jesus never seems to leave discussions in the abstract.) Gloating over others' suffering or worrying about its cause is not what we should be concentrating on. Rather, are we ready to die?

We can die at any moment. We know we *must* die because our world is a world defined by death. Jesus wants his hearers to escape the eternal death that may come at judgment. Have we repented? How have we responded to the claims of Jesus? Have we welcomed his claims as the Messiah and begun to live our lives in accordance with his principles? Then we need not fear judgment for rejecting him. Jesus explains what action he wants from individuals and from nations in the parable that follows (Lk 13:6-9). Are we fig trees that never bear figs? God will patiently tend us so we have time to show in our actions that we obey the Messiah's principles. No, not all death is from personal sin; but yes, judgment does come from rejecting God incarnate. We can avoid that "death" by repentance.

Jesus' disciples raise the question about sin and suffering on another occasion. If all suffering comes from sinful behavior, what about someone who was blind at birth? "Rabbi, who sinned, this one or his parents, since he was born blind?" (Jn 9:2). Jesus could have answered that his parents sinned or that babies are conceived in sin. Rather, he responds: "Neither this one sinned nor his parents" (Jn 9:3). What a shock the disciples must have had! Jesus again immediately goes on to address the responsibility he and his disciples have: "It is necessary that we work the works of the One having sent us" (Jn 9:4).[3] In other words, we need to do all we can to heal others.

Jesus therefore teaches his disciples of the first century and his disciples of every century that all suffering cannot be reduced to a punishment for behavior displeasing to God. Instead, the person evaluating continually needs to ask, *what is my responsibility before God?*

However, some suffering can come to us as a direct or indirect punishment for our sins. And we need to become aware of this possibility.

Punishment Is Part of a Covenant

Punishment for sin is the penalty for violating one half of a covenant. We still have covenants today as a part of our daily lives. We call them contracts. A recent example of the negative side of covenants happened to a woman in a town not far from us. A local newspaper ran a feature article on her, since she was singlehandedly picketing a local bank because it had repossessed her home. She had had only a few thousand dollars left to pay on her home mortgage. Seeing so little left to pay, she took out two additional mortgages, one to improve her home and the second to buy a business, adding them to another loan she already had. When the business failed, taking with it all the money, she could not keep up her side of the contract. After a time, the bank said it was sorry, but they had made an agreement together, and she had failed her part of the agreement. The bank was compelled to foreclose.

God gave us a first covenant with our first human representatives, Adam and Eve. According to their contract, they could freely enjoy Paradise as long as they did not eat from the tree of the knowledge of good and evil (Gen 2:16-17; 3:16-17). Breaking that first covenant, as we read in chapter one, has had collective effects. The good Paradise we once lived in has become a marred Paradise. But that marring did not end God's covenants with humans. If we ever wonder whether we humans of later centuries might have chosen better than Adam and Eve did, we need only read the rest of the Scriptures.

Down through history, humans are continually breaking their side of covenants, breaching God's contract, precipitating judgment. At one point we are almost blotted out because of our great wickedness. However, one righteous family saves us and is given a promise, symbolized by the rainbow, that never again will inhabited earth be blotted out.[4]

The Ten Commandments do not occur in a vacuum. They are part of God's requirements as a result of God's great compassion: "You have seen what I did to the Egyptians, and how I bore you on eagles' wings and brought you to myself. Now therefore, if you obey my voice and keep my covenant, you shall be my treasured possession out of all the peoples. Indeed, the whole earth is mine, but you shall be for me a priestly kingdom and a holy nation" (Ex 19:4-6 NRSV). The Ten Commandments themselves begin: "I am the LORD your God, who brought you out of the land of Egypt, out of the house of slavery" (Ex 20:2 NRSV). God acts on our behalf, expecting love and obedience as a result. Again and again God promises that if humans "listen carefully to the voice of the Lord your God, and do what is right in his sight," then we will not be punished by illness or war or destroying animals or natural disasters.[5]

"Punishment for sin" sounds like a negative action that comes from a vindictive and impersonal God. However, punishment always flows from a covenantal relationship that could have been positive. God is never unjust or impersonal.

Externally Inflicted
Sometimes the Bible describes punishment for sin as directly caused by God, at other times as self-inflicted. Often the external and internal causes work simultaneously, God's sovereignty and human will working together.

Nations can be judged by God. For instance, Isaiah describes God as friend or enemy, defense attorney or prosecutor according to what the people do. When the house of Israel rebelled, God "turned to be their enemy, and himself fought against them" (Is 63:10 RSV). A large part of the Old Testament is a defense for why Israel and Judah were taken into exile by the Assyrians and Babylonians. They had continued year after year in the same types of sins that the original inhabitants of Canaan had committed: burning their children, disobeying God's laws of justice and worshiping other gods. "Yet the LORD warned Israel and Judah by every prophet and every seer" (2 Kings 17:13 NRSV). (See also Jer 25:4; 35:15; 2 Chron 36:15; Lk 11:50-51.) Ahijah, Shemaiah, Jehu, Joshua, Obadiah and Micaiah are all mentioned during the first years of the divided kingdom. Elijah and Elisha are active during the second half. Amos proclaims that God has known only Israel "of all the families of the earth; therefore I will punish you for all your iniquities" (3:2 NRSV).

Hosea preaches that Israel has said, "Our God," to the work of their hands (14:3). Micah reminds Judah and Israel of the false idols they built: "What is the transgression of Jacob? Is it not Samaria? And what is the high place of Judah? Is it not Jerusalem?" (1:5 NRSV). Huldah preaches to the leaders of her time that God has been provoked to anger because God's people have abandoned God and made offerings to other gods (2 Kings 22:16-17). Jeremiah keeps warning the people of his time—so much so that even the attacking Babylonians hear about him (Jer 40:2-6; 39:12).

Near the time of his arrest, Jesus told a crowd that Jerusalem, a city that represented the religious people who rejected God's message, would soon be rejected:

Jerusalem, Jerusalem, the city that kills the prophets and stones those who are sent to it! How often have I desired to gather your children together as a hen gathers her brood under her wings, and you were not willing! See, your house is left to you, desolate. For I tell you, you will not see me again until you say, "Blessed is the

one who comes in the name of the Lord." (Mt 23:37-39 NRSV)
Luke tells the reader that King Herod wanted to kill Jesus (Lk 13:31).
Jesus warns that the city and its people will be judged for not welcoming him.

Individuals as well as nations can be judged by God. When Jesus
was on earth, he spoke of a future time, after he ascended to the
Father, when he would be an intercessor for our prayers. He used two
different words for "ask": "In that day in my name you will *ask (aiteō)*
for yourselves, and I do not tell you that *I* myself *will ask (erōtaō)* the
Father concerning you; for the Father himself loves you, since you
have loved me and you have believed that I myself came from God"
(Jn 16:26-27). The New Testament in Modern English and the King
James Version try to show that the Greek has two different words by
translating one "ask" as "pray": "You shall *pray* in my name . . . *I will
ask* the Father" or "ye shall *ask* in my name . . . *I will pray* the Father."
In the Gospels, *aiteō* is used when people ask questions of Jesus or
of one another, but only Jesus "asks" *(erōtaō)* of the Father.

Erōtaō can mean not simply to ask a question, but also to interrogate or challenge. The implication is that only Jesus is on an equal
footing with the Father to question, challenge or judge a human request. When we ask something in Jesus' name, Jesus will not challenge
that request before the Father if we love Jesus and believe Jesus came
from God. Conversely, if we do not love Jesus and if we do not believe
he came from God, then Jesus will challenge the Father concerning
us. Peter, quoting Psalm 34:15-16, writes a similar point: "For the eyes
of the Lord are upon the righteous, and his ears [are open] to their
prayer, but the face of the Lord is against those doing evil" (1 Pet
3:12).

Even believers are sometimes judged by God for extreme disobedience. For instance, Ananias and Sapphira did not have to sell their
land and donate the proceeds to the rest of the Christians in Jerusalem. However, they wanted to look like sacrificial givers. They decided
to sell their land but tell the church that they sold it for less, so they

could hold some money back but get credit for giving it all. Peter gave Sapphira an opportunity to be honest: "Tell me whether you and your husband sold the land for such and such a price" (Acts 5:8 NRSV). Neither Ananias nor Sapphira was honest. Because they lied ultimately to God, they died.

God's interaction with the priest Eli is very sobering when we consider that Eli was a devout man who was disturbed with what he heard about the actions of his sons Hophni and Phinehas. They were treating the offerings of the Lord with contempt by eating the meat before the fat was burned (1 Sam 2:12-17). Hophni and Phinehas were sleeping with the women who had come to minister at the entrance of the tent of meeting (1 Sam 2:22). Eli rebuked his sons: "Why do you do such things? For I hear of your evil dealings from all these people" (1 Sam 2:23 NRSV). However, he did not remove them from their priestly duties. Eventually he was punished—*killed*—for not restraining his sons (1 Sam 2:27-36; 4:11-22).

God does sometimes judge people during their lifetimes. And God will judge people definitively at their death or at Christ's Second Coming.

The Lord Jesus will return in the same way he departed, from the heavens: "inflicting vengeance on those who do not know God and on those who do not obey the gospel of our Lord Jesus. These will suffer the punishment of eternal destruction, separated from the presence of the Lord and from the glory of his might" (2 Thess 1:8-9 NRSV). The writer of Hebrews writes that humans are appointed "once to die, and after this judgment" (Heb 9:27). Similarly, the Christ who came "once to offer" to bear the sins of many will appear without sin at his return (Heb 9:28). Some people might hope that their death is merely a new opportunity to return to earth to try again to do better. However, God has decided that one lifetime is sufficient time for people to discover that indeed by ourselves we humans are incapable of being perfect. We need God's help. Moreover, we can today be acceptable in God's judgment if we believe that Jesus is God incarnate, who lived among us, died on our behalf and rose again from the dead to live forever. Jesus is both a means and a model of purification.

God is a just God. Therefore God does punish evil. However, since God is also merciful, God takes no pleasure in the death of humans or animals or nature. Judgment is never an inexplicable act which happens to the innocent person. Judgment follows warnings. God's goal is repentance, change of behavior. God wants to forgive. The priest Eli is first warned by a prophet of God (1 Sam 2:27). Peter warns Sapphira. God poignantly tells Ezekiel: "As I live, says the Lord GOD, I have no pleasure in the death of the wicked, but that the wicked turn from their ways and live; turn back, turn back from your evil ways; for why will you die, O house of Israel?" (Ezek 33:11 NRSV; see also 2 Kings 17:13; 18:12). Even Pilate was warned by his wife not to kill Jesus: "Have nothing to do with that innocent man, for today I have suffered a great deal because of a dream about him" (Mt 27:19 NRSV).

When God reveals the first lengthy description of God's attributes to Israel, God declares first of all: "The LORD, the LORD, a God merciful and gracious, slow to anger, and abounding in steadfast love and faithfulness, keeping steadfast love for thousands, forgiving iniquity and transgression and sin" (Ex 34:6-7 RSV). Peter repeats this truth about God. God is not slow to bring judgment "but is patient with you, not wanting any to perish, but all to come to repentance" (2 Pet 3:9 NRSV). Repeatedly, God's "steadfast love" is praised throughout the Bible. God "does not deal with us according to our sins, nor repay us according to our iniquities. For as the heavens are high above the earth, so great is his steadfast love toward those who fear him; as far as the east is from the west, so far he removes our transgressions from us. As a father has compassion for his children, so the LORD has compassion for those who fear him" (Ps 103:10-13 NRSV). God is love (1 Jn 4:8, 16). Therefore, God wants people to change their behavior, and God gives warnings. However, God's love does not nullify God's justice.

Internally Inflicted

Whenever someone chooses evil, that person is judged by the evil ramifications of that personal decision. God works in this process. For instance, wisdom, personified as a woman elder at the place of judgment, the city gates, warns that those who reject God's ways or wisdom "shall eat the fruit of their way and be sated with their own devices" (Prov 1:31 NRSV). The people who "wantonly ambush the innocent" while they themselves lie in wait will be killed in their own ambush (Prov 1:11, 18). Similarly, Paul writes of people who began by worshiping idols and then "God delivered them over to the desires of their hearts to impurity" (Rom 1:24).

An evil choice can be the deliberate choice of evil or simply the lack of choosing good. Repeatedly in Proverbs, suffering or calamity results from ignoring wisdom's counsel:

The prudent see danger and take refuge,
   but the simple keep going and suffer for it. (Prov 27:12 NIV)
If you had responded to my rebuke,
   I would have poured out my heart to you
   and made my thoughts known to you. (Prov 1:23 NIV)
The simple believe everything,
   but the clever consider their steps.
The wise are cautious and turn away from evil,
   but the fool throws off restraint and is careless.
   (Prov 14:15-16 NRSV)

In the same way as God's sovereignty and human freedom are not contradictory possibilities of either/or but happen concurrently and cooperatively, God's external infliction of punishment and a human's internal self-infliction of punishment usually happen concurrently and cooperatively.

One day when the religious leaders of his time were questioning Jesus' authority, Jesus told them a parable about someone who planted a vineyard and rented it to tenants while he went to live in another country. In the story the tenants never want to pay their rent but instead beat up each of the collectors. When the owner sends his own "beloved son," the tenants kill him so that they might own the farm themselves. "Therefore, what will the owner of the vineyard do to them? He will come and he will kill those tenants, and he will give the vineyard to others" (Lk 20:15-16). Jesus then quotes Psalm 118:22: "The stone which the builders rejected, this one has become the head of the corner. Everyone falling upon that stone will be broken to pieces; upon whom it may fall, it will crush him" (Lk 20:17-18). At the conclusion of this story, the religious leaders actively began to talk about finding a way to have Jesus killed without the intervention of the large crowds.

This parable includes all the elements we have discussed so far. The story clearly indicates that God judges sin (in this case sin is the rejection of God's messengers). God also gives repeated warnings before anyone is judged: three servants and the heir come to receive the owner's share of the produce. Judgment is both externally inflicted and self-inflicted. God will kill the tenants and give the vineyard to others (external), yet "everyone falling upon that stone will be broken to pieces" (self-infliction), yet "upon whom (the stone) may fall, it will crush him" (external). When the tenants chose not to follow the contract they had signed with the owner, they began their own process of self-judgment. Similarly, people who reject Jesus' claims as the Messiah who is God incarnate have chosen to "fall upon" the Rock Jesus rather than to "rest upon" the Rock Jesus. They incur God's judgment as the Rock Jesus who could have been a shelter or defense attorney becomes an avalanche or prosecutor. Self-inflicted judgment and externally inflicted judgment work cooperatively.

Does this parable refer to a nation or to individuals? The use of the metaphor of a vineyard suggests that Jesus speaks of the nation Israel.[6] The parable concludes that the owner will give the vineyard to "others," namely, Gentiles (Lk 20:16). Yet individual choices are also important in the last extended metaphor: "everyone" falling, it will crush "him." A nation is made up of individuals who can use their freedom for good or evil. What was true of the nation Israel—it lost God's favor because it rejected God's presence—was and is also true of individuals: each of us, too, can lose (or not gain) God's favor if we reject God's presence.

What is the point of this parable? God wants to be merciful. However, God cannot be merciful if the tenants do not give the owner a share of the produce and if they continually reject the owner's messengers.

James develops this same concept of punishment. Judgment is two pronged: self-inflicted and God-inflicted. In James's time wealthy people were underpaying the laborers. Not only will they be judged by Jesus at his return, but the gold and silver they so desired and hoarded will have "rusted and their rust will be a witness against you, and it will eat your flesh like fire" (Jas 5:3). What a great irony that James personifies money and gives it human abilities to be a witness against its owners! If people had never hoarded their money, underpaying their workers, they never would have had this witness to testify against them.

In the same way, wealthy Christians at Corinth had been eating the *agapē* meal without equally sharing the best with the poorer Christians. They were eating and drinking "without discerning the body." Therefore, they were eating and drinking "judgment against themselves" (1 Cor 11:29). For this reason, Paul adds, "among you many are sick and ill and some have died. But if we judged ourselves, we would not be judged" (1 Cor 11:30-31). These wealthy Christians were profaning Communion, a symbol of unity, by using it as an opportunity to be unjust to other Christians. Their own eating and drinking were acts of self-inflicted judgment. God's infliction of suffering was a warning for them to change so that they would "not be condemned along with the world" (1 Cor 11:32).

Punishment for Sin Has Communal Repercussions
What we are only beginning to understand, despite the mammoth

indoctrination of individuality we have received as Westerners, is that when certain people are punished for sin, other innocent people may suffer along with them. These innocent people are not punished for others' sins. In the book of Ezekiel God explicitly states: "It is only the person who sins that shall die."[7] However, others are affected by our choices. In this way, God "visits the sin" of parents upon their children and grandchildren. That is why the child of a drug user or a promiscuous parent might be born with AIDS. When the Israelites had chosen not to believe God could protect them from the tall and terrifying inhabitants of Canaan, why did Caleb (who *did* believe it) and his children have to wander around also for forty years? Caleb's daughter, Achsah, may have been fifteen. If so, she had to wait until she was fifty-five before she could "settle down." And Jeremiah, God's prophet who was willing to accept Babylon as God's instrument of justice, had to go off to Egypt with the very last remnant of disobedient people (Jer 43:4-7), probably to die there, his prophetic message rejected.

God is one God in three Persons—unity and community. Therefore, throughout the world we will find, reflected in creation, unity and interrelationship. Even as God's steadfast love spreads around to "the thousands," the inverse also results (but to a lesser degree): parental sins affect children, grandchildren and great-great-grandchildren. The consequences of evil choices can affect others.

The application for us should be: Beware what you do. Your sin will not only find *you* out (Num 32:23), but also your *family* and maybe your *friends and compatriots.*

Response to Suffering as Punishment for Sin

In summary, one reason we have suffering in the world is that individuals and nations are judged for their sins. However, this is not the only reason for suffering. God warns before judging, because God prefers repentance and life to judgment and death. God works with the inevitable result of people's evil choices (self-inflicted punishment) to condemn them (externally inflicted punishment).

God is not a malicious, vindictive god waiting and hoping to inflict punishment on us should we stray from the narrow path. God is a merciful God and a God of love. However, since God loves goodness, righteousness and justice, God loves purity. Purity demands judgment. Because, deep in our hearts, we love evil, we do not like the judgment which condemns evil in ourselves, although we may cheer when the evil of others is condemned.

G. K. Chesterton reportedly took some children to see Andrew Lang's version of a fairy tale in which the ending had been altered so that an evil cat was reprimanded and punished rather than slain. As they left the theater, the children were outraged at this miscarriage of justice. Chesterton noted that children are innocent and naturally want justice, while adults are not and therefore prefer mercy.

Notice something very basic here: *Suffering from punishment is the only type of suffering that we humans can avoid.* The drama of the New Testament is that it narrates the ultimate answer to sin. For instance, the Gospel of Matthew begins by reminding the reader, steeped in Old Testament events, of Judah and Tamar and David and Bathsheba, "wife of Uriah," *synecdoches* or representatives of the many sinners of the past. It then builds up to the climax that Jesus, God-with-us, will save people from their sins (Mt 1:21-23). No one need die from sin. Nevertheless, we still must obey God and lovingly and gently discipline those under our authority. Discipline should always be seen as a step toward repentance. It is not an end in itself. We should also work on loving and promoting justice. Unlike the suffering caused by living in a fallen world (which may be limited only by adjustment to a life of mortality), the suffering caused by punishment can be eliminated by heeding and making warnings, avoiding wrong moral choices and asking for forgiveness of sins.

We Christians cannot escape all the suffering caused by a fallen world, but we must try to escape the suffering caused by sin. As Peter expresses it: "If you are reproached for the name of Christ, you are blessed, because the spirit of glory and of God rests upon you. But let none of you suffer as a murderer, or a thief, or a wrongdoer, or a mischief-maker; yet if one suffers as a Christian, let him not be ashamed, but under that name let him glorify God" (1 Pet 4:14-16 RSV). Peter's letter challenges us today not to do wrong, because then we will be ashamed of our suffering. On the contrary, suffering for the name of Christ should be an occasion for pride and joy, as we will discover in the next chapter.

What if someone else suffers because of the evil he or she has done? We should never be gleeful when someone receives God's judgment: "Those who are glad at calamity will not go unpunished."[8] Instead, we should identify with the sinner and structure our lives so as to make it less likely that we ourselves will make the same wrong choices.

If someone has repented of past wrong choices, they may still have to suffer the consequences of their self-inflicted judgment. In that case, we need to treat them with the same care and love as someone suffering simply because they live in a fallen world. A friend of ours used to be an alcoholic before he became a Christian. He decided one day to stop drinking. He became a devout minister. Unfortunately, years later he still has residual problems with his liver.

Recognizing Punishment Is Difficult
In genuine self-inflicted punishment, someone does something wrong, often over time, and the judgmental consequences naturally follow. Because we live in a fallen world, self-inflicted punishment is not necessarily a clear result of sin. For example, we have a friend who would always choose to do the very thing he hated to do or could not do or feared to do. He was afraid of becoming a homeless alcoholic, so he would spend hours with homeless alcoholics. And after a while, sure enough, he started dressing like one.

Or, sometimes people will try to punish others by punishing themselves. Youth sometimes dream that if they were dead, everyone they know would regret not having treated them better. "When they see me in my casket, then they'll be sorry!" Alcoholism has a mixture of motives. Certainly the Bible speaks clearly against drunkenness. For example, the apostle Paul writes: "Do not get drunk with wine" because then you cannot be filled with the Spirit (Eph 5:18). Therefore, even repentant alcoholics might still suffer damage to their livers.

However, people will sometimes drink to escape unhappy situations. When we lived in Newark, we discovered that several of the alcoholic men who stayed in cheap hotels or at the graveyard were drinking as part of a long-range plan to kill themselves or to punish others. One man we knew drank in order to spite his ex-wife. In effect these people are not simply experiencing the consequences of their own wrong choice. They are embracing judgment or self-inflicted punishment for its own sake. These "death wishes" are part of an aberrant reaction to a fallen world, possibly a failure to accept responsibility or limitations. In other words, we need to be discerning as we analyze the appropriate cause for suffering so that, therefore, we can respond most appropriately.

Today one of the most difficult answers for Christians to give is whether the acquired immune deficiency syndrome (AIDS) is a clear punishment from God for sin or not. The church is divided on its views, some members contending clearly yes, some no, with the bulk of Christians very confused. The main reason for confusion, as we have seen from this chapter, is that all sufferers from AIDS do not fall into a single category. The answer has to have several facets.

Indeed, plagues themselves are difficult to categorize. Second Samuel 24 clearly tells us of God's punishment of Israel by plague (though David in 24:17 pleads for the people as innocent sheep, in the face of verse 1). Because of revelation, the people knew that they were being punished, yet the innocent suffered along with the guilty, if not by death, at least by bereavement.

But what about the pneumonic/bubonic plague of the Middle Ages? One-quarter to one-third of the population of Europe died. God has not, to our knowledge, revealed any clear reason why rats developed such a disease, transmitted by fleas and fatal to humans. And what of succeeding plagues? Certainly, the church has been periodically corrupt. But even those reforming the church have succumbed to plague. North America's Protestant theologian Jonathan Edwards and his married daughter Esther died of inoculation during a smallpox epidemic. His wife Sarah succumbed, largely due to grief, within a few months.

Today the AIDS plague threatens, potentially fully as devastating in its effects as the Black Death. Is this a punishment by God?

The Bible is clear in condemning promiscuity, adultery and homosexual acts, chief means for the spread of AIDS (Lev 20:13; 1 Cor 6:9-10). Romans 1:24-27 contends that those committing "shameless" acts receive among themselves "recompense" which "reveals their error" as self-inflicted punishment. Certainly, as a punishment that returns to one's person as recompense for homosexual and heterosexual sins, the plague of AIDS today falls on those guilty of breaking God's law—but, like the punishing plague in the time of David, it attacks the innocent as well: hemophiliacs, patients infected by dentists, doctors infected by patients or blood samples, victims of rape, children born to drug abusers—its devastation is no respecter of persons.

For those guilty of breaking God's law, AIDS can be seen as a ramification of sin, just as gluttony brings about the conditions that cause heart attack or an excess of alcohol causes cirrhosis of the liver. In an intensified physical way AIDS for some is a ramification, a natural consequence and punishment, for sin.

For others, the innocent, the victim, AIDS is a result of living in a world cursed by the sin of others. For these victims the world is not fair. But that is the whole point. Sin eliminated fairness when it turned the world askew. In this sad condition we all suffer the effects of our own and sometimes others' punishment. That is why we work for our own and others' repentance: to eliminate sin and alleviate punishment.

Hymn of the Comforted

Jesus, we thank you. Jesus, we praise you.
Jesus, we give you our love forevermore.
Jesus, we thank you. Jesus, we praise you.
Jesus, we give you our love forevermore.

He came into a world of sorrow,
The Prince of grace and truth.
He left a scepter for a staff,
Emptied and humbled, and offered to suffer,
And taken and broken wholly for us.

Jesus, we thank you. Jesus, we praise you.
Jesus, we give you our love forevermore.
Jesus, we thank you. Jesus, we praise you.
Jesus, we give you our love forevermore.

We suffer in a world of sorrow.
The Prince of comfort comes.
And in our dying he is there,
Emptied and humbled, and offered to suffer,
And taken and broken wholly with us.

Jesus, we thank you. Jesus, we praise you.
Jesus, we give you our love forevermore.
Jesus, we thank you. Jesus, we praise you.
Jesus, we give you our love forevermore.

WILLIAM DAVID SPENCER, AÍDA BESANÇON SPENCER, 1980

4

ADVANCEMENT
OF GOD'S REIGN:
PERSECUTION

*A*ll evil persecutes Christians. The death of Bill's sister and his father's accident were in their own ways general examples of the way in which the evil one persecutes all people—the undeserving as well as the deserving. But when we use the word *persecution,* this is not what we normally mean.

For us, *persecution* often evokes pictures of Christians sent to prison camps or shot down by firing squads. The church has suffered, is suffering and will suffer in such physical ways. Jesus predicted such persecution. At the end of the age, "They will hand you over to be tortured and will put you to death, and you will be hated by all nations because of my name" (Mt 24:9 NRSV).

Life-Threatening

Eusebius, the early church historian, recounts many stirring accounts of Christians who were put to death. One example, in the second century, during the reign of Roman Emperor Marcus Aurelius, was Blandina of Gaul. She was "filled with such power" that those who took turns torturing her morning and night gave up because they were so exhausted. She was then hung on a post, but this, instead of further terrorizing the believers, reminded them of Jesus, "the One who was crucified for them." Finally she was taken to a sports event. The crowd submitted her and a fifteen-year-old boy, Ponticus, "to every horror and inflicted every punishment in turn," attempting to make them renounce their Christian faith. The crowd admitted that "never yet had they known a woman suffer so much or so long."[1]

Everyday

However, intense physical suffering is not the only kind of persecution. A friend of ours, Bruce McDaniel, who volunteered to be a war medic in Vietnam in the 1970s, once remarked that the staff sergeants used to say, "It's the little things that are killing us," referring to the details of cleanliness that were needed for a perfect barrack. In his manuscript "My Buddies Will Keep Me Alive," he relates some of the other concerns the soldiers had: How can the children get water and soap to wash their sores? How can I keep lugging all this equipment? What can I do about ripped trousers? Can I make it to the latrine? Did everyone take their salt tablet and malaria pill today? How can I keep awake during guard duty? Where are we being taken? Will they shoot at me while I am walking? Succeeding in a war, a potentially life-threatening cataclysmic event, is achieved by mundane everyday successes. In the same way, succeeding in a large-scale national persecution, a potentially life-threatening cataclysmic event, is achieved by mundane everyday successes. Decisions to speak up for Christ or not to do so occur in everyday events. The "big events" are merely made up of many small decisions.

After completing the Master of Divinity and beginning full-time service, Aída began looking for a specific educational goal to give a focus to her work. Colossians 1:27-28 became that helpful focus: "Christ among you, the hope of glory, whom we ourselves make known by exhorting [the will of] every person and teaching [the intellect of] every person in all wisdom, so that we may present every person mature in Christ." Paul worked for the same goal (Col 1:29). So our goal, like Paul's, is that we may present others to God on the day of judgment as fully mature Christians.

That seemed clear enough. We began to pray regularly that we too would become mature in Christ, that we would take on Christ's image (Rom 8:29), because Christ could not be proclaimed or made known if we ourselves did not know who he was. However, we had not appropriated the significance of the context of those words in Colossians 1:29. Five verses earlier, Paul speaks about bearing in turn his share of Christ's afflictions—and he rejoices that he has suffered for the sake of the believers. This was not exactly what we had in mind for ourselves!

We began to experience difficulties in our ministries, difficulties that were out of our control. First, although we never lacked necessary food or shelter, our employing board never seemed to be satisfied with our work. Much was being accomplished in service, but little was being recognized. Not until a year later did we discover an enemy on the board who had been stirring up discontent. This married minister had been committing adultery with his secretary. Although we had no idea that this was occurring, apparently we represented orthodoxy or right doctrine to him—the type of people who would have complained if they had known.

Ever since we were married, until our present move to the suburbs, we have chosen to live in the city. For four years we lived in Newark, New Jersey, which was identified as a black city because, at the time, a majority of its residents were African in heritage. Commuters doubled its inhabitants every workday.

In order to be able to keep doing our ministries and to share our salaries with others, after we lost both our cars, one through theft (it had good tires) and one through an accident (a new driver hit us head-on at a slippery turn), we decided not to buy another car but simply to use mass transportation.

Simple enough? Did you ever realize to what extent people in cars in the United States can harass walkers? Once a driver turned against a light, almost hit us, then glared at us for being in his way! People (in the suburbs) kept telling us that we *must* have a car, as if something were wrong with us. Then we noticed that some people began to treat us as second-class, ignoring our comments, giving us disdainful looks, not respecting us. Even more specifically, one woman once told us that if our denomination ordained homosexuals it would not matter, since they would all go minister in the cities anyway. To our shock we realized that we were being treated as second-class because we were living in a city that represented second-class people and the poor. (Also some suburbanites, we discovered, come into the city to commit their sins and project blame on the city, not on themselves.)

Suddenly we realized the import of our prayer. We had been praying to become more like Christ. Christ *suffered!* Christ was *persecuted!*

The "little things" from the arsenal of evil were beginning to disrupt our ministry too. Wanting to become more Christlike is opening oneself to the harassment of evil. This is why Paul writes about suffering (Col 1:24) in the same context as he writes about maturing in Christ (Col 1:28). Christ did die for our sins. Therefore, he was a *crucified Messiah*. Christ's being crucified is not only an act which God did to bring us into the Lord's presence (although that is true) but also an act which indicates the very nature of God. If being a crucified Messiah who ends up victorious is God's nature, then we too must follow that example. In other words, if we follow Jesus by imitating Jesus, we must follow a Messiah who has been crucified.

Why Must We Suffer?

God does not want us to suffer. Nevertheless, because God became victorious over the powers of evil through suffering, we must follow that same route. When we attempt to advance God's reign, we too will suffer, for three interrelated reasons.

First, persecution or resistance from unbelief will come as we promote God's cause, because our world is indeed a fallen one. When evil is resisted by good, pain may result.

Second, our desire as Christians is to become more Christlike. As we become more and more like our Messiah, we will suffer as he did. Suffering because of identification with Christ is a blessing or privilege. Sometime we might suffer or die for someone else's benefit as Christ did for ours. In that case becoming more Christlike has resulted in vicarious suffering.

Third, one way to advance God's reign is to become more cleansed of the evil within us. If we welcome Christ's gift of salvation for us, we are justified (or seen as pure) in God's sight. But then we need to become pure in reality. Growth sometimes is painful. This third aspect will be discussed in the next chapter.

What unites these reasons is that *we have chosen to advance God's reign.* God's reign is modeled and represented by Jesus' life when he was on the earth. The biblical language about "reign" or "kingdom" is an extended metaphor. It is true, but metaphorically explained. God's country has citizens but it has no earthly boundaries. *Immigrants* can enter by repentance, turning away from their native country (Mt 4:17). God's country, though, is always "near." Genuine *citizens* of God's country obey the *ruler,* God. True members are both righteous and just because in the Greek language "righteousness" and "justice" are one word, *dikaiosynē.*

The reign of God is exhibited not by unnecessary regulations, but by (1) justice, which characterizes our *Judge,* (2) peace, because we are reconciled with the true *Ruler* and other *citizens* of this country, and (3) joy, because we look forward to a celebratory *banquet* in the great hall of the *King* when our fallen world has been replaced with a new world (Rom 14:17).

An indirect result of promoting God's reign which we have been warned to expect will be suffering. Jesus warned his disciples: " 'Servants are not greater than their master.' If they persecuted me, they will persecute you" (Jn 15:20 NRSV). We should never choose to suffer for its own sake. But if our suffering is a result of promoting God's reign, the suffering must be endured and even joyfully acknowledged. God ironically works despite such suffering to bring victory.

Almost any book in the Old or New Testament can be studied to find illustrations for this category of suffering. As one extended illustration, we will focus on a few chapters in 1 and 2 Corinthians and compare Paul's teachings to those of Jesus, especially in the Gospel of Luke, written by Paul's coworker Luke.

"Spiritual" is a characteristic that many people desire today. No Christian wants to be "unspiritual." For some people, "spiritual" is asceticism, the opposite of matter or the body. For others, "spiritual" is having many spiritual gifts, especially the gifts of speaking in tongues or angelic languages, or of doing miracles. But what does Paul mean by "spiritual" and "unspiritual"?[2]

For Paul, to be "spiritual" is to be propelled by the Holy Spirit. Being "spiritual" cannot mean asceticism or the deprecation of the body. Matter, or the body, is significant to Paul. Paul claims he has a right to food and drink and he is making an extended effort to collect money for the starving Jerusalem Christians (1 Cor 9:4-14; 16:1-3). The future to which he looks forward is the resurrection of the *body*, not the immortality of the soul (1 Cor 15:21, 44).

Being "spiritual" cannot be limited to spiritual gifts, because Paul could *not* address the Corinthians as "spiritual" even though he also writes that they had every spiritual gift they needed (1 Cor 1:5-7; 3:1). The Corinthians were "infants," not "mature adults." Who then is the "spiritual" person? The spiritual person is the one who lives out in community "Christ crucified" (1 Cor 2:2).

Crucifixion Living in 1 Corinthians

Paul begins his letter to the Corinthians with an exhortation for unity (1 Cor 1:10). They were not united, because they were choosing favorite leaders and boasting about them. They were creating a competitive environment. Some people preferred Paul; others, Apollos; others, Cephas; and others, Christ (1 Cor 1:10-13; 4:6). The Corinthians did not understand that their "leaders" needed each other, that they were interdependent. The interdependence of these leaders was a model to everyone in Corinth (1 Cor 12:4-31). Paul and Apollos were only "servants" of God—together they were planting a garden, one sowing the seeds, the other watering them. Neither of them had the power to cause the growth of these plants (1 Cor 3:5-9).

The Corinthians had been "suffering," in other words, fighting, but their suffering had nothing to do with promoting God's reign. The arguments they were having came from *misunderstanding* God's kingdom.

After Paul makes his appeal for unity, he explains what is truly entailed in the power of the cross of Christ. It is not eloquent speeches. It is not miraculous signs. It is preaching Christ crucified (1:18-23). What does it mean to "preach Christ crucified"? One begins by identifying with and becoming one of those whom God chose: the foolish, the weak, the insignificant, the rejected, whom Paul calls the "not being" (1 Cor 1:27-28). Paul echoes Jesus' words in Luke 10:21. What Paul calls "weak" and "insignificant," Jesus has already described as "infants," the unlearned. Infants can be easily hurt, are rarely consulted in decision-making, and often are to be "seen but not heard." The Corinthians in particular should have identified with the "weak" since the city of Corinth lacked an aristocracy. However, in this newly rebuilt city, social distinctions were developing from newly discovered wealth. The culture was pulling the Christians away from godly wisdom. The Corinthians were identifying with the powerful and newly wealthy (1 Cor 4:8).

Preaching Christ crucified also affected Paul's teaching, preaching and leadership style (1 Cor 2:2-5). The Messiah *had* to suffer. The rulers of this age did not understand that fact (1 Cor 2:8). Luke records in his Gospel that the large crowds who followed Jesus began to diminish as he began to teach the necessity for the true Messiah to suffer (Lk 9:43-62). At this point Jesus also taught his disciples that true followers must follow his own example and "take up their cross daily" (Lk 9:23). Even when Jesus summarizes the meaning of his life, he repeats the same point: "Was it not necessary that the Messiah suffer these things and enter into his glory?" (Lk 24:26).

Paul understood that if he were to *proclaim* a crucified Christ, he would also have to *live* a "crucified life." People will follow our actions as well as, or even more so than, our words. The end (belief in Christ) and the means (living in a Christlike manner) must be identical. For the Corinthians to live as "wealthy rulers" or comfortable Christians, then, would contradict the meaning of citizenship in God's reign. In contrast, Paul and Sosthenes and Apollos, God's apostles, lived "sentenced to death" (1 Cor 1:1; 4:9). Paul uses the image of a large Greek amphitheater, open to the air. The apostles walk in a conquering triumphal procession in the position of prisoners. Taken captive, they walk into the arena observed by all: "the world and angels and humans" (1 Cor 4:9). God chose the weak (1:27), and now these genuine apostles look "weak" (4:10). God chose the insignificant (1:28), and now these genuine followers look "unhonored" (4:10). God chose the rejected, the "not being" (1:28), and now, Paul adds: "Until the present hour also we are hungry and we are thirsty and we are insufficiently clothed and we are beaten and we are homeless and we work hard working with our own hands" (4:11-12).

Why should Paul and his colleagues do such things? The answer comes in the next sentence: "Being insulted, we bestow a blessing, being persecuted, we are patient, being slandered, we encourage" (4:12-13). Paul has rephrased Jesus' teachings: "Blessed are the poor, for yours is the reign of God," "Blessed are the ones being hungry now, for you will be satisfied," "Blessed are you whenever people might hate you and whenever they might set you apart and insult and reject your name as evil for the sake of the Heir of Humanity," "Bless those cursing you, pray concerning those insulting you. To the one striking you on the cheek, offer also the other" (Lk 6:20-22, 28-29). In effect, what Paul writes here is that if someone begins to obey the laws of God's country, then one will begin to resist the evil around one which violates those laws. And when one begins to resist evil, evil may very well retaliate. That is persecution. But we should not be surprised, because that is what happened to our leader. And we should discover that we are identifying with our Messiah such that our suffering, then, is a blessing or privilege. We can rejoice because our reward is "great in heaven" (Lk 6:23).

Paul's display of his life of suffering as an imitation of Christ is his "power" (1 Cor 4:19).[3] True apostles establish their authority by the suffering they undergo for the sake of the One who commissioned them. (It is not self-inflicted suffering.) Paul's sufferings prove that his words must be from God because he is in no earthly position to be powerful. He looks like the "refuse of the world," the "scum" of all things (4:13). Paul *has* to rely on God in such situations.

Paul's sufferings also prove his genuine intentions. He has gained nothing, in an earthly sense, from preaching Christ crucified. He is not wealthier, he is not more politically powerful, he does not have more honor. He is entitled to have all his needs at least for food and shelter fulfilled. But Paul does not accept money from the Corinthians because he believes it would become an obstacle to their appropriating his message (1 Cor 9:6, 11-12; 2 Cor 12:13). Proclaiming the good news has cost Paul a lot. He is suffering vicariously for the benefit of the Corinthians.

However, this type of suffering is not limited to apostles or to leaders. Paul exhorts all the Corinthians: "Become my imitators" (1 Cor 4:16). Paul's "ways" (1 Cor 4:17), his mode of conduct as a teacher, are his sufferings. His sufferings are both the *content* of his teaching and the *methodology* of his teaching. Timothy was also such a teacher. Both of them preached verbally the fact of Christ's crucifixion and lived out physically the life of "crucifixion."

Paul's example, by reflecting Jesus' example, authenticated his own preaching of the reign of God. Jesus too had challenged his hearers that only people who renounced all they had and bore their own cross could be his disciples (Lk 14:25-33). The good news of Jesus *must* cost us something in terms of money, belongings and honor if we genuinely follow the Jesus of Nazareth. Jesus also explains: "If the world hates you, be aware that it hated me before it hated you" (Jn 15:18 NRSV). Paul's display of his life of suffering necessitates and demonstrates the presence of an external strength and authenticates his words as a genuine believer. Yet, even as God raised the Messiah, God would also raise the apostle. The Corinthians did not understand what Paul had been telling them. Or, if they understood, they did not accept and appropriate his teachings. In the months that followed, they went on to encourage leaders who had nothing to do with suffering, who claimed to do impressive miracles, who took their own authority too seriously, who said that their generous salaries (paid by the Corinthians) were in themselves proof of their commission. These so-called superapostles began to attack the unimpressive, "weak" leadership styles of Paul and his coworkers.[4] Paul wrote the second letter to the Corinthians in order to quell the revolt.

Crucifixion Living in 2 Corinthians

In many different ways Paul continues to develop the principles he has already stated in 1 Corinthians. The distress of living in a fallen world can be increased if we choose to act sinfully or not in accordance with God's laws. However, resisting the natural order of this world in obedience to God can and will result in difficulties. Those difficulties, however, are signs of genuineness.

"Living sentenced to death" is not simply being persecuted or beaten by non-Christians. It entails also identifying with insignificant people, enduring economic difficulties, working hard, being slandered and resisting evil with good *for the sake of* advancing God's reign. Jesus' teachings, if truly appropriated, affect people's leadership styles, making leaders interdependent.

Three times in 2 Corinthians Paul includes lists of personal sufferings which demonstrate his authenticity, power and authority as a genuine apostle. In each list he continues to show what "preaching Christ crucified" means. In 2 Corinthians 4:7-10 he focuses on why genuine believers must have difficulties. God's presence is a "treasure." The "clay containers" in which this treasure is hidden are a life of difficulties arising from external and internal opposition to Christian ministry: "in every way experiencing trouble," "being uncertain," "being persecuted," "being thrown down" (2 Cor 4:8-9). The extraordinary power of God prevents the natural human result. Trouble need not degenerate into destruction. Uncertainty need not degenerate into despair, persecution need not leave one abandoned, nor does being hurled down necessarily produce death.

Paul concludes by citing the example of Jesus and how identification with Jesus affects our own lives, literally: "At all times the death of Jesus in the body we are carrying about, in order that also the life of Jesus in our body may be revealed" (2 Cor 4:10). In the *midst* of difficulties is where we will experience God's deliverance. Paul concludes that he experiences these difficulties so that the Corinthians may grow in their faith: "death among us is working, but life among you" (2 Cor 4:12).

If in 1 Corinthians 4:9-13 Paul describes the present difficulties of apostles, in 2 Corinthians 4:7-10 Paul explains the paradox of their ministry, God's powerful presence prevents their being overwhelmed by difficulties. In 2 Corinthians 6:3-10 he goes on to explain that genuine leaders who obey God will be commended by their difficulties. Servants of God are: "in great perseverance, in difficult circumstances, in troubles, in difficulties, in blows, in prisons, in insurrections, in toil, in wakefulness, in hunger, in sincerity, in knowledge, in long-suffering, in goodness, in Holy Spirit, in genuine love, in truthful word, in power of God" (2 Cor 6:4-7).

The Corinthians thought they had the Holy Spirit, but they did not have the genuine love that the Spirit brings. The weapons of attack and defense which Paul and his coworkers grasped were: "through glory and disgrace, through slander and good repute, as impostors and yet truthful, as failing to understand and yet understanding, as dying and behold we live, as being scourged and not being killed, as grieving and always rejoicing, as poor but many enriching, as having nothing and everything possessing" (2 Cor 6:8-10).

Again, in this list, Paul explicitly writes about persecution from the resistance of unbelief. The persecution takes the form of attempted disgrace, slander and the charge of being impostors. And Paul and his coworkers do become confused, grieving, poor and physically scourged in the process. But they remain moral, and by persevering in their desire to please God they eventually are privileged to learn of the many they enriched and of the happiness they had in possessing the essentials.

In 2 Corinthians 11:23-29 Paul illustrates a third reason why difficulties are necessary for him and his coworkers. Not only do difficulties prove that their words are from God and their intentions are genuine, they also prove that they are being obedient to God. True servants of Christ do not enslave, exploit, seize, put on airs, strike others or boast in their heritage (11:20, 22). Rather, says Paul, they live a life of "weakness": "in troubles to a greater degree, in prisons to a greater degree, in misfortunes to a much greater degree, within death many times, by Jews five times I received forty lashes less one, three times I was beaten with a rod, once I was stoned, three times I suffered shipwreck, a day and a night I have spent on the open sea, in journeys many times, in dangers from rivers, in dangers from robbers, dangers from one's own race, dangers from Gentiles, dangers in the city, dangers in the wilderness, dangers at sea, dangers among false brothers and sisters, in trouble and hardship, in sleeplessness many times, in hunger and thirst, in fastings many times, in cold and nakedness, apart from what I leave unmentioned, there is the daily pressure on me, the concern for all the churches" (11:23-28).

A synonym for "power" in 2 Corinthians 4 is "weak" in chapter 11. Paul advocates a way of living which would be seen by the super-apostles as "weak." This life of weakness (11:30) is a sign of a true servant of Christ. It includes physical discomfort from the persecution of false believers for preaching "Christ crucified." Physical discomfort may also come from traveling about, from natural disasters, robbers, hard work, living without all physical necessities. This life of weakness also includes mental anguish because of responsibilities and passionate concern for the spiritual well-being of believers. No one can boast about difficulties if God is the One who sustains one in those difficulties.

Paul does not use "weakness" as a metaphor for individual deficiencies or incompetence (though many seem to make that assumption). He writes about the cost of following Christ which may affect one's whole way of life and the esteem (or lack of it) with which others regard one. We want to live in comfort. Paul wanted to live in comfort. However, if we are genuine believers we will become more and more like God. Paul sets his example in the context of Christ's example: Christ "even was crucified out of weakness, but he lives out of the power of God" (2 Cor 13:4).

The fictional character Diamond in George MacDonald's *At the Back of the North Wind* expresses the dilemma well. The child Diamond can be close to the face of the great North Wind by being held in her arms, but then he receives the full force of the gale; or he can ride on her back, and then he is not buffeted around so much. He chooses to be held in her arms because "I begin to think there are better things than being comfortable."[5] Similarly, being in God's presence is more than compensation for the difficulties a genuine believer may sustain.

Responses to Crucifixion Living

To summarize, what does it mean to be spiritual? The spiritual person is the one who lives out in community Christ crucified. As one lives in imitation of the pattern of the crucified Lord, then one can better comprehend and hear the concerns and insights of the Spirit.

One danger in living out Christ crucified is that one might begin to become ascetic. We might begin to see Jesus as always suffering, always hanging on the cross, and forget that that cross is now empty, Jesus is alive and victorious. The early church understood that persecution would result from advancing God's reign. However, some believers wanted to suffer even if unnecessarily. For example, Ignatius writes, in his letter to the Romans: "I am writing to all the churches, and I give injunctions to all, that I am dying willingly for God's sake, if you do not hinder it. I beseech you, be not 'an unseasonable kindness' to me. Suffer me to be eaten by the beasts, through whom I can attain to God. . . . Then shall I be truly a disciple of Jesus Christ, when the world shall not even see my body" (IV. 1, 2). Ignatius certainly borders on desiring suffering for its own sake, almost implying that if he is bodyless, he is all the more pure. He was martyred in A.D. 108, killed by animals.

For Paul suffering was not a permanent state. He did not suffer disgrace in all the churches. Nor was he always in physical discomfort. He explains to the Philippians: "I know also to be lowly, I know also to abound; in every and in all I have learned also to be satisfied and to hunger, also to abound and to need" (Phil 4:12). He expected the Philippians to send him money (Phil 4:10-19). Because Paul did not seek suffering as an end in itself, he was free to escape the governor of King Aretas in Damascus by being lowered out through a window in the city wall (2 Cor 11:32-33). Another misinterpretation of living out Christ crucified would be to decide that spiritual gifts or miracle workers are wrong. Paul said he spoke in angelic languages and performed healings more than even the Corinthians (1 Cor 14:18; 2 Cor 12:12).

However, the desire for comfort and the desire to awe others should not become ends in themselves. To hear God's Spirit we must live, like

Paul and his coworkers, a prophetic life wherein we are ready to follow our crucified Lord; and we must listen to others who live such lives. Paul saw his difficulties as proof of his apostleship, proof of his power and proof of his genuine intentions.

Even as Paul warned the comfort-seeking Corinthians, he warns all comfort-seeking believers of today. In order to advance God's reign, we will encounter pain. As we resist evil with good, as we act for others' well-being rather than our own, as we encounter persecution for promoting God's reign, as we live in an economic style that may be discordant with our society's, we will suffer.

Such suffering is worth it because we are becoming like our Savior. Therefore, it is a privilege. We also will experience God's power in an undeniable way. We will not be overwhelmed by guilt but eager to receive God's commendation (1 Cor 4:5; 2 Cor 10:18). Now we may be persecuted, but in the long run we will be victorious. "The life of Jesus" will be revealed (2 Cor 4:10). The One who raised the Lord Jesus from the dead will also raise us with Jesus and present us acceptable in God's presence (2 Cor 4:14). Paul calls these difficulties "light and momentary" compared to the eternal glory God has prepared for us (2 Cor 4:17). Our salvation can never be taken away from us, nor can God's love be snatched away.

Community Is Essential

Identifying suffering that comes from a genuine attempt to further God's reign is absolutely crucial. Such suffering should not be avoided *if* by avoiding it one ceases to further God's reign. Paul began his 2 Corinthians 6 list with the overarching term "great perseverance" (6:4). Believers need to persevere through the midst of such suffering *by relying on God and on community with other believers* (2 Cor 1:9-11).

We evangelicals are quick to challenge others to rely on God, but not always so quick to be God's instruments of encouragement. When Paul writes about his life of difficulties he always somewhere refers to the plural: "*us* apostles," "*we* have become," "*we* hunger and *we* thirst," "*we* have this treasure," "*we* are commending ourselves as servants of God," "*we* will live with [Christ] to serve you" (1 Cor 4:9, 11; 2 Cor 4:7; 6:4; 13:4). He is not alone in his difficulties; he is sustained by his coworkers.

For example, when Paul has to leave the Christians in Thessalonica, he sends Timothy "to strengthen" and "encourage" their faith so that "no one be disturbed or upset in these difficulties" (1 Thess 3:2-3). Paul, Timothy and Silas did not leave the Thessalonians alone, saying, "If their faith is genuine, they can withstand anything!" They sent someone who himself would not be persecuted, young Timothy, to care for them as much as they would allow him. Paul exhorted Timothy to strengthen him, too, in difficult times: "Share in suffering as a good soldier of Christ Jesus" (2 Tim 1:8; 2:3). Unlike Demas, Crescens and Titus, Paul asks Timothy to endanger his life by coming to visit him in prison (2 Tim 4:9-14). "Everyone wanting to live a godly life in Christ Jesus will be persecuted," he notes, but Paul wants Timothy to continue in what he has learned and believed (2 Tim 3:12-13). Jesus, too, preferred to work in community. "Being alone" for Jesus might mean he had only hundreds of disciples (Lk 9:18). The seventy-two are selected from among them (Lk 10:1). When he contemplated his death he asked three of them, Peter, James and John, to stay with him (Mt 26:36-38).

Paul and his coworkers honored Christians who had persevered in difficulties: "We ourselves boast among the churches of God in behalf of your steadfastness and faith in all your persecutions and the afflictions which you have endured" (2 Thess 1:4). Similarly, Paul wrote the Philippians to welcome and honor Epaphroditus because "for the work of Christ he approached near death, risking his life in order to complete your lack in your service to me" (Phil 2:30). In contrast, when others are unjustly maligned, we might be tempted not to say a word so that our reputation is not damaged. But we need not honor a "crucified" Messiah if we are not willing also to honor a "crucified" disciple.

Community is important in suffering. In the fall of communism in the former USSR, we see dramatically the power of community in suffering. Christians for over half a century laid down their lives, suffering together as they underwent persecution for the name of Christ. The accounts of perseverance are as dramatic as those from the early church. The united prayers and witness of these valiant Christians, together with the heroic opposition of Jews and other dissenters, eventually showed up godless communism as the empty utopian sham that it is, toppling it in the regard of the Soviet-bloc people, communist and noncommunist alike. A new era of freedom has been bought by these efforts—but the price in pain was (and is) expensive indeed.

Directly, for serving Christ, or indirectly, for simply being alive in this Christ-hating world, Christians suffer. For we are called to live lives conformed to Jesus, picking up our cross daily and following our Lord (Mt 16:24; Mk 8:34; Lk 9:23). Evil, which made our Lord suffer, will assault us too. We must expect this and be prepared spiritually, emotionally and communally for it. When the authors first learned the truth about the interrelationship between the Messiah's sufferings and the disciples' sufferings, we wrote "Hymn of the Comforted." We learned that even as we follow Jesus' example, resisting evil for good, we will then delight in his comfort because "in our dying he is there . . . taken and broken wholly *with* us."

Baptizing the Graven Image

With our bellies still bitter from the golden water,
And the wailing in the camp for our brothers slain,
With the swords of the priests now bent from the slaughter,
And the plague scars on us like the mark on Cain,

To us abashed, to whom god broken
Was not much more than a bitter dining,
Comes he to whom great God has spoken
And on whose shapely face is shining.

What we tried to do with our feeble hands,
His God has done with our tears and lives.
What cannot be made now makes demands,
And we are the image shaped by God's knives.

WILLIAM DAVID SPENCER, JULY 1985

5

ADVANCEMENT
OF GOD'S REIGN:
TESTING

*O*ne spring when we were senior-high Sunday-school teachers, we joined our youth group on a retreat. As we began to talk about Jesus' imminent return, a return which could happen at any moment, one young woman shared that she wanted to die now. She pointed to Philippians: "My desire is to depart and be with Christ, for that is far better" (1:23 NRSV). She told us about her many problems with her family. We were dismayed that now she had religious reasons for potential suicide. Of course, we pointed out to her that Paul's sentence does not end at verse 23 but goes on to state: "but to remain in the flesh is more necessary for you. Since I am convinced of this, I know that I will remain and continue with all of you for your progress and

joy in faith" (1:24-25 NRSV). Outside of the fact that Paul was not
writing about taking his own life but of the possibility of having his
life taken from him by the Roman authorities, she, like Paul, needed
to think about her ministry to others, not merely the easiest way out
of her problems.

We often emotionally wish that God would transport us by helicop-
ter up and out of this world with all of its difficulties. But God allows
us to remain for two reasons: (1) so that we can minister to others,
doing all we can with God's aid to help people begin the road of
salvation and advance along that road toward maturity; (2) so that we
ourselves can advance, growing in Christlikeness. God's reign is promoted not only outwardly but also inwardly. This inward advancement is necessary because God is a God who examines and judges.
Humans are not pure, and the fallen world we live in also is impure.

God is so frequently described as the One who knows hearts (Lk
16:15; 1 Jn 3:20; 1 Kings 8:39) and examines our hearts (1 Thess 2:4)
that early Christian speakers coined a new Greek word to describe
God: *kardiognōstēs*,[1] the "knower of hearts" (Acts 1:24; 15:8). Why
does God examine human intentions, motivations and thoughts? Because God examines all, even God's own self: "The Spirit examines all,
even the depths of God" (1 Cor 2:10). "The one examining the hearts
knows what is the thought of the Spirit" (Rom 8:27). God is an examining or searching or investigating God. Therefore, we humans,
too, were created with an examining spirit: "For what person knows
the things of a person except the spirit of the person, the one within?
Likewise also the things of God no one knows except the Spirit of
God" (1 Cor 2:11). "The human spirit is the lamp of the LORD, searching every innermost part" (Prov 20:27 NRSV).

God Searches for Love

For what does God search? God searches our spirit to ascertain whether we love God, working all to good "to the ones loving God" (Rom
8:28). God allows us to remain in a sin-full world in order to put to

proof our love. God allows the very possibility of evil and suffering because God wants voluntary active love from us humans, even as God voluntarily and actively loves *us*. Moses has written that God would even allow the presence of false prophets in the midst of the Hebrew people in order to "put to proof" the Hebrew love, "to know whether you indeed love the LORD your God with all your heart and soul" (Deut 13:3 NRSV).

"To know," biblically, is not simply cognitive, abstract knowledge. It is also active behavior, and it is experiential. God "knows" we love God if we demonstrate that love in action. The account of God ordering Abraham to take his "only son Isaac," whom he loved, to Moriah and "offer him there as a burnt offering" (Gen 22:2 NRSV) is a mystifying account if we do not remember that biblical "knowledge" is often experiential. God wanted to observe Abraham's act of obedience. As Abraham followed each of God's commands, God "knew" Abraham's love. God had ordered Abraham: "Take now your son, your only one, whom you love, Isaac, and go to the land of Moriah" (Gen 22:2), and Abraham did so. Isaac was his only heir. Had God ordered Abraham to kill Isaac? Literally, the sentence continues: "and *lead him up* there for a burnt offering." '*Ālâh* signifies "go up, ascend, climb" and in the tense used "to cause to go up, to lead or bring up."[2] God does not command Abraham literally to "offer" or "kill" Isaac as a burnt offering. Rather, God commands him: "lead him" there or cause Isaac to ascend one of the mountains of Moriah. Abraham may have noticed this vagueness, because he tells the young Isaac, "God will provide for Godself the lamb for a burnt offering, my son"—yet he binds Isaac on top of the wood on the altar (Gen 22:8-9).

God came to know Abraham's love. And in the process Abraham came to know God's love as well. "Your son, your only one, whom you love," God's description of Abraham's love for Isaac, is not very different from God-the-Father's love for God-the-Son, the Heir of Humanity ("son" was often the "heir")[3]: "You are my Son, my beloved, in you I am well pleased" (Lk 3:22). Likewise, Abraham learned "the LORD will provide" (Gen 22:14 NRSV); the Lord "will see" to his needs. This "testing" in effect became not only a search into Abraham's love but also a means for Abraham to identify with God. Abraham had the privilege of identifying with God's relationship to the Messiah, a father's offering of an only heir for the sake of others.

God Searches to Purify

God also searches our spirit to purify us. God is not only an examining or investigating God, but also a pure God. God is a holy God (Lev 11:44-45). Metallurgy is a consistent metaphor which the Biblical writers use to describe the effect of God's holiness on humans. For instance, Solomon writes: "a refining pot is for silver, and a furnace is for gold, and purifying is for hearts by the Lord" (Prov 17:3). In the same way as a refining pot and a furnace each have their intended goal of purification, so too our hearts or wills will not become as glorious or as valuable as silver and gold, if they are not purified or examined by God.

How does God go about "purifying" us? That purification may often be done by letting us experience difficulties. The psalmist uses the same Hebrew word, *bāḥan* ("purify") in 66:10 as was used in Proverbs 17:3. Again God's action is described as the refining of silver. The nature of that refining is described in verse 12: "You let people ride over our heads" (Ps 66:12 NRSV). External adversity or oppression by others is the "test." However, the end result is deliverance: "Yet you have brought us out to a spacious place" (Ps 66:12 NRSV; see also 2 Pet 2:9). This purified silver not only is more beautiful without its impurities, but it is also stronger and more useful (e.g., Prov 25:4; Is 28:16).

The uses of silver and gold have many analogies to God's uses of people. In ancient and in modern times silver has been used for money (e.g., Is 7:23), jewelry (Song 1:11) and alloys. Alloyed with gold, silver becomes softer and is more useful for conducting electricity. Silver conducts heat and electricity better than any other metal. Silver alloys are used in dentistry to fill teeth since silver can prevent further decay. Silver solders are used in missiles for high-temperature bonding.

Gold is almost never found by itself but mixed in gravel or quartz deposits. Gold ore must be refined. Since it is soft it is the most malleable metal, but it is also one of the heaviest. It is very durable. It is an excellent conductor of heat and electricity. To be used for jewelry it must be alloyed with silver, copper or nickel because by itself it is too soft.[4]

Similarly, people's wills have been made durable by God. However, they may have beliefs or securities they hold onto in times of comfort, which should be abandoned (or "purified") if they want to persevere (be "durable") during economic adversity. People who have persevered during difficult times become less rigid and more open (or "soft") toward other people. They themselves become better "conductors" of God's work, bringing "health" to others.

When James writes about trials (e.g., 1:2), he too writes about external difficulties that happen to people. "Trials light upon" us in the same way as robbers "light upon" *(peripiptō)* travelers (Lk 10:30). When he wrote in the first century, before the war with Rome in A.D. 70, many wealthy landowners were unjustly oppressing the poor.[5] These rich people were given preferential treatment for seating at the synagogues (1:9-11). They also were inadequately paying their workers (5:1-11). James strongly calls them to account: "Listen! The wages of the laborers who mowed your fields, which you kept back by fraud, cry out, and the cries of the harvesters have reached the ears of the Lord of hosts" (5:4 NRSV). Until the landowners change, the harvesters have to endure. The rich are their "trial."

Peter describes as tests or trials the difficulties that Christians were experiencing as a result of the Roman persecution (1 Pet 4:12). He encourages them to rejoice because they were "sharing Christ's sufferings" (1 Pet 4:13). Paul also uses "trials" to describe his pursuit by the unbelieving Jews who were attempting to kill him (Acts 20:19). In other words, the difficulties that arise from advancing God's reign can be seen as tests. Will we persist in our trust of God despite these difficulties?

As we are attacked by the evil without, we will also be attacked by the evil within. Will we be those who receive God's word with joy, but then fall away in a time of testing (Lk 8:13)? Our goal is to become mature and to help others become mature (Col 1:28). The stage before maturity is perseverance or steadfastness, as James exhorts: "let steadfastness show itself perfectly in practice, so that you may be mature and complete, in nothing having need" (Jas 1:4). We should not seek persecution. We should not seek difficulties. But if they occur, God can work with us to enable those difficulties to become a means of purification. Even in the midst of a fallen world, God can be victorious!

Bill's parents experienced severe testing from this evil world through familial, physical and financial adversity. Ultimately, after years of suffering in the aftermath of those blows, Bill's father became embittered, finally dying estranged from the remains of his nuclear family and from his extended Christian family. Bill's mother, however, endured through testing. Today, in her eighties, she is a sprightly senior citizen who bikes a mile or more on her great three-wheeler, gives children a dollar for each year of their life on their birthdays, and sees her service to the church as sweeping up after community meals. Her disposition is very sweet, but one must repeat endlessly during a conversation:

"What day is this?"

"It's Thursday, Mom."

"Thanks."

"Did you enjoy lunch?"

"I don't know."

"Can you remember what you had?"

"No," she laughs. "But Billy—it is Billy, isn't it?"

"Right, Mom."

"Billy, what day is it?"

"Thursday, Mom."

"Oh, yes, yes."

"Want to go for a bike ride, Mom?"

"That would be nice."

"Which way shall we go today?"

"You pick it."

"Want to go this way?"

"O.K. But, Billy—it is Billy, isn't it?"

"Right, Mom."

"What day is it?"

"It's Thursday, Mom."

People ask how one can repeat endlessly and not lose patience. The reason is that one remembers what another was like. In her day Mother Spencer was a business whiz, increasing sales to an impressive volume in the Macy's chain. Her bosses tried her out for a time as an executive, but neither was happy with the arrangement. She was a natural in sales, garnering the store's coveted "Ambassador" status, and always the leader in her department, on her floor, in her store. She could also be extremely perceptive when she concentrated, having a knack for understanding and dealing with people.

As she lay in the hospital after her Christmas collapse, the doctors studying her brain X-rays could see the hardening that was causing her loss of short-term memory. None of this is her fault. The mind and the body worked together to protect her from the pain of her life, and now she has a natural anesthesia easing her final years. When asked how she is doing she always responds, "I'm persevering!" Her memory may be robbed of all else by the ravaging of age and the passing of time, but the key trait that sustained her in the faith—enduring through testing—stays staunchly on.

God Trains Us

Another metaphor the Bible uses to describe God making humans holy is "train." Because God loves us, God trains us (Heb 12:6). The victorious Jesus declares to the church in Laodicea: "I, as many as I love, I show fault and I train. Therefore, be earnest and repent" (Rev 3:19). Jesus does not "show fault and *punish*" people for their own sakes. No one would repent if all he or she could expect was punishment. Paul uses the noun *paideutēs* in this manner in Romans 2:20: "a *corrector* of the foolish, a teacher of children" (NRSV). For example, Pilate concludes that Jesus is innocent of the crimes charged against him. Therefore, he wants to "have him flogged *(paideuō)* and release him" (Lk 23:16 NRSV). Or Paul writes that Christians are "disciplined" so they may not be condemned along with the world (1 Cor 11:32). Because God loves us, God shows us our faults so that we can change our behavior. In Revelation 3:19 Jesus uses the verb *paideuō*. *Paideuō* is the type of action taken by a *paidagōgos* or "pedagogue." A pedagogue would often be an educated Greek slave bought by a wealthy family to escort their child *(pais)* to school, converse in Greek and supervise the child's conduct. "Training" was also used to describe the personal apprenticeship of a student and teacher at the university level (Acts 22:3). In the same way as a pedagogue would help a child become more ethical and intercultural, God supervises us, trains us, so that we may be more moral and communal. Paul uses the same metaphor to describe the effect of God's grace: "training *(paideuō)* us to renounce impiety and worldly passions, and in the present age to live lives that are self-controlled, upright, and godly" (Tit 2:12 NRSV).

Often that training can come through the means of other humans. Paul exhorts Timothy not to quarrel but instead to instruct *(paideuō)* his opponents, so that "perhaps God may grant to them repentance into knowledge of truth and escape out of the devil's trap, after being captured by him into that will" (2 Tim 2:25-26). The devil's "trap" is the enticement of "foolish and ignorant controversies" (2 Tim 2:23). God's pedagogue here can be another believer who compassionately treats the ensnared person as uninformed and immature (not as uneducable or recalcitrant), humbly teaching that person with the end goal of repentance or escape from a trap. "Trainer" or "disciplinarian" *(paidagōgos)* is an apt metaphor for the law. Laws and being disciplined are activities needed for the immature. But when people become mature they are no longer appropriate since they are internalized by love (Gal 3:23—4:7). Our goal is to become mature as individual Christians and united as gatherings of Christians so that we may reflect our mature, or perfect, Parent, the one God.

One person in whom we can see great strides toward maturity is the apostle Saul/Paul. We often forget that several believers helped him along his way as his advocates toward a goal of maturity. We first learn about him in Acts. He has letters giving him full authority to imprison Christians.

Jesus is the first to offer Paul an opportunity to repent, and Paul must listen: "Saul, Saul, why do you persecute me?" (Acts 9:4). However, God does not simply leave Saul blind and confused. God continues as his advocate. "Ananias," God calls in a vision in Acts 9:10-18, "Rise, go to the street called Straight, and seek out in the house of Judah a Tarsian named Saul. . . . This one is a chosen instrument by me to carry my name before Gentiles, and also rulers, and Jews."

Faithful Ananias goes and becomes Saul's second advocate. God has handed Saul over to Ananias's care.

Did you ever wonder why Ananias was chosen by God? No doubt he was a prominent leader in the church and so the others would have trusted him. But as well, he had to have had compassion, for we see compassion expressed in this gracious extension of the family of Christ to Saul, *"Brother* Saul." And he said this to a person who was a notorious persecutor of Christians, a person he might normally be terrified to meet.

Notice, for example, the kinds of things Ananias did *not* say: "Saul, you sniveling murderer! Now see what all your evil has done. God has ordered me to heal you, but you're gonna get yours. God told me God's going to make you suffer for persecuting the saints! I'm glad I'm not in your sandals, that's for sure!"

The Scripture does not record Ananias telling all immediately in graphic detail to poor, blind, confused, terrified Saul. God would handle that in God's time. Instead, Ananias consoles him. "Brother Saul," he explains, "the Lord has sent me—Jesus, who appeared to you in the road when you were coming—that you may see and be filled with the Holy Spirit." He calms Saul's fears, explains the gospel to him, heals his sight and introduces him to the family of Christ. What a wonderful Christian brother Ananias was. The third advocate of Saul was Barnabas. Barnabas received Saul soon after Ananias and the Damascus Christians had to help Saul over the wall at night. Saul fled to Jerusalem, but the reaction there was the same as Ananias's initial one: fear.

Acts 9:27 tells us Barnabas "brought him" and "declared" to the believers, interceding for Saul until he was accepted. Joseph of Cyprus of the tribe of Levi had been nicknamed "Barnabas," which means "Son of Encouragement," by the apostles (Acts 4:36). And this good man, full of the Holy Spirit and faith, certainly lived up to his name! Not content simply to introduce Saul to the faithful, Barnabas followed up on him when he visited Antioch again, exhorting all there to remain purposefully steadfast in their faith. He took a side trip to Tarsus, Saul's home, to see what had happened to Saul since he had left Jerusalem, his aim being to encourage Saul in the faith (Acts 11:23-25).

Barnabas is following God's example when he takes Saul and brings him to others, intercedes for him in Jerusalem, then follows him up in Tarsus, brings him to Antioch and starts team-teaching with him. In fact, what breaks up their team eventually is Barnabas's advocating for yet another young Christian—John Mark. When Mark gets homesick during a missionary journey, Saul (by now called Paul) is disgusted and refuses to take him again. Barnabas cannot convince Paul to give the younger man a second chance, and they split up (Acts 15:36-41).

Paul learns a poignant lesson in negative reinforcement from this incident and its aftermath. By his refusal to encourage John Mark he is deprived of Barnabas's companionship and is proved wrong about John Mark. By the time of Paul's last imprisonment, we find him begging Timothy to get hold of Mark and bring him to join Paul, for "he is helpful to me in ministry" (2 Tim 4:11). On the other hand, Barnabas's faithful encouragement pays off handsomely. Eusebius, the great historian from the fourth century, tells us that this same Mark was the one who wrote down Peter's report of Jesus, which today we call the Gospel of Mark, and strode out himself as the first missionary to evangelize Egypt.[6]

Further, think of the alternatives. What might have happened to John Mark if Barnabas had not given him a second chance? Slinking around Antioch, defeated, a pitiful loser who would live out his life of shame as a failed missionary. If the tradition is true, how many Egyptians would have had to wait before another brave Christian took the gospel to them, because Mark had been given no second chance?

What would have happened to Christian Public Enemy Number One, Killer Saul, if nobody had reached out to advocate for him? As a blind sufferer, he might have stumbled out his days in darkness of sight and spirit, wondering how he could have ended up so wrong when he had tried so hard to do right. Instead, he lived to write down the prescriptions for joyful living in the church: bearing each other's burdens, suffering and rejoicing with each other (1 Cor 12:26).

What may happen to each of us if a Paul does not exhort us, an Ananias does not console us, a Barnabas does not advocate for us? How can any of us become truly mature if we do not educate one another, treating each other with compassion, humility and patience?

God Does Not Tempt

We can become confused in this matter of testing, purification and training. That God "tests" us can never mean that God directly "tempts" us. If God were to place opportunities for sin before us which we have not the ability to avoid, God, in effect, would be impelling us to sin.

James points out that although external difficulties can become "trials," people's own desires are what cause them to succumb. We should not blame God, for God "tempts no one. But each one is tempted, being dragged away and allured by means of his/her own desire" (Jas 1:13-14).

Some of the desires which can cause temptations are desires for economic or social superiority (money, power), selfish ambition, jealousy, immorality and testing God.[7] In the context of the passage where Paul describes the evil desires of the early Hebrews (desires for evil, idolatry, immorality, testing God, grumbling), Paul explains that along with the testing God also provides humans with a way out so that we may be able to endure (1 Cor 10:6-13). God has a means of escape for even our internal desires! Paul certainly is not stating in 1 Corinthians 10:13 that God tests or tempts us. The tests Paul describes are internal evil desires.

These types of internal temptations are sometimes spurred on by external tempters. The people tempted Aaron to make gods for them while Moses delayed on Mount Sinai. And then Aaron tempted the people by commanding them to donate gold (Ex 32:1-2). People can become traps to one another. A *skandalon* is one kind of trap. The *skandalēthron* is the stick in the trap on which the bait is placed. When touched by an animal, it springs up and shuts the trap onto the animal.[8] Peter, metaphorically, became a "stumbling block" *(skandalon)* to Jesus when he began commanding Jesus not to go to Jerusalem and undergo suffering (Mt 16:21-23). Jesus was righteously indignant against anyone who would cause a believer to be tempted: "Woe to the world because of stumbling blocks! Occasions for stumbling are bound to come, but woe to the one by whom the stumbling block comes!" (Mt 18:7 NRSV). Believers who truly love one another can never cause stumbling because they live in the presence of God, who causes no one to stumble because God is love (1 Jn 2:10; 4:8).

God does use a type of "trap" which may look negative but in reality is positive. "Christ crucified" is a stumbling block to some modern miracle seekers, just as it was to some of the ancient Jews (1 Cor 1:23). The cross is also a stumbling block to those who desire to maintain regulations as a means of justification (Rom 9:33; Gal 5:11). In the previous chapter we discussed "crucifixion living" as one reason for suffering. "Christ crucified" is not in itself a cause for temptation. It is God's means of bringing deliverance. "Christ crucified" *becomes* a trap only to those who snarl at the concept like gluttonous animals. But to the humble believer the nourishing meal can be eaten for one's good health without fear of ensnarement.

Summary
In summary, God leaves us in this fallen world so that we can serve others and ourselves. Resistance from unbelief can come from others. We call that persecution. Persecution results in one type of "testing," the purification of believers. "Testing" may be simply God's verification of our love. No resistance from unbelief is involved (at least initially). Resistance from unbelief can come from our own immaturity.

We call God's working with us another type of testing, "training." The internal resistance from unbelief can be still another type of "testing." We can call it "temptation." God can sovereignly work with all such "testing" to advance God's reign, to search for love and faith and to strive for purification.

But we can become agents of evil if we misunderstand testing. If we become the tempters, we are working against God's reign. If we conclude God wanted a world full of temptations, we blaspheme God by misunderstanding God as a lover of evil, suffering and deceit. God is not a tempter. God is the One who gives generously of every good and perfect gift. God has no evil side (Jas 1:17). If we ever wonder how God can go about examining so much, we need only look at ourselves to see how much we examine ourselves and each other, because we humans are created in God's image, the One who examines. May we also become pure as God is pure!

George MacDonald develops the imagery of a purifying fire in his *Princess* stories. The young miner Curdie, coming up to visit his grandmother, discovers a great fire of roses. This aged princess with youthful face, wanting to put Curdie to one more trial, asks him to thrust his hands into the fire of roses she has in her tower. He finds that this painful process results in the removal of all the rough, hard skin from his daily work in the mine. Now he is able to discern a person's spiritual state by simply holding the person's hand. According to the princess, many people are "going to the beasts." The rose-fire makes Curdie's hands so knowing and wise that from then on he will "be able to know at once the hand of a man who is growing into a beast; nay, more—you will at once feel the foot of the beast he is growing."[9]

We too can see our lives on earth as a fire of roses through which, if we persist, we may learn to become more discerning. Heaven forbid that we should turn into animals that snap at traps. Our prayer should be that we will become more and more human, creatures fully mature in the image of our Creator.

Mercy the Medicine

Mercy is the medicine
that flows from the love of God,
like a strong heart that beats blood
down through the arteries and capillaries of humanity,
a healing transfusion that nourishes
a sick and tired earth,
pumping, pumping multiple beats a minute
on through the centuries;
God's healing mercy moves through
the caring touch of strong vessels,
conduits of mercy
that help Christ's body strengthen and grow.

WILLIAM DAVID SPENCER, 1987

6

RESPONDING TO SUFFERING BY PROMOTING GOD'S REIGN

So far we have studied three main reasons for suffering, because diagnosis must precede prognosis. Much poor advice that people give one another comes from not taking the time and care to diagnose suffering.

Should people claim to be persecuted by Satan if they become sick from overwork? No, they have forgotten they live in a fallen world as a mortal being. Should we say God is punishing us if we are sick? Some of the Corinthians should have said this, but many people would not be accurate in saying so. In other words, illness from sin can be very specifically localized. The sin can be easily discovered. Other illness should not be seen as punishment.

Should someone claim that if you live truly close to God you can escape all suffering? Never. Jesus has promised that his followers *will* at some time suffer as he did. Nor should anyone claim that if you suffer greatly, you must be a great Christian. People who are not Christians can suffer greatly too. In other words, reducing all suffering to one cause or misdiagnosing the cause of a specific person's suffering can lead to greater damage and unnecessary pain. "Where do you want her body sent?" "Maybe it's all for the best. Maybe she would have wandered away from the faith." "They must have all done something wrong." How many times do our responses to suffering not heal, not teach, not bring justice, but, in fact, lay further burdens on those who are suffering?

God incarnate, Jesus, proclaimed God's reign (or kingdom) by teaching, preaching and healing. Good news was brought to earth. God worked in the midst of a fallen world to overcome that fallenness. Jesus taught that we humans need not act in a fallen way because God can give us the wisdom and the power to live according to God's "constitution"; that reconciliation with God is necessary so that we might be both individually and corporately just, thus receiving God's covenantal blessings, not punishment; that people can be physically, emotionally and spiritually delivered from the ill effects of a fallen world.

The "reign" of God is one of the major biblical concepts that helps us understand God's presence and activity among people. From the prophets' repeated exhortations to the Israelites to trust in God as their "Sovereign," as opposed to foreign allies,[1] through John the Baptist's and Jesus' preaching, through the ministry of the early church,[2] God's reign is a pivotal theme.

When people create idols, whether carved figures or false securities such as money, success or wrong political alliances, they forget that God is the only ruler worth trusting. Gideon proclaimed: "The Lord will rule over you," *we* will not rule you (Judg 8:23). When the Israelites wanted a king, in order to be like the other nations, God interpreted that choice as a rejection of God (1 Sam 8:7, 20). The continual moral downfall of the Israelite nation is a proof of God's original warning:

> Where now is your king, that he may save you? Where in all your cities are your rulers, of whom you said, "Give me a king and rulers"? (Hos 13:10 NRSV)

Jesus taught us to pray to God, "let your reign come" (Lk 11:2). The Greek word "reign" or *basileia* occurs about 160 times. In the New Testament the only significant words which occur more often are *God, heaven, Lord, belief* and *Spirit.*[3] *God* and *heaven* both occur in the same phrase, "the reign of *God"* or "the reign of *heaven."* God's reign is a helpful model for our response to suffering. When God came to a suffering earth in the person of Jesus, God responded to that suffering by promoting this reign.

Responding adequately to suffering takes the skills of many people in many disciplines. Some help by teaching. What is God's reign? How can we become members of that reign? How can we promote it? Others help by proclaiming God's reign. Proclaiming God's reign involves working for justice among needy people. It also involves exhorting people to become personally just or "righteous" by affirming Jesus as the means for righteousness. The Greek New Testament word for "justice" *(dikaiosynē)* is also the same word that can be translated "righteous." That is why God's reign includes both individual and communal "justice" or "righteousness." Healing is a third way Jesus promoted God's reign. Sometimes healing is done by command in Jesus' name, but even more frequently by prayer. God who is sovereign is invoked.

In this chapter we will summarize the biblical teachings on *teaching, proclaiming* and *healing* as three basic means of responding to suffering. Usually, when we think of responses to suffering, we remember only the healing types of responses. However, Jesus used all three activities as means to bring in God's reign to this fallen world.

Teaching

This book itself is an example of teaching as a response to suffering. Our desire is to promote God's reign. Ignorance or wrong information can cause unnecessary pain. Warning is one way to educate. Because God is compassionate, we can be compassionate as well by assuming ignorance before we go on to judge someone. How many years did God keep on teaching (and warning) the people of Israel before they were exiled? Over seven hundred years, if we begin with God's warning to Moses. Over two hundred, if we begin with God's warning to Solomon and Jeroboam.[4] Many a prophet wanted a quicker punishment (at least of the other nations!).

The surprise in the account of Jonah is that we are not told until the end why Jonah had been fleeing from the presence of the Lord. Jonah had not been trying to escape God's judgment because of personal sin. He was not without faith that God could fulfill God's word of judgment. What he could not tolerate was God's asking him to predict the enlarging of Israel—and then to accept the forgiveness of its political enemies! He wanted these Assyrians, who invaded Israel, whose god Asshur was a god of war, whom Nahum later denounced for their "endless cruelty," who killed pregnant mothers by ripping out their babies, to be punished to the maximum.[5]

However, God forgave even the Assyrians, when they repented—just as Jonah had feared. For Jonah knew that unlike Asshur, God is "gracious and tender, delaying anger, and abounding in steadfast love, and ready to relent from punishing" (Jon 4:2).

Jesus also taught about the right and wrong reasons to suffer. The Sermon on the Mount is an extended example of what Jesus taught: be forgiving, not unnecessarily angry, reconciling, loyal to your spouse, loving to your enemies, generous, praying, obedient; let God take care of you (Mt 5—7). In effect, some of our suffering on earth can lessen if we obey Jesus' teachings. Jesus also paved the way for ultimate release from death in the resurrection, which became an essential element in the early church's teaching.[6] But some suffering will *increase* if we teach what Jesus taught. When the man healed of his blindness tried to explain his understanding of Jesus' power to heal him, the religious leaders forcibly threw him out (Jn 9:34).

Therefore, one of the first ways we might respond to someone's difficulties is education, if someone's difficulties are caused by not knowing how to live in a godly way. Education takes patience. It is a gradual process. One of the revivals recorded in the Old Testament was caused by education (2 Chron 17:7-10). King Jehoshaphat courageously sought only God. But he went one step further. He sent his own governmental officials and some priests to teach all the people in Judah the content and application of God's law. As a result, the countries surrounding Judah did not begin any wars with Judah.

Jesus had many disciples, but he began with twelve of them (probably as a symbol of his ministry to the twelve tribes of Israel). They were first appointed simply "to be" with him and, as well, to preach and to have authority (Mk 3:14). Not until later were they sent out two by two (Mk 6:7). Jesus waited even longer before he began to teach them about the difficulties that the Messiah must endure (Mk 8:31; Jn 6:60-71). Then he appointed seventy-two others (probably symbolizing the seventy-two elders who received God's Spirit [Num 11:16-29]) whom he also sent out in pairs (Lk 10:1).

Jesus taught in both formal and informal settings.[7] What he taught depended on whom he was teaching. For instance, with the crowds he used parables, which he then explained to his disciples (e.g., Mk 4:33-34). The Holy Spirit continues today to do what Jesus did while on earth: teaching believers all things, even teaching us what to say when we are persecuted (Lk 12:12; Jn 14:26).

Aída teaches her class on "Suffering and Joy in the New Testament" every other year. Inevitably, someone from the class will stop her afterward as did one particular student. He said that his wife had had a miscarriage. This course had helped him cope with the loss of the child. Apparently, the couple became able to focus on supporting each other emotionally, being able to face this loss for what it really was, a suffering which was part of living in a fallen world.

Proclaiming

If teaching *(didaskō)*[8] has to do with causing others to learn, proclaiming or preaching *(keryssō)* has to do with bringing reconciliation to warring factions. An ancient "preacher" was a herald *(kēryx)* or messenger vested with authority, who conveyed the official messages of kings, magistrates, princes or military commanders, or who gave a public summons or demand.[9] Angels are messengers from God, such as the mighty one who proclaimed with a loud voice: "Who is worthy to open the scroll and break its seals?" (Rev 5:2).

The philosopher Philo uses Hermes as an example in his *Embassy to Gaius* XIII. A messenger, like Hermes, "should be very swift-footed, travelling with well-nigh the speed of wings in the zeal which brooks no delay. The news of things profitable should be carried quickly, bad news slowly if it is not permitted to leave it untold." Hermes "assumes the herald's staff *(kērykeion)* as an emblem of covenants of reconciliation, for wars come to be suspended or ended through heralds *(kēryx)* establishing peace; wars where no heralds are admitted create endless calamities both for the assailants and the defenders."

Heralds could bring news of a treaty or reconciliation negotiated by rulers. The apostle Paul builds on this imagery in Romans 10:14-15 when he recalls the importance of preachers being sent, quoting Isaiah 52:7: "How beautiful are the feet of the one bringing good news." From this perspective, proclamation can be seen as bringing reconciliation and peace between warring factions.

The content of the good news ("Repent, for heaven's reign has come near")[10] has two main components. First, we need to understand that each of us is responsible for—is the cause of—some suffering. Each of us sins; we fail to obey all of God's law. Therefore, each of us must "repent." We must recognize that in God's presence we need to change.

Second, we need to welcome God's reign because it has come near.

Thus, reconciliation or peace with God requires self-evaluation and action. God's reign has both a vertical and a horizontal dimension. As we become reconciled to the ruler God, we then become ourselves emissaries of that same ruler. We too must bring good news to the poor, proclaim release to captives and the recovery of sight to the blind, let the oppressed go free. Today is the year of God's jubilee (Lk 4:18-19). We saw from chapter four that Paul "proclaimed" "Christ crucified" (1 Cor 1:23). That proclamation affected his words, teaching, preaching, leadership style—all his actions. Becoming a means of reconciliation, biblically, is certainly not avoiding all suffering at all costs. God's reign is intended to be lived out in this world now, as well as in the world to come.

Whenever we appeal to others to be reconciled with God, we are doing what we can to help them avoid temporal punishment from sin and eternal separation from God. Whenever we speak up on someone's behalf who we think has been unjustly treated, if we remember "repentance" as the first aspect of the good news, we will then evaluate first our own sins and be more merciful with those we are calling "oppressors."

The summer after he finished seminary, Bill worked in West Philadelphia setting up block associations for the presbytery of Philadelphia. Block associations were families in the same neighborhood who were committed to solve their joint problems together. The U.S. was in the aftermath of riots that had torn through its cities in the late 1960s, and Philadelphia, which had not had a cathartic release like Los Angeles and Newark, seethed like a boiling pot. The neighborhood to which Bill was assigned was the territory of a motorcycle gang that had taken over a house directly across from the church building.

A month previous to his arrival, a gang-related murder had been committed. Bill and Herb Greenspan, who was then a seminary student at Westminster, were assigned to visit every house in the neighborhood to see if they could set up block associations. When they began knocking on doors they discovered why there was reluctance.

The blocks appeared to be divided into black and white sides. Each side thought of the other as oppressors.

"Ever since those blacks moved out here," moaned the whites, "this neighborhood has changed. Now I don't let my kids out on the streets. It's not safe. I'd move away if I could afford to, but I can't."

"This is a horrible neighborhood," lamented the blacks. "I saved up my money and moved out here to get a better home for my kids and I can't let them out on the streets—the way those whites look at us—I'm so sorry I came. I'd move away if I could afford to, but I can't."

"You know," Bill and Herb would say, "we were just down at the end of your street and your neighbor said the exact same thing. Look, if you and all the people on this block could get together in some nonthreatening place, in a home or at the church, and just talk about things, about the neighborhood, and hear what your neighbors had to say, would you come?" Overwhelmingly the answer was yes.

Bill and Herb "proclaimed" God's reign by helping these "warring" neighbors to be reconciled to each other. As messengers of God they helped people hear the truth that both white and black neighbors had the same point of view. They further offered them the opportunity to become Christians, which would give them greater unity.

Healing

Healing needs to be one component of a total program to advance God's reign: teaching, proclaiming *and healing*. Jesus taught, proclaimed and cured (Mt 4:23; Lk 9:11). Jesus commanded the Twelve while they were "going" to preach, to heal, to raise the dead, cleanse lepers, cast out demons (Mt 10:7-8; Lk 9:1-2).

One of the dangers that Francis MacNutt perceives in his ministry is the pitfall of people welcoming illness as a gift from God. Illness is never a gift. Illness, whether from physical disease or demonic possession, is something Jesus attacked here on earth. It is a result of sin or demonic activity. It is not God's intention:

I find as soon as I start to talk about praying for healing, someone usually brings up the words of Jesus in the Garden of Gethsemane, "Not my will, but thine be done," with the implication that sickness is probably God's will, and so we should accept it. This wrenches the words of Jesus out of context, for he is praying about his impending crucifixion which, as we have said, is a suffering brought upon him from without, and is not sickness. Why is this Gethsemane passage always brought up instead of the sayings of Jesus that more directly pertain to healing, such as "Cure those in it who are sick and say 'The Kingdom of God is very near to you' " (Lk 10:9)?[11]

In effect, what people are doing here is confusing suffering for Christ's sake with suffering from a fallen world.

The good news, the reign of God that has come near, includes both physical healing and casting out demons. Jesus and his disciples knew there was a difference between curing illnesses and casting out demons (Mk 6:13; Lk 13:32). And after Jesus' resurrection, Jesus' disciples continued to teach, proclaim and heal.

For example, Paul, Timothy, Silas and Luke arrive at Philippi. They begin to teach the women at the place of prayer about God's reign (Acts 16:12-14). Lydia and her household become believers and are baptized. When Paul is harassed by a woman who is demon-possessed, he commands the demon to come out of her (Acts 16:16-18). At Ephesus, as well, Paul teaches, proclaims and heals. He heals people from illnesses and drives out evil spirits (Acts 19:8-12). Two parallel infinitives ("to depart" and "to come out") are used by Luke to describe two different actions: "illnesses to depart from them and evil spirits to come out" (Acts 19:12).

Thus, in this section, we are going to discuss healing and exorcism as two means to promote God's reign. In the next chapter under the heading of "joy" we will go on to look at the healing that comes from healthy and caring interpersonal relationships.

If God's reign begins in the Old Testament, so does healing. The prophets were used by God for some dramatic healings. Elijah heals the son of the widow of Zarephath (1 Kings 17:17-24). Elisha's reputation is international. An Israelite prisoner of war boasts about Elisha, and Naaman, commander of the enemy army of Aram, comes to Elisha to be healed of his leprosy (2 Kings 5:1-19). Jesus' healings are proclaimed so extensively that thousands of people come to follow him wherever he travels.[12] Since the church is the body of Christ (Eph 5:23), it too continues this ministry of healing.

Spiritual Gifts of Healing

In the lists of spiritual gifts Paul inserts several categories that include healing: miracle workers, healings and the gift of faith. "Miracle workers," literally "powers," are mentioned in Paul's letters to Corinth (1 Cor 12:10, 28-29). No one person in the New Testament is described by this title, but we have several examples of persons who did miracles. Jesus, of course, is a miracle worker.[13] (Jesus is a model for *every* spiritual gift.) Paul explains that as an apostle he did "signs and wonders and mighty works" (2 Cor 12:12).

However, the main point of 2 Corinthians is Paul's intent to convince the Corinthians that such supernatural shows are not most important in proving God is present in a particular person. The real proof is a leadership style of humility. Examples of such miracles are physical healing of sickness and casting out demons (Acts 19:11-12). Stephen, who was appointed to make sure the Greek widows were fed, also did great wonders (Acts 6:8). Philip, the evangelist, did great miracles as well. He cast out demons and healed the sick (Acts 8:6-7). The goal of these deeds of power, healing and exorcism is to encourage people to repent (Mt 11:20). Ironically, in the book of Acts those who perform these awesome signs and wonders are later persecuted.[14]

Thus, a miracle worker is someone with the God-given power or strength to perform miracles such as healing and exorcism in order to cause people to repent. As with any spiritual gift, it has its counterfeits. Simon the sorcerer, with his magical tricks, amazed the people at

Samaria, but he himself became amazed by Philip (Acts 8:9-13). Satan can cause miracles too (2 Thess 2:9). Even people who do great deeds of power in the Lord's name will not enter God's eternal reign if they have not been obedient to God (Mt 7:21-23).

A separate gift is the gift of "healings" (1 Cor 12:9, 28, 30). "Healing" *(iama)* may refer to a remedy or medicine—any soothing or pacification—or to the result of a remedy.[15] The noun *iama* is used only in 1 Corinthians and in the plural, "healings." Luke is an example of a physician *(iatros)* who may very well have assisted Paul by giving him remedies for his persistent eye problem.[16] Paul recommended wine as a remedy for Timothy's frequent stomach ailments (1 Tim 5:23).

The related verb *(iaomai)* can add more biblical examples of healing. Jesus healed without remedies by the power of God. Sometimes he touched the diseased ear or tongue or people touched him.[17] Peter and Paul also healed people, sometimes by command, sometimes by prayer and touch.[18] Therefore, a healer is someone who heals by using remedies, medicines or God's power through command, prayer and laying on of hands. Or, better stated, a healer is an instrument of God's power (whether prayer or medicine is used). Who is healed? According to one healer we know, Rocco Rezza, the person in whom God chooses to manifest God's work (Jn 9:3).

Persons with the gift of faith (1 Cor 12:9) also may be healers. Paul explains "faith" as the ability to remove a mountain (1 Cor 13:2). Paul seems to be alluding to Jesus' conversation with Peter and the other disciples (Mk 11:21-25). Jesus talks there about commanding a mountain through a prayer that has faith. Therefore, we can conclude that what Christians popularly call the gift of prayer is probably Paul's "gift of faith." A group of elders is promised this "prayer of faith" (Jas 5:15) as a means of healing. Elijah is one example of a person with the gift of faith (Jas 5:17). The content of faith is of course God's power, not human resolution (1 Cor 2:5).

These spiritual gifts are proofs of God's joy which God gives individuals in order that they may give joy to others by strengthening them spiritually. *Charisma* is a "gift" from the same root as the noun *charis,* "joy," and the verb *chairō,* "I have joy."[19] The intention of these gifts is to demonstrate the variety or diversity of the church yet its unity in the Spirit. The gifts prove our need for interdependence.

When Paul asks: "Do all work miracles? Do all have gifts of healings?" (1 Cor 12:29-30), he uses the negative interrogative: "All do not work miracles, do they? All do not have gifts of healings, do they?"[20] If everyone had every gift, we would no longer need one another. Nevertheless, Christians with gifts of power and healing sometimes expect every genuine Christian to have these same gifts. And Christians without these gifts sometimes declare that no one can have gifts of power and healing. Our spiritual gifts, unfortunately, sometimes become microscopes with which we view the world. We end up seeing everything from one small focus, blinded to the broader view around us.

Healing by Individuals and Elders

What happens when we have a church with many sick people but no one with the gift of healing? First of all, any believer can pray for healing. For instance, King Hezekiah was a devout man near death who in tears prayed for his healing and whom the Lord healed: "I have heard your prayer, I have seen your tears; indeed, I will heal you; on the third day you shall go up to the house of the LORD." God promised Hezekiah that he would live fifteen more years (2 Kings 20:5-6 NRSV; Is 38:2-6). John reminds us of Jesus' promise: "that if anyone might ask for one's self according to [God's] will, he hears us" (1 Jn 5:14). We know that God's will is for healing. Therefore, why should not our prayers include prayers for health? However, at times God wants to hear two or three witnesses to confirm a resolution.[21] In that case, our requests need to be shared with the body of Christ.

Second, the Lord has the appointed leaders of a congregation serve as the representative will of a group.[22] The elders are the two or three witnesses who agree (Deut 19:15). This representative will, the elders together, has the gift of healings that might elsewhere be given to one person, a healer, or to a miracle worker. James gives instructions on how this means of healing may be done, with the purpose of exhorting the Jewish church that, having thrown off all evil deeds, in humility they must receive the implanted word (1:21).

After telling his readers that the Lord is compassionate and merciful but also just to punish those who oppress the poor (Jas 5:7-12), James discusses four topics: suffering, happiness, sickness and deception. Each of these themes has a verb and a pronoun ("any," *tis*). He especially connects the first three themes because each begins in parallel form:

Suffering (v) any *(tis)* among you?

Happy (v) any *(tis)?* (5:13)

Sick (v) any *(tis)* among you? (5:14)

My brothers, if any *(tis)* among you might be deceived (v). (5:19)

A compassionate and merciful God would not only be concerned for justice on the grand scale but also be personally concerned for each person and for the Word to be implanted in each one's everyday affairs.

First, James asks if anyone among his readers is suffering bad things, such as enduring oppressive working conditions (5:4-11). Paul uses the same word *(kakopatheō)* when he refers to his imprisonment, probably the final one before his death (2 Tim 2:9). How can someone endure? James commands that person to continue regularly to pray (present imperative).

Second, James asks if anyone is cheerful *(euthymeō)*. *Euthymeō* comes from *eu* (good) and *thymos* ("soul, spirit, as the principal of life, feeling and thought, esp. of strong feeling and passion").[23] In other words, do you feel happy? Are you in good spirits? As Paul told the other passengers: "And now I urge you *to feel cheerful,* for there will be no loss of life among you, except of the ship" (Acts 27:22). James again commands the happy person to continue regularly to sing *(psallō,* 5:13). *Psallō* originally referred to "plucking off, pulling out, causing to vibrate by touching or twanging." It later came to refer to singing to the accompaniment of a harp.[24]

James certainly does not want people who are happy to hide that fact. If we take James literally, they should even go so far as to sing to the accompaniment of stringed instruments. If we take him metaphorically, when we feel happy we should express our feelings outwardly in some appropriate way. Paul uses *psallō* as a type of prayer to God and of communication to one another: "Be filled in the Spirit, speaking to one another in psalms *(psalmos)* and hymns and spiritual songs, singing and playing *(psallō)* in your heart to the Lord" (Eph 5:18-19). We can learn from Paul's letter that "singing" might be another type of *prayer.*

The first word in James 5:13 for prayer, *proseuchomai,* is a prayer addressed especially to God.[25] The second word in James 5:13 for prayer, *psallō,* is praying in an appreciative way, which helps ourselves and others become more filled with the Holy Spirit. According to Colossians 3:16 it can also help believers teach one another. Being in God's presence is clearly one way to relieve suffering and enjoy good news.

However, when James goes on to write about illness, more than one person must become involved: "Is anyone sick among you?" (5:14). James uses a word for being sick, *astheneō,* which elsewhere in the New Testament refers to having illnesses such as blindness, lameness, paralysis, fever, and eye and stomach ailments. Sometimes these illnesses are chronic or life-threatening.[26] The synonym for "sick" *(astheneō)* is *kamnō* in James 5:15. In the apocryphal writings *kamnō* refers to death or extreme weariness, as if from much labor. Josephus also uses it to refer to the child of Jeroboam who is ill and about to die.[27]

A sick person's answer to illness is not only prayer for oneself. Rather, James instructs that such a person call the elders of the church and that the elders pray over the sick person after having anointed *(aleiphō)* that person with oil *(elaion)* in the name of the Lord. When people pray for their own suffering they should do so, as a habit, over time. The present imperative usually refers to an action done over time. In contrast, the elders need only pray once, since James uses the aorist imperative.[28]

Sick persons must act on their own behalf by calling for the elders, since James commands the call with the aorist *middle* imperative. In other words, the sick person's faith is shown by calling for the elders. Elders should never force their call on a sick person if they are not wanted. Thus, the procedure that James recommends is:

1. The sick person calls the elders.
2. The elders anoint the sick person with oil in the name of the Lord.
3. The elders pray over the sick person.

Anointing with Oil

Why is oil used? James does not explain, but we think the oil in this passage is a symbol of healing or celebration. Olive oil was an everyday commodity. Oil, wine and grain were three prized staples of the ancient Hebrew and Greek societies. Olive oil *(elaion)* was mixed into and poured onto foods, used to light lamps and applied to the skin after a bath or before exercise. Oil was so important that some people could make a living selling it alone. It was also used as a symbol of holiness or dedication and of celebration.

In James it probably did not symbolize holiness or dedication. Usually in the Old Testament the verb *chriō* ("touch the surface of a body slightly")[29] was used when anointing a priest or ruler. The sense of being "set apart" was so great that if a priest were to leave the tent of meeting after he had been anointed with oil, he would die (e.g., Lev 10:7). James uses no modifier in his letter to show that what he has in mind is a special anointing oil.

Olive oil was also a symbol of celebration. Not anointing oneself with oil was a sign of mourning (2 Sam 14:2). Anointing one's face with oil was a pleasant action (Ps 104:15; Eccles 9:8). Anointing the foreheads of one's guests with oil was an honor which Jesus regretted not having received (Lk 7:46; Ps 141:5). In that case, using oil would symbolize restoring the sick person to the "cheerful" state *(euthymeō)* of 5:13. The prayer-vow of faith would then act on that symbol. The elders would indeed believe that God would heal the person.

Olive oil could also be poured over bruises or wounds to quicken healing, as the Samaritan in the parable did, pouring oil and wine on the wounds of the attacked man before he bandaged him (Lk 10:34).[30] In the same way, we might rub a first-aid ointment on a wound today. James may be treating the oil as a healing medicine or a symbol of healing.

The practice of anointing the sick occurs in one other reference in the Bible. Jesus commands the twelve disciples to promote God's reign by healing sick people, raising dead people, cleansing lepers and casting out demons (Mt 10:8). After proclaiming that people should repent, the disciples went on to cast out many demons and anoint with oil many who were sick (Mk 6:12-13).[31]

Probably this is the very practice that James follows in his command to the sick. In that case, prayer for the sick is clearly one way in which God's reign is furthered. Since olive oil is mainly helpful for skin ailments, we find it unlikely that it could have been so helpful for *all* weak people, for Mark tells us "they were healed" (Mk 6:13). While the oil itself perhaps healed some skin infirmities, the key to general healing is that oil is applied "in the name of the Lord," followed by prayer (Jas 5:14). Thus, when the elders anoint a sick person with oil, they may be using the first stage of the healing process, using a natural medicine, while asking for God's full compassionate healing care. With God's sovereign care, natural medicine works to its maximum. The oil can also be a symbol of the healing about to follow. The elders are symbolically telling the sick person, "In the same way as this oil can heal your skin, God has the power to heal any part of your body or spirit." Or, even more specifically, the oil could itself symbolize God as the Divine Healer (Ex 15:26).

Whose Prayer of Faith?

James then promises: "and the prayer of faith will save the one being sick and the Lord will raise that one; and if that one had been doing sins, they will be forgiven to that one. Therefore, keep confessing to one another sins and keep praying in behalf of one another, in order that you may be healed. Much can accomplish a working prayer of a righteous person" (5:15-16).

Whose prayer of faith is this? It is the prayer of the *elders*.

Bill has been seriously ill several times during our marriage, and he has asked the elders of different congregations to come and pray for him. We have noticed that God has responded to all these prayers to some degree. The most dramatic answer came one night when a group of faithful African-American Christians prayed for him. His high fever disappeared in one night. Another group of elders began to ask Bill if healing were possible. Their prayers yielded only minor improvements. The type of prayer that James describes has the strength of a vow, as when Paul cuts his hair at Cenchreae because he was under a vow (Acts 18:18; Jas 5:12).

The faith-full prayer will have two consequences: It will save the one being sick, and the Lord will raise him or her (5:15). *Sōzō* was used in the Bible to refer to "salvation" from death, natural disasters and political oppression. In the New Testament frequently the word was used of "salvation" from eternal death and, sometimes, from sins. To "save" someone was to act on the person's behalf, protecting him or her from a person, thing or event that could destroy the person physically, emotionally or spiritually. Some of the potential causes of death are demons (who cause death of the human personality) and illness. "Save" clearly refers to healing in several New Testament passages.[32] For instance, the woman who has been suffering from hemorrhages for twelve years says to herself: "If only I might touch his garment, I will be healed *(sōzō)"* (Mt 9:21). Luke tells us that Jairus's daughter died. Jesus declares that if Jairus believes, his daughter will be brought back to life ("saved") and she will rise up from the dead (Lk 8:49-55).

Similarly, in James's letter, the person in the continual state of illness (*kamnō* appears as a participle) will also be brought back from death and will rise up from the bed. Possibly the reason James chose to use "save" as opposed to "heal" is that he wants the elders to be instruments of physical *and* spiritual salvation.

James now adds a condition: "and if he [or she] may have been doing sins." James does *not* say, "the prayer of faith will save . . . *because* he [or she] has been doing sins." Again, all illnesses are not necessarily caused by sin. Rather, he uses the subjunctive mood ("may") which is the mood of doubt, indicating hesitating affirmation, conditions not assumed to be true, probability, expectation, something likely to occur. "If" states clearly that the person *may* have sinned. The perfect participle "have been doing" highlights that these sins had been begun in the past and continued over time. In other words, he is not writing about some new or temporary sin. What is the possibility of being forgiven? These sins *"will be* forgiven." James assures the sick person who is about to rise up that any sins will definitely be forgiven. The future indicative tense, unlike the subjunctive, asserts positively what will occur.[33]

James restates his point in the next sentence in chiastic order: salvation from sickness (A), forgiveness of sins (B) (5:15), forgiveness of sins (B), salvation from sickness (A) (5:16). The present imperative highlights the fact that confession of sin must be a continual practice. James now uses the present imperative for *pray* (v. 16) to show that prayer for one another should also be continual. Probably James no longer limits the practice of prayer to the elders. He begins 5:16 with the particle *oun* ("therefore"), a coordinating conjunction, which shows that James is making somewhat of a transition to a new subject.[34]

As well, he writes about "one another." Prayer is not simply vertical (elders for the sick); it is also horizontal. Here is the priesthood of believers in action, confessing publicly what is within *(exomologeō)* and praying prayers of faith for one another. James's use of the present imperative ("pray," *proseuchomai,* 5:13), aorist imperative ("pray," *proseuchomai,* 5:14) and present imperative ("pray," *euchomai,* 5:16) is quite striking, probably indicating that when an individual moves from prayer for oneself, the first step to bring in outside help should be calling the elders.[35] After the elders pray, in themselves symbolizing the whole church, then the whole church itself continues to pray regularly for the sick person.

Ironically, most people wait to ask the elders to come until all else has failed. Sometimes sick people feel that they do not want to impose on busy elders; they may feel that they would be embarrassed if they were not healed; they may feel that prayer by the church at large is sufficient. However, as James 2 points out, faith is obedience. If James commands us to call the elders when our own prayers do not suffice in a continuing illness, then we will be faithless if we do not act on this prescription. Moreover, the elders' prayer is more likely to be effective early in the illness.

In verse 16 James uses "heal" *(iaomai),* the verb form of the spiritual gift of healings, to highlight that "save" (v. 15) also means "heal" (v. 16). Forgiveness of sins has no doubt of fulfillment (v. 15). Healing does have some doubt of fulfillment: "You *may be* healed" (5:16). James uses the aorist passive subjunctive. As we saw, the subjunctive is a mood of doubt. The passive indicates that something will be done to one. Spiritual salvation is always sure. Everyone who believes can be sure he or she will have eternal salvation and rise from death (1 Jn 5:13). Physical healing is possible, even probable, but not absolute. For example, Paul was never healed of his eye condition. He left Trophimus ill in Miletus. Prayer did not help Timothy's stomach ailments.[36]

Effective Prayers

Why can someone be healed? James 5:16 reads literally, "Much can accomplish a working prayer of a righteous person," or "a working prayer of a righteous person can accomplish much." When a righteous person forcefully asks for something (James uses another synonym for prayer, *deēsis),* that working or effective prayer has much strength. Unlike the King James Version's rendering, James's original does not use "man" here. The power is not in the gender but in effective requests. James switches to the singular here even though he has earlier used the plural ("keep confessing," "keep praying"), because he is introducing an illustration:[37] "Elijah was a human with the same nature as we have, and in prayer he prayed in order that it not rain, and it did not rain upon the earth three years and six months; and again he prayed and the heaven gave rain and the earth yielded its fruit" (5:17-18). James highlights what we might doubt: Elijah was a human just like us!

Why did James not cite Elijah's healing the son of the widow at Zarephath (1 Kings 17:17-24)? Instead he cites the events in the midst of which this healing takes place, the drought and rain (1 Kings 17:1-16; 18:1-46). In the same way, as James throughout his letter cites agricultural and natural imagery of growth and lights to symbolize the goodness of God's work, he cites the example of rain for its double significance. The God who has power over and concern for nature also has power over and concern for humans. For instance, the Father of lights is like a sun shower pouring down good and perfect gifts which then result in good fruits. God causes life and growth and nutrition without any movement of turning shadow (1:17-18). Again in 3:17-18, God's wisdom comes from above, resulting in an overabundance of mercy and good fruits and a harvest of righteousness.

So here too James wants, first, to illustrate the power of effective prayer by a miraculous event, the stopping and giving of rain, and, second, to remind readers of the working of God's grace in the world by referring to rain, God's gift to the just and unjust. He alludes to his earlier use of "save" for "heal" in 5:15. A total healing is both physical and spiritual.

Jesus knew that forgiving sins and healing people are both hard to do, forgiveness being the harder: "Which is easier to say to the paralytic, 'Your sins are forgiven,' or to say, 'Rise up and take your mat and walk'?" (Mk 2:9). Jesus does both. Since the church is Jesus' body on earth, it too can do both.

James ends his letter by continuing to write on the theme of sin: "The one having turned a sinner from his way of error will save his life from death and will cover many sins" (5:20). Being able to save someone from spiritual death is a great act indeed. Yes, physical healing is possible, but spiritual healing is greater.

A Different View

That is James's teaching according to our study. But some devout Christians have had their doubts. John Calvin posited:

> The reality of this sign continued only for a time in the Church, the symbol also must have been only for a time. . . . That the gift of healing was temporary, all are constrained to allow, and events clearly prove: then the sign of it ought not to be deemed perpetual. It hence follows, that they who at this day set anointing among the Sacraments [referring to Roman Catholics at extreme unction], are not the true followers, but the apes of the Apostles, except they restore the effect produced by it, which God has taken away from the world for more than fourteen hundred years. So we have no dispute, whether anointing was once a sacrament; but whether it has been given to be so perpetually. This latter we deny, because it is evident that the thing signified has long ago ceased.[38]

Even though Calvin is renowned for his exegetical sensitivity, here he gives an experiential argument: "It is evident that the thing signified has long ago ceased." In other words, Calvin argues, I have never seen the Lord heal someone through the prayer and anointing of a group of elders, therefore, *despite* what James teaches, I will not believe that God can heal today.[39] Calvin has "no dispute" that healing has occurred. And if demonstrable healing were evident to him, he would believe.

Today the Holy Spirit has potently returned the experiential level which Calvin challenged. Reports of healings come from China, South America and other areas, from the Order of St. Luke in the mainline churches, from the charismatic movement in both mainline and independent churches. Everywhere are more and more Christians who do think the spiritual gifts of healing continue today. Some, such as Emily Gardiner Neal, Francis MacNutt and Agnes Sanford, write about physical healing from disease. Others, such as Ruth Carter Stapleton and some in the Order of St. Luke, write about the inner healing of the psyche, the healing of memories and of bitterness. Some believe that no medicines should be used at all. Others believe that God interacts in all human health, using medicine, prayer, even death.[40]

If the experience is evident in the church today, the rite needs to be evident as well. James 5:13-18 teaches us what that rite is and to whom it belongs. It does not belong to glib and glittering televangelists. It is the gift of God to the collective eldership in real, not fast-food commuter, churches in authentic workaday communities. The biblical writers, like James and Paul, were not remote. They were pastors dealing with daily pain and suffering, and they passed on God's message of healing from a true perspective of divine working and human pain. James 5:13-18 provides God's answer for healing through the given eldership of each Christian body.

How do we conclude? We see no suggestion in Paul's or James's letters that the gift of healing was to be considered as any different than, for instance, the gift of teaching. If we take James's advice to be humbly obedient (chap. 3), why not take his advice to pray for healing (chap. 5)? Healing is available today through believing healers, prayers, miracle workers and elders. Bill's own experience with prayer for healing is very similar to that of Francis MacNutt: "The most important thing I have learned in the past few years about praying for healing is that *usually* people are not completely healed by prayer, but they are *improved.*"[41]

Bill was hospitalized in 1989 with complications after an operation to save his life. He asked his elders to come weekly to anoint him with oil and pray for him. Each time they came, he would slightly improve. Over two months he became well enough to leave the hospital. He is now able to live a physically normal life. However, he is not completely "healed." He must still rest every afternoon and watch his diet. Chronic conditions seem to be the most difficult to heal. Jesus seems to speak about a similar situation in Mark 9:14-29. The boy who has had an evil spirit from childhood has a chronic condition which the disciples cannot remedy. Jesus replies: "This kind is not able to come out except by prayer" (Mk 9:29).[42]

In addition, Jesus would pray for the means, not just the end result. For example, after Jesus saw the crowds helpless as sheep without a shepherd, he did not tell the disciples to pray, "God, help the crowd"; he told them to pray for the means to help them, for more workers (Mt 9:36-38). MacNutt recommends that prayer and medical analysis should work hand in hand.[43] As the doctor would explain what was needed next, in order for Bill to heal, the elders would pray for that need, until finally he was released from the hospital.

On the other hand, during a service of healing, Aída and another elder prayed for a woman with scars on her uterus. The doctor feared her fetus might attach to one of these scars. At the very moment of prayer she felt warmth, but she did not say anything. Three months later she contacted us with news of her safe delivery of a healthy child. We can pray with full confidence that God *can* heal people, through prayer and also with helpful medicines, but God may not choose to heal some specific person. We do not know why. However, in many, many instances we have witnessed the improvement of people's conditions. As with spiritual salvation, where one is either being saved or being killed (2 Cor 2:15), so too with physical salvation: It is better to be "improving" than it is to be getting worse.

Many times, though, we will credit healing to everyone or everything else rather than God. Our problem is that we seem to allow ourselves only two competing categories: miracle or nature. We think we must either be miraculously healed (completely and permanently) *or* healed through natural means. We are always asking God for a sign, a *miracle*. What should be more *natural* than that the God who created nature should work in, over and through nature to bring about God's will? So let us pray, not expecting a "miracle," but rather expecting what is natural, that the God who created this world is still capable of working through it. The line between "miracle" and "natural" for God is artificial, and so it should be for us.

Casting Out Evil Spirits

The same type of thinking which questions spiritual healing also questions exorcism, summoning God's power over the powers of evil and healing people from the ravages of occupation by the powers of evil. Demons have been mentioned in the Bible since Saul became possessed by one (1 Sam 16:14). And they are in evident operation through the lifetimes of Jesus and Jesus' disciples. Exorcism is one aspect of the healing process, as we saw earlier, one component of a total program to advance God's reign.[44]

In the same way that some believers do not think spiritual healing continues today, some also doubt exorcism. Rudolf Bultmann gave a classic description of this post-Enlightenment assumption in his 1951 Shaffer Lectures at Yale University Divinity School and Cole Lectures at Vanderbilt University:

> The whole conception of the world which is presupposed in the preaching of Jesus as in the New Testament generally is mythological; i.e., the conception of the world as being structured in three stories, heaven, earth and hell; the conception of the intervention of supernatural powers in the course of events; and the conception of miracles, especially the conception of the intervention of supernatural powers in the inner life of the soul, the conception that men can be tempted and corrupted by the devil and possessed by evil spirits. This conception of the world we call mythological because it is different from the conception of the world which has been formed and developed by science since its inception in ancient

Greece and which has been accepted by all modern men. . . . Modern science does not believe that the course of nature can be interrupted or, so to speak, perforated, by supernatural powers.[45]
In the U.S., this same view was prevalent until the movie and book *The Exorcist* came out in 1971, becoming a box-office hit and literary bestseller. The everyday person, even in a so-called scientific society, evidences eagerness to learn about evil spirits. And a lot has been discovered. Now, even our local police force is being trained to recognize demonic activity, as one aspect of law enforcement. In the Philippines, in South America, across the United States, occult activity has been discovered to be epidemic. It had been thriving in secret, but worldwide media popularity has brought it to light.

Even though *The Exorcist* is about demonic possession, the ideas in it are not always biblical. *The Exorcist* is, of course, a work of fiction. Its author, William Peter Blatty, was educated in Jesuit schools and at Roman Catholic Georgetown University. The premise of the book can be observed in these two quotations from it, the first one quoted by Blatty from a book on witchcraft:

The demoniacal form of possession is usually thought to have had its origin in early Christianity; yet in fact both possession and exorcism pre-date the time of Christ. The ancient Egyptians as well as the earliest civilizations of the Tigris and the Euphrates believed that physical and spiritual disorders were caused by invasion of the body by demons. The following, for example, is the formula for exorcism against maladies of children in ancient Egypt: "Go hence, thou who comest in darkness, whose nose is turned backwards, whose face is upside down. Hast thou come to kiss this child? I will not let thee. . . ."

And then those exorcists . . . Karras frowned. They often themselves became the victims of possession. He thought of Loudun. France. The Ursuline Convent of nuns. Of four of the exorcists sent there to deal with an epidemic of possession, three—Fathers Lucas, Lactance and Tranquille—not only became possessed, but died soon after, apparently of shock. And the fourth, Pere Surin, who was thirty-three years old at the time of his possession, became insane for the subsequent twenty-five years of his life.[46] The idea being implied here is that demonic evil precedes the idea of good. Evil is somehow the reality in the world, good a later idea to counteract it. Evil is primal, a priori and exceedingly powerful.

As anyone can see from the ending of *The Exorcist,* the demon is not cast out by the ritual or by commands in God's name. It is enticed out by the lure of possessing a priest. It is tricked out. The commands in God's name are not powerful enough to move it. This is what gives *The Exorcist* its terror: that *good* is not powerful enough to overrule evil!

The Exorcist is fiction. On the other side is Dr. Kurt E. Koch with his studies and particularly his casebook, *Christian Counseling and Occultism.* Koch was a minister and psychotherapist who for twenty-five years specialized in treating occult phenomena. At the outset of his study he observes:

> Under this view of things it should become theologically impossible to publish informative literature with such titles as: *Under the Spell of the Devil* or *Powers of Darkness.* This much speaking about demons can, in the case of unstable psychic constitutions, induce demonic enslavement. Out of the New Testament we have only a positive premise and no negative regarding this enigmatic kingdom of occultism, namely, the premise that Christ also holds the last decisive word in this labyrinth of unsolved questions. Christ is the "end of the demons." This fact is clearly testified by the verbal usage of the early church, which spoke of only *One* Lord and Master, the Lord Jesus Christ.
>
> In connection with our study it must be clear in advance that the proclamation of the Gospel is the premise of every assertion about the domain of occultism. The herald shout that Christ is the Victor over all secret powers and dark rulerships spells the dominant focus, the Christo-centric presupposition to this study.[47]

Koch says that possession or oppression is most likely to come to:

1. People who have dabbled with mediums in seances or with other forms of the occult.

2. People who have gone to shepherds or other purveyors of so-called white magic for healing.

All spiritualistic activity leaves psychical residue on the person involved. For example, Koch observes, a young man was conjured by a shepherd and thereby factually received healing of an organic disease. However, from that time on he had manic attacks, blasphemous thoughts against God and Christ and an abnormal sexual depravity.[48]

Koch observes that Christians have immunity from possession. Psychologist T. K. Oesterreich quotes possessed persons who in the presence of missionaries shout out, "I'll have nothing to do with that one," which is, of course, in direct contrast to the insidious invitation to do battle of the demon in *The Exorcist*. He also observes that Christian South Africans were not subject to possession epidemics and only Christians who had fallen back in heathenism became possessed. Finally, he quotes a possessed woman who was appointed to take pestilence to a Christian village but upon reaching the village suddenly froze in terror and cried:

Look there; there he stands, the God Jesus with outstretched arms, protecting His people like a shepherd His lambs! Back! Go back!

He is a great God! I can go no farther. If I advance, I will die!

Oesterreich also gives the history of a possessed woman who converted to Christianity and "the demon vanished while it explained, 'that is no place for me!' "[49]

Though Oesterreich is quoted continually as an authority in *The Exorcist,* none of these affirmative quotations appear—only his creepy descriptions of the phenomena and the constant blasphemies aimed at Christ. Rather than the prolonged struggle of *The Exorcist,* this is the kind of effective exorcism Oesterreich reports:

On Sumatra and Nias the Christians have had the courage over against possessed persons calmly to command in the name of Christ that the evil spirit depart, for it was a matter of fact to them that then the demon would leave the poor man. And when he had departed, they made no fan-fare about the matter. They had the firm trust in the mighty Jesus that He would manage His enemies. Koch credits a revival and pristine Christian lives and observes, "no wonder that genuine exorcisms occurred there."[50] Resistance, of course, has been observed. The possessed hates communal prayers, flips the Bible into a corner, has bursts of fury, of anger and of blasphemy. But even when the demon resists as in Mark 9:29 and Jesus observes to his disciples, "this kind cannot be driven out by anything but prayer," the end result is the same. Jesus rebukes his disciples for their little faith (Mk 9:19, 23). For if they had sufficient faith (mustard-seed size), they could move mountains!

And the approach *The Exorcist* takes should be rebuked as well. For the name of Christ is *all-powerful,* and before him *all* knees will bow!

Personal Encounters

We ourselves saw demon possession mainly as a theoretical possibility until we encountered the real-life situation. Demon possession is not something hard to recognize; any sensitive Christian can easily sense the strong presence of evil. Aída remembers when she was a community organizer. She had heard of a nearby spiritualist but had never met her. One day she sat alone in the office working. She heard no sound, but she felt a strong sense of evil, and she knew at that moment that the spiritualist must have entered. Aída stood up and looked over the divider wall. There she was: a middle-aged woman with a hard-looking face.

Several years afterward, Bill was involved in a summer urban ministry. Among his teammates was a college student who claimed to be a Christian but who did not see himself as a sinner in need of repentance before God. After a time, this young man began to predict disasters every time the team began to pray. Late one night, disturbed by his lack of communal concern and refusal to pray, his housemates went to confront him and found him chanting by his window while his unsuspecting roommates tossed in fitful sleep. They called his name. As he turned, his eyes opened in a malevolent glare, and he rushed forward, brushing larger and stronger college men aside as he pushed past them. They found him outside, and the minister in charge commanded him to choose God or Satan. Bowling over backward, he passed out. When he revived he seemed a different person, gentle and normal. Eating with him a week afterward, Bill learned that he had been led to Christ at a secular Midwestern campus, but, while believing in Jesus, he had doubted the existence of evil. Standing by a lake on campus, he asked the devil to show himself real if he indeed was real. At that moment he felt as if someone had poured ice into him, as if he had made a grave error but was helpless to rescind it or restore himself. In that condition he came to the urban ministry team.

A third incident occurred when Bill was a campus minister. One college student began gathering what he called a "family" about him. At home in New York City he had been introduced to a demon and had learned to summon it by writing its name on a paper, burning the four corners and calling it by name. At first he enjoyed the notoriety that came from using the strange powers the demon gave him, most notably the prediction of a serious car accident involving students, which gave him enormous respect on campus. But as the demon came more and more to take over his personality, he became terrified of the evil presence within him and tried to remove that demon by himself. Unbeknownst to the unsuspecting "family," he summoned the demon and sought freedom. He was seized by a fit, destroying his dorm room, becoming very ill—and all over campus the "family members" experienced seizures, the degree of severity in direct proportion to their length of time in the "family." At this point he asked a Christian on the dorm floor to ask God to remove the demon. Bill, as chaplain, was sought out and we met with many other Christians for prayer in the basement of the building where the deliverance was being done. With the guidance of the chaplain of a nearby psychiatric institution, this demon was cast out by the Christian students enlisted by the possessed student. Dozens of us heard and Bill saw the fury as the possessed man threatened the others by swinging about a very heavy cross. We saw one other minister, who did not believe in demons, become temporarily insane.

In both incidents of removal, the possessed person was released by a word of command. Both, we learned, had invited the devil to enter them, in the same manner as people might invite the Lord Jesus to enter them. Jesus' message had been "Repent, for God's reign is at hand." Repentance is absolutely crucial for someone to be Christian.

Similar to the New Testament events, both possessed men became unusually strong physically and spiritually negative toward Christ. Both collapsed as soon as the demon left. People who doubt the devil's existence or who doubt God's power to drive out evil do best to stay away. Psychological dissonance between what they believe is true and stark reality may drive them temporarily insane. In the same way, the sons of Sceva were overpowered and wounded when they tried to remove an evil spirit "by the Jesus whom Paul proclaims" (Acts 19:13). Jesus had warned that an empty house is no protection (Mt 12:44-45). Only being filled by the Holy Spirit will protect one. In both incidents the possessed person was released by a word of command: "Come out in the name of Jesus Christ!" (Acts 16:18).[51]

Summary

Responding to suffering is a mammoth task. We have chosen to tackle it by focusing on suffering as one way to understand the promotion of God's reign. Jesus, as God incarnate, is described as teaching, proclaiming and healing. And Jesus' disciples can use these categories to orient their own response. But before any of us take action, we need lovingly to observe each individual case so that we may learn how best to respond. A warning, an explanation—that was how Jesus began. Teaching can give sound information when needed.

Being God's messenger also entails bringing reconciliation to warring factions by model and by word. Doing what one can to heal illnesses and cast out demons is not an unusual activity; it is one aspect of promoting God's reign in this world. God has equipped the church to act on these challenges by giving us teachers, preachers, miracle workers, healers, prayers and elders—diverse people with one goal, to glorify God's name.

Moving

Two unmatched socks,
one brown and one black.
The black one is shorter
like the pile of boxes dwindling in the hall.
Dust in the cracks we never did clean,
clean now of everything but sunlight.
The second-to-last truckload pulls away.
I reach for the last ceramic pot,
fingers clumsy from exhaustion,
priest of the packing ritual,
benedictor of the boxes,
high liturgist of the newspaper.
Its shattering tells the true tale,
for like movers the doctors draw the sheets.
And we are marked for transit,
three jigsaw pieces of our home
to be reassembled in another town
in another time.

WILLIAM DAVID SPENCER, 1990

7

MYSTERY

*W*hen Bill was in a hospital several years ago for two and a half months, he outstayed fifteen other roommates. They were very different from one another. The first was a man in his early sixties, near retirement, who had reared foster children all his life—a life of giving to people who could not give back to him. He had had an industrial accident and was down with phlebitis and pneumonia as well as an injured leg. Another was a young French entrepreneur who had picked up malaria in Africa. Another was a lobsterman with a ruptured disc. Another was a builder who had had an eye accident with a grass cutter. A number were diabetics who were losing more and more control of their extremities, developing wounds that would

not heal for months. Then there was the young Spanish man hurt on
the job, and the executive whose expenses in his new home business
had caused his insurance to lapse and who was now down with pneumonia that would not heal—and on they went!

They were all different, but they all had one thing in common. They
all asked the same question: "Why me?" All of them said, in effect,
"I'm a good person. Why did this have to happen to me?"

This made us think of the old Sidney Poitier and Bill Cosby movie
Uptown Saturday Night in which Richard Pryor plays the sleazy detective Sharp-Eye Washington. Poitier is in a place where he shouldn't
have been and has his wallet stolen. He cannot go to the police, so with
his last bit of cash he hires Sharp-Eye Washington. Immediately that
crooked detective makes off with his money. Poitier pursues and ac-
costs him. "I trusted you!" he complains. "How could you cheat me?"

Sharp-Eye replies, " 'Why me?' Why *not* you, brother?"

Well, long before any of us were around, the great man Job asked
the same question of God: "Why me?" And God seems to have given
Job a similar reply, when in the midst of his suffering Job tried to
make sense of what happened.

So far we have looked at many clear biblical reasons for suffering:
our world is fallen, sin is punished, promoters of God's reign may be
persecuted and growth can be painful. In this chapter we learn that
*we do not always discover in this world why a specific righteous per-
son has suffered.*

A Wrong Response Is Corrected

The book of Job is an extended dialogue between friends dealing with
a problem: If God blesses the righteous and punishes the wicked (Prov
3:33-35; 10:25), then if someone is not blessed, that person must be
wicked. Job's three friends cannot think beyond this one reason for
suffering—punishment. In every conversation, they always go back to
this one principle: Job must have sinned, since he is suffering. Eliphaz
the Temanite asks in every one of his three speeches:

Think now, who that was innocent ever perished? Or where were the upright cut off? (Job 4:7)[1]

The wicked writhe in pain all their days, through all the years that are laid up for the ruthless. (15:20)

Is not your wickedness great? There is no end to your iniquities. (22:5)

Then Eliphaz directly accuses Job of economic oppression, insensitivity to the poor, the widow and the orphan (22:6-11).

Bildad the Shuhite begins more directly in his first speech but ends with a more abstract approach:

If you are pure and upright, surely then [the Almighty] will rouse himself for you and restore to you your rightful place. (8:6)

Surely the light of the wicked is put out, and the flame of their fire does not shine. (18:5)

How then can a mortal be righteous before God? How can one born of woman be pure? (25:4)

Zophar the Naamathite completes the three-fold witness of these elders:

If iniquity is in your hand, put it far away, and do not let wickedness reside in your tents. Surely then you will lift up your face without blemish; you will be secure, and will not fear. (11:14-15)

Do you not know this from of old, ever since mortals were placed on earth, that the exulting of the wicked is short, and the joy of the godless is but for a moment? (20:4-5)

Job agrees with his friends' understanding of suffering. Job himself notes: "Does not calamity befall the unrighteous, and disaster the workers of iniquity?" (31:3).

Job's friends are correct. What they say is true. However, their advice simply is not true in Job's case. They are correct in their understanding that God does reward those people whom God loves with long life and material blessings:

The fear of the LORD is the beginning of wisdom, and the knowledge of the Holy One is insight. For by me your days will be multi-

plied, and years will be added to your life. (Prov 9:10-11 NRSV)
This promise for long life extends even to children who respect their
father and mother, a promise from one of the Ten Commandments
(Ex 20:12). If "the fear of the LORD prolongs life, . . . the years of the
wicked will be short" (Prov 10:27 NRSV; 11:19). As well, "The LORD
does not let the righteous go hungry, but he thwarts the craving of the
wicked" (Prov 10:3 NRSV; 13:25).

Righteous believers who are generous with their income will be
generously taken care of by God:

Honor the Lord from your wealth
and from the first of all your profit;
and your storehouses will overflow with abundance
and your wine-vats will burst with wine. (Prov 3:9-10)

Giving God from the first of one's profit results not only in similar
future profit but in an abundance of return. In the New Testament
Paul continues this theme. For example, he reminds the Corinthians,
after quoting Psalm 112:9, that "the One providing seed to the one
sowing and bread for food will supply and multiply your seed and
increase the harvest of your righteousness" (2 Cor 9:10). God supplies
both "seed" and "righteousness," material provisions and spiritual
provisions. Even as this same Paul could write about God providing
for material needs, he could also write, even to the same church, that
he endured "sleeplessness many times, hunger and thirst, abstention
from food many times, cold and nakedness" (2 Cor 11:27). God does
promise at least enough food and shelter for our basic needs (Lk 12:29-
31).

If the end result is provision, the ways to that end may be rocky.
As David writes:

Many are the misfortunes of the righteous,
but from them all the Lord will deliver them. (Ps 34:19)

David wrote this psalm when he feigned madness after seeing Ahime-
lech the priest. David might be referring to the events recorded in
1 Samuel 21, which recounts his escaping Saul, who is trying to kill

him because he fears David wants to rob him of his kingship. David has no safe place to go and pretends to be mad before King Achish so that he will not be killed. He uses a play on words, *rabbôṯ rāʻôṯ* or "many misfortunes," to bring out the burden of adversities in his own life.

Eliphaz, Bildad and Zophar may especially have had in mind such truths as the ones contained in these proverbs:

Poverty and disgrace are for the one who ignores instruction,

but one who heeds reproof is honored. (Prov 13:18 NRSV)

Misfortune pursues sinners,

but prosperity rewards the righteous. (Prov 13:21 NRSV)

Job has misfortune; therefore, his friends conclude, he must be a sinner. Many people consider the book of Job to be an early book, possibly occurring during the patriarchal period.[2] In that case Job's friends may not have had these specific Davidic and Solomonic writings before them. However, the same truths had been communicated during the patriarchal years. Because people were so evil, God destroyed them with a flood, all except Noah's family (Gen 6:11-22). Abram and Lot were so materially blessed they could no longer dwell near each other (Gen 12:2; 13). Jacob's flocks did so well in breeding that Laban and his sons began to resent him (Gen 31:1-2). Joseph succeeded wherever he was: overseeing Potiphar's estates, overseeing the chief jailer's prisoners, overseeing Egypt's preparation for famine.[3] The Israelites were oppressed by the new Egyptian ruler because he envied and feared their success in numbers and power (Ex 1:8-10).

Why did Hitler's Germany choose the Jews to persecute? The hardworking German Jews had succeeded financially because they were industrious, communal and mutually supportive, forging out a better standard of living than many of their "Aryan" peers. Envy and greed—wanting to have for free what the Jews had gained by toil—fed into the motivation to persecute, just as they had motivated the Egyptians in ancient times.

The righteous may be rewarded with temporal blessings, but temporal benefits do not prove one is righteous, nor does a lack of temporal benefits prove one is *not* righteous. (Not all truths can be reversed.) Abram and Sarai had to wait a century for one child (Gen 21:5). Lot was taken by neighboring kings from Sodom and Gomorrah and later lost everything he had (Gen 14:12; 19:16-29). Jacob had to leave his closest family in fear of his life (Gen 27:41-45). Joseph succeeded, but in prison, after being almost killed by his own family! Because God blessed the Israelites, they were ruthlessly oppressed by the Egyptians.

One observation comes out clearly in the book of Job. Job is blameless. Job is not "tested" in the sense of "purged" of his own evil. Eliphaz suggests: "How happy is the one whom God reproves; therefore do not despise the discipline of the Almighty" (Job 5:17 NRSV). However, God declares three times that Job is completely righteous. The narrator begins: "[Job] was perfect and upright and he feared God and turned aside from evil" (1:1). God declares: "There is no one like [Job] on the earth, a perfect and upright man fearing God and he turns aside from evil" (1:8; 2:3).

Job was someone perfect or wholesome, completely mature spiritually. He walked a straight path toward pleasing God because he revered God, and he never turned off that path to follow any temptation of evil. Job helped the poor, was sympathetic with those suffering, just with his servants and moral with all:

I delivered the poor who cried,
    and the orphan who had no helper.
The blessing of the wretched came upon me,
    and I caused the widow's heart to sing for joy.
I put on righteousness, and it clothed me;
    my justice was like a robe and a turban.
I was eyes to the blind,
    and feet to the lame.
I was a father to the needy,
    and I championed the cause of the stranger.

I broke the fangs of the unrighteous,
   and made them drop their prey from their teeth. (29:12-17 NRSV)
Did I not weep for those whose day was hard?
   Was not my soul grieved for the poor? (30:25 NRSV)
Even though he was wealthy, he never trusted in his wealth. He never
was secretly enticed to worship other gods. He never rejoiced at the
downfall of his enemies (31:9-40). Years later when God spoke to
Ezekiel (14:14, 20), Job was grouped with Noah and Daniel as one of
three exemplary righteous people.

Job's three friends were silent for one whole week upon first seeing
Job, because his suffering was so great (2:13). Yet Job called them
"worthless physicians" who "whitewash with lies," "miserable comfor-
ters are you all." "If you would only keep silent, that would be your
wisdom!"[4] Apparently Job thought one week of silence was not
enough! Because they thought Job must have sinned, they had no
empathy over time for him. All they had was contempt for his misfortune (12:5).

God agreed with Job even at the end. God vindicated Job before
his so-called friends:

My wrath is kindled against [Eliphaz] and against [Bildad and
Zophar]; for you have not spoken of me what is right, as my servant
Job has. Now therefore take seven bulls and seven rams, and go to
my servant Job, and offer up for yourselves a burnt offering; and
my servant Job shall pray for you, for I will accept his prayer not
to deal with you according to your folly; for you have not spoken
of me what is right, as my servant Job has done. (42:7-8 NRSV)

Aaron and his sons needed only one bull and two rams to be conse-
crated or made holy (Ex 29:1). These fellows needed seven times the
sacrifices because of their great error. And ironically God gave only
to Job the prerogative to bring about their forgiveness.

A Right Response Is Affirmed
The young Elihu, son of Barachel, has a mysterious place in this

dialogue. He is not reprimanded by God. Job never has the opportunity to answer his comments.[5] Elihu restrains himself until finally he
blurts out six chapters' worth of advice! Elihu agrees with everyone
else: God does repay people "according to their deeds" (Job 34:11).
However, he does not dwell upon whether Job has been unrighteous.
Instead, he focuses upon Job becoming unrighteous now:

> Beware! Do not turn to iniquity;
>
> because of that you have been tried by affliction. (36:21 NRSV)

Elihu also refocuses Job's sight onto the greatness of God:

> Surely God is great, and we do not know him;
>
> the number of his years is unsearchable. (36:26 NRSV)

God "gives songs in the night" and "teaches us more than the beasts
of the earth" (35:10-11 RSV). Elihu, though, is wrong when he claims
that

> surely God does not hear an empty cry, nor does the Almighty
> regard it. How much less when you say that you do not see him,
> that the case is before him, and you are waiting for him! (35:13-14
> NRSV)

"We cannot draw up our case because of darkness" (37:19 NRSV).
God "does not regard any who are wise in their own conceit" (37:24
NRSV).

God does hear the cry of Job. God hears his case. God regards even
those who are unwise. Even Elihu was not aware of how responsive
God is. But God's response is to question Job: "Who is this obscuring
counsel with murmurings without knowledge?" (38:2). God apparently
perceives Job's comments to be mere ignorant mutterings which
eclipse true wisdom. God then proceeds to describe God's greatness.
God is the One who not only created and maintains the world but even
takes care of the wildest, remotest animals:

> Who provides for the raven its prey,
>
> when its young ones cry to God,
>
> and wander about for lack of food?
>
> Do you know when the mountain goats give birth?

Do you observe the calving of the deer? (38:41—39:1 NRSV)
God has the tenderest concern for lives that humans do not even know
exist. God also has created beasts of great power: the war horse whose
"majestic snorting is terrible," the eagle which makes its home on a
high rocky crag, the hippopotamus whose limbs are "like bars of iron"
and Leviathan whose back is made of rows of shields.[6]

Even though Job has had a personal relationship with Almighty
God, in contrast, he feels that what he has had previously has been
only a second-hand knowledge of God. He replies to God by rephras-
ing God's own question and describing himself: "Who is this veiling
counsel without knowledge?" (42:3). Job deletes the insulting "murmurings" or "mutterings" and replaces God's "obscuring" or "spreading darkness" (38:2) with a less strong term "veiling" or "covering."
Yet he does agree he was ignorant and unwise. He concludes:

By the hearing of the ear I heard of you,

but now my eye sees you;

because of this I despise myself,

and I grieve with dust and ashes. (42:5-6)

Job feels undone (another translation for "despise") in God's presence.
No matter how mature and straight he has been, in God's perfect
presence he has to repent. And when Job is in God's presence, somehow the whole question of how a righteous person can suffer becomes
meaningless.

A Temporary Question

In our limitation as humans, we may not be able to answer the question of why suffering has come to one righteous person and not to
another. However, remembering and focusing upon God's nature and
dwelling in God's presence will bring us to the attitude we need to
maintain and which, itself, will help maintain us.

God is compassionate and merciful and sovereign and just. We need
to *trust* that God is good even in the midst of adversity. The mystery
is that when we are in God's presence, then the very question we are

now asking is no longer necessary. Since while we are on this earth we are not completely in God's presence—"we know only in part," "we see in a mirror, dimly" (1 Cor 13:9-12)—we cannot fully understand this answer. The introduction to the book of Job mentions the war or conflict in heaven, the accuser's desire to test Job's faith. However, Job is never told about that by God. All that Job knew, as described by our narrator, is that when he entered God's presence he no longer needed to ask his question.

"We have just learned of the home-going of your little girl and are deeply saddened and feel for you in your great sorrow," wrote the Bowery Mission director to Bill's grieving family at Carol's death. "We shall always remember her and her sweet testimony and musical talent. We cannot understand this sudden and tragic termination of a life so young and beautiful and full of promise." That a child so sweet and full of goodness should die is baffling. Its mystery has confounded the greatest theologians. "The Lord has certainly inflicted a severe and bitter wound in the death of our infant son," mourned the great John Calvin, though he knew fully well that God is love and that every good gift comes from God (Jas 1:17). To our skewed, sinful human vision that sees only in part (1 Cor 13:12) some of our suffering will remain an inexplicable mystery to us until God wipes all the blinding sin from our eyes and, made perfect in heaven, we finally see all clearly. For now our ultimate concern when we find that asking "Why does this happen?" fails is substituting the question "So, what can I do?"

Job prayed for his inadequate counselors; the Lord restored to him a new family and an extended estate (42:10-13). Job lost ten children and he regained ten. Three of those new children were daughters who are the only children mentioned by name and who, contrary to Jewish practice, received inheritances along with the brothers (42:13-15).

Not until this year did Aída realize that for Mother Spencer she was like one of Job's second set of daughters. How did Job feel about those first children? Did the second set really replace them? The text does not say. But Aída has no doubt that she is a second daughter, in a

sense replacing her mother-in-law's first daughter, Carol. Almost every week now her mother-in-law accidentally calls her Carol, although
she knows she is Aída. Aída is treated with gratitude that far out-
weighs her own grace. She is a new daughter by marriage. Her mother-
in-law always appreciates and speaks well of her daughter Carol. But
she no longer is overwhelmed by the tragedy of her death. Aída is not
Carol, but she is a welcome substitute appreciated for her own sake.

In theory the possibility of having ten new children replace ten
former ones seems grotesque. How can any human being be replaced?
In practice, no human being can be reincarnated in another human.
Yet a substitute can help one turn to the present and to the future,
away from being engulfed by regrets of the past.

Wrong and Right Responses Today

Job shouts out to his friends: "Will you plead the case for God? Will
it be well with you when he searches you out?" (13:8-9 RSV). When
Job's friends tried to plead God's case, even God was disgusted with
them.[7] We too should not reduce all the causes for suffering to one.
Correct diagnosis must precede response. Sometimes, however, diagnosis should not be shared. When you are not sure what to say, shut
up! Be silent, empathetic and loving. Even Job's misled friends sat
with him in mourning seven days and seven nights without speaking.
And we don't need to defend God. Let a person question God! God
can defend God's own actions!

Because this world is fallen, humans, even good Christians, suffer.
Sometimes the appropriate question might be why we do *not* suffer
more. Why *not you,* brother or sister? Those who live a life displeasing
to God may suffer the ramifications of their own sin. Those who strive
to advance God's reign will suffer resistance from those who hate the
faith or from the supposedly religious. The attempt to become more
holy may result in pain. However, the Bible does not tell us why a
particular righteous person might suffer. Yes, we do know that Job
was given an opportunity to prove his faith in God. But ultimately the

answer to Job's pleadings came only in God's presence. Thus, all problems with suffering begin and end at the same place: who is God and what is God like? God is love. God is just. God is sovereign yet concerned for each of us. We need to remember this.

The book of Job is one more reminder to us not to entice people into becoming believers by promising them a hassle-free life. Rather, we need to invite people into God's reign because *God* is the one reigning. There is no one or nothing more trustworthy than the living God.

Job is also a reminder to us that we must not evaluate people's belief by their evident success, nor should we enjoy the difficulties which suddenly come upon the "successful." If someone should suddenly be caught in a great sin, we should take the occasion as an opportunity to assess our own life. Could we too commit such a sin if we are not careful? We have noticed that when people overwork, they seem predisposed to some illness or sin. Some people get colds or other health problems, others become irritable, others overeat or undereat, others might steal, others might regress to homosexual behavior, others might become fearful and refuse to change, others might commit adultery. These illnesses or sins are still displeasing to God, even if they are predispositions. For the person watching they are a reminder that any one of us can fall if we are not careful.

Job's three elders "fell" in the very process of counseling Job! Might they have envied Job's great success and favor all along? Why did they travel, possibly a great distance, to see him?[8] The narrator does tell us that when they saw Job they wept aloud and threw dust upon their heads in mourning (2:11-13). But as soon as they opened their mouths, they began to accuse him: "Think now, who that was innocent ever perished?" (4:7 NRSV). What would our response have been?

In the New Testament, James describes Job as "persevering." We can be misled by translating *hypomonē* as "patient." How can James tell his readers, "Ye have heard of the *patience* of Job" (Jas 5:11 KJV)? According to *Webster's Dictionary patience* is, first, "the will or ability to wait or endure without complaint," and, second, "steadiness, endurance, or perseverance in performing a task." Its synonyms are "resignation, endurance, submission, perseverance. *Patience* refers to the quietness or self-possession of one's own spirit; *resignation* to his submission to the will of another."

Job complained for many speeches! The last thing he was was "quiet," "self-possessed" or "resigned" to his suffering. He was *angry!* And, according to his understanding of God's work, with good reason. Job did *persevere,* though. He knew he had lived right and he could not be suffering because he was being punished for evil deeds. He persevered until God the great Judge came to vindicate him (and confront him as well). Similarly, James writes to righteous believers who are being underpaid by their employers (Jas 5:1-6). These laborers are the people James calls to be longsuffering, to endure or hold out, to continue in their faith in a just God until the Lord comes to judge these unjust people. "Behold, the Judge, before the doors, is standing" (Jas 5:9). Jesus stands just outside the house, about to enter. The time will not be too long because God is very compassionate and merciful (Jas 5:11).

Thus, we can learn from Job's perseverance that *perseverance* does not negate honesty with God or the expression of one's feelings. Jesus' parable of the persistent widow and the tyrannical judge has a similar message (Lk 18:1-8).[9] When Luke writes that we should "at all times pray," he cannot mean we must keep bombarding God with prayers in order to get results, as if heaven were some kind of steel fortress with double-bolted doors. That type of prayer is the "many words" of the Gentiles (Mt 6:7).[10] That type of persistence is needed only when one deals with *unjust* judges who respond to powerless people only because they become weary of their continual asking of the same questions ("Vindicate me from my opponent!"). God is a just, compassionate and impartial Judge.

Jesus' point is, rather, that persons who suffer unjustly, who may become weary and thus lose their faith in God, need to "at all times pray," in other words, continue in devout communication to God, expressing trust in God that the righteous will be vindicated. Devout communication does not contradict sharing one's feelings, because the "elect" are "crying out" (Lk 18:7).

A Variety of Responses
During those ten weeks in 1989 that Bill spent in the hospital, we observed many differing reactions from visiting Christians. Some came for one or two weeks hoping for a "prayer miracle." When Bill did not immediately get better, they stopped coming because it threatened their faith. Others also came for one or two weeks to share their "prayer allotment." They seemed to give Bill a certain time allotment by which to get better. If he was not better by then, they were impatient to go on to other matters. Some came only once to deliver a message, teach a lesson or lay blame. One person said that Bill's suffering was his lot in life. He would get better when he learned God's lesson. Bill had had this health condition for seventeen years. He thought anything he could have learned had been received long ago! Similarly, many interpreters think that the apostle Paul's "thorn in the flesh" was a recurring eye condition (2 Cor 12:7; Gal 4:15).[11] He did learn a lesson: that God's grace was sufficient. But his eyes never did get better.

Other people came to lay blame. Like Job's friends they wondered, had Bill sinned? "Sin" now is no longer limited to wicked deeds but it can be wrong eating habits, insufficient psychological wholeness or lack of faith. Had Bill been eating the right foods? Had he been overly tense? Had he insufficient faith? Once the blame was assigned, Bill could be left to work on the cause. However, they did not stay around long enough to get an accurate diagnosis. Bill had just come back from an extended sabbatical feeling great and in wonderful spirits. He was relaxed. He had been eating the right foods. But a cumulative blockage from seventeen years of illness had finally taken its toll.

Further, according to James's instructions, *the elders* are the ones who must have the united prayer-vow of faith. The sick person's faith is exhibited by calling for the elders of the church (Jas 5:14-15).

Still, some believers kept coming back week after week after week. They trusted in God's compassion and justice. They did keep crying out to God, not in order to force God's unfeeling hand, but rather to express trust in God and to show obedience to God by being in Bill's presence over time.

Bill himself trusted God at this time by continuing his normal ministry. As energy permitted, he kept writing; he even taught a class in the hospital (with the doctor's permission), plugging two intravenous feeding machines into the walls, and he spoke well of God to the other patients and to the staff, evangelizing at each opportunity, reading a devotional passage and praying each morning with each roommate who would permit him to do so. We do not think that God made Bill ill *so that* he could speak well of God in the hospital. Rather, we think that because this is a fallen world, Bill became ill. We do not know why *he* became ill. Nevertheless, Bill, through God's power, was able to advance God's reign even in the midst of this adversity.

The book of Job reminds us that a correct diagnosis of suffering may not always be clear to us humans. Often, however, the response to all reasons for suffering may be identical. The suffering person should ask, *What should I do now? How do I get out of this? How can I serve God now?* And the one helping should ask, *What can I do to ease that suffering? How can I be God's helper to the person(s) in adversity? How can I help bear their burden?*

Letting Others Help

If Bill's father's experience had similarities to Job's early story, Bill's mother is very different from Job's wife. What kept her in the faith for so many years? She never suggested her husband curse God and die. Instead, she drew on her spiritual resources, keeping contact with the Christian community over the years, allowing them to ease her burden.

We need not only to help others, but also to let others help us. For some people that is even harder because then they become dependent on others. At least Job did not send his friends away! (If we had been in Job's place, *we* certainly would have wanted them to leave!) And then, not only should we allow others to ease our burdens, but also we might have to forgive them for doing that "lifting" in a more burdensome way. In other words, if their counsel is worthless, we may need to forgive *them!* Still, community is one of God's best resources for persevering through adversity. That is why God was so upset with Eliphaz, Bildad and Zophar. What should have been a means of life became a means of death.

We can bring life to others and help them persevere if we do not reduce all suffering to one cause, if we encourage people to dwell on God's nature, to trust God and to stay in the Christian community, thereby availing themselves of the resources to persevere, and if we ask and act on the action-oriented question: What can be done now?

Nursing One Another

Whose are the hands of Christ,
Steady, strong, and deft,
Working with Paradise,
Transfiguring the bereft?

I call and Christ is there,
Wise and kind and good.
She calls and trembling here,
I don the fallen sacred hood.

WILLIAM DAVID SPENCER, 1987

8

JOY IN THE MIDST
OF SUFFERING

*T*his letter came to Bill's parents one morning not long after his sister drowned on the playground swim trip:

City of Plainfield, New Jersey
Office of the Mayor
City Hall
July 16, 1954

Dear Mr. and Mrs. Spencer:

We were all deeply grieved to learn of the tragedy that took the life of your daughter, Helen Carol. Such events are always hard for us to comprehend and certainly at such times only a deep and abiding faith in God can help.

I want to extend to you my most heartfelt sympathy on the occasion of this great loss.

Very sincerely yours,
Carlyle W. Crane
Mayor

"We were all deeply grieved." Being communal is not something that a Christian *does* or should *do*. True community is something that Christianity *is*.

Without community, pain is ultimately unbearable, joy is unattainable. At its core Christianity is communal. Mutual appreciation and cooperation among Christian brothers and sisters are what God has ordained for the body of Christ to bring God's reign into the world, and they are the chief means by which God increases our joy.

To avoid producing a study that was simply theoretical, we have been following and interpreting a true story about a typical North American family—father, mother, daughter, son—who suffered. Nothing about them was unique. And nothing about their pain was unique.

The daughter drowned accidentally on a playground outing. Such a catastrophe can happen to any child on any summer's day. The father was maimed for life in a mishap on the job. Work-related injuries occur day and night all over the world. The son developed a lifelong chronic disease while carrying on an exhausting urban ministry. City pastors do not burn out or burn up for nothing. All ministry, after all, is grinding. The mother maintained the family through each crisis as best she could, regretting each loss but helpless to stave off the next. Nothing here to make any reader say, "What a bunch of heroes! How much better their life is than mine!" Instead, theirs is a story every reader has encountered at one time or another, has seen in the neighborhood, perhaps has experienced in his or her own family. Nothing unique about human suffering. Nothing unique about this family's pain, except for one immutable fact: that Jesus Christ suffered along with them.

But if this family's suffering was not unique, neither are the resources for enduring unique to them. What preserved the mother through each crisis was that, unlike the father, she found Christ's comfort by depending on the resource of Christian community. And in its care ultimately she found joy again.

Joy has always been God's intention for humanity. Scripture abounds with joy; it is the *telos* of all good theology. In the pages that follow we will first survey the scriptural words for joy and examine their theology of communal love, then see how Scripture suggests we can develop joyful relationships with God and with one another. What a delightful task confronts us! As Jesus' disciples did, we will discover that not all theology that is sound is grim.

Scriptural Words for Joy

We sneer at the syrupy concept of a "Pollyanna," the sickeningly cheerful overoptimist who always sees the bright side of everything. That stereotype is revolting because it trivializes pain.

The real Pollyanna story was a Christian serial novel by Eleanor H. Porter, appearing first in 1912 in the respected *Christian Herald.* As with most primary sources, it is much better and more true-to-life than its popular stereotype. Chapter twenty-two, "Sermons and Woodboxes," paints an all too realistic portrait of a burned-out minister, "sick at heart" at the "wrangling, backbiting, scandal and jealousy" in his congregation. Despite the fact that he has "argued, pleaded, rebuked, and ignored by turns" and "prayed—earnestly, hopefully," he is facing two deacons at war with each other over a triviality, three key women quitting because of "a tiny spark of gossip . . . fanned by wagging tongues into a devouring flame of scandal," jealousy causing schisms in the choir, "open criticism" of two officers, an alienated youth group, and then the resignation of the Sunday-school superintendent and two teachers.

These and a general spirit of disheartenment have driven the minister into the woods to contemplate miserably that "the church, the town, and even Christianity itself was suffering" and the "few conscientious workers . . . still left . . . pulled at cross purposes, usually; and always they showed themselves to be acutely aware of the critical eyes all about them, and of the tongues that had nothing to do but to talk about what the eyes saw."

Anticommunity like this is shamefully often the nature of our churches. Instead of hospitals, we run charnel houses for our wounded, tossing them to the side to die in heaps when the arrows of evil fell them. No wonder some Christians hesitate to seek fellowship. We expect to be devoured, not comforted, by one another. And disappointed clergy often respond exactly as this minister intends to do— with a blistering tirade: "Woe unto you, scribes and Pharisees, hypocrites . . . a bitter denunciation."

At this point the orphaned daughter of missionary parents, Pollyanna, encounters him. She instantly sympathizes with his pain, because she has known the suffering of ministry only too well: "Father used to feel like that, lots of times, I reckon ministers do—most generally." And then she gives him her dead father's last legacy, " 'most always he said, too, that he wouldn't *stay* a minister a minute if 'twasn't for the rejoicing texts. . . . Of course the Bible didn't name 'em that. But it's all those that begin 'Be glad in the Lord,' or 'Rejoice greatly,' or 'Shout for joy,' and all that, you know—such a lot of 'em. Once, when father felt specially bad, he counted 'em. There were eight hundred of 'em."[1]

Out of suffering comes the glad discovery of joy. C. S. Lewis called joy "the serious business of Heaven."[2]

Well over twenty different words are used in Scripture to convey the word *joy*. Thirteen key ones (and related forms) are in the Old Testament and six key ones (and related forms) in the New Testament.

A brief representative survey reveals *gîl* in Psalm 43:4, praising God as my exceeding joy (with its related form *gilah* in Is 35:2, rejoicing with joy and singing), *hedwâh* in Nehemiah 8:10, where the joy of the Lord is our strength, *ṭûb*, related to goodness, the joy of heart (Is 65:14), *māśôś*, the joy of one's way or manner of life (Job 8:19, Is 32:14), *rinnâh*, the morning joy that follows the night of weeping (Ps 30:5, [6 Hebrew]) and *rānan*, the ringing cry of joy (Ps 98:8), *śimḥâh*, the mirth or shouting aloud for joy in Ezra 3:12, *śāśôn*, the joy of salvation that needs to be restored (Ps 51:12 [14]), *terû'âh*, implying shouting or offering sacrifices with joy (Ps 27:6), *śûś*, God's rejoicing in people (Is 65:19), *pāṣaḥ*, breaking forth in joy, singing together (Is 52:9), *'ālaz*, exult, the faithful exulting joyfully in glory (Ps 149:5). We also find *'ālaṣ*, exulting, letting those that love God's name be joyful (Ps 5:11 [12]), *rûa'*, making a joyful noise (Ps 66:1), *re'ēh ḥayyîm*, living joyfully with the wife of one's youth (Eccles 9:9).

In the New Testament we find *agalliasis*, gladness, as when John the Baptist leaped for joy in Elizabeth's womb (Lk 1:44), *euphrosynēs*, the Acts 2:28 Greek translation of Psalm 16:8-11, the joy of God's presence, *chara* (or *chairō*, the verb, in 1 Thess 3:9), rejoicing with exceeding great joy (Mt 2:10), (or, in Philem 7, having great joy and consolation from the encouragement of others), *kauchaomai*, rejoicing (taking pride, boasting) in God through our Lord Jesus Christ (Rom 5:11), *skirtaō*, leaping for joy (Lk 6:23), *oninamai*, having joy as in profiting or benefiting, as in Philemon 20.

When we analyze these words, we find two general categories emerging. Nehemiah 8:10 and Ezra 6:22, for example, employ different words but note that *the source of the joy described is the Lord.* This is the joy of salvation that David pleads be restored after his sin with Bathsheba has plunged him into the misery of conviction (Ps 51:8, 12). When one has that joy, even when everything is destroyed and one is suffering from such pains as starvation, one is still able to rejoice in the Lord of one's salvation (Ps 13:5; Hab 3:17-18), for at God's right hand are pleasures forevermore (Ps 16:11). Therefore,

1 Peter 3:14 can enjoin us to be happy if we suffer for righteousness's sake (see also 2 Cor 6:10; 8:2). This joy gives us strength and overcomes misery in our lives. Thus, we discover a joy that is the result of God's favor. It is the assurance of security in the Lord.

This joy is unrelated to circumstances. When the people cried in terror because they had broken God's law after the exile, they were commanded to rejoice! When Habakkuk faced losing all earthly goods and security, he had joy in God. When Peter writes from experiencing suffering, he maintains joy. This, we see, is eternal joy, resting in one's purity before God through Christ. It is unrelated to circumstances. It is sometimes euphoric. It is at other times quietly present, a sense of eternal well-being and security. Bill experiences it as a plateau just at the edge of his consciousness. When he looks at it with inner eyes, he sees it descending profoundly deep, bottomless. Nothing lies below it—it goes down forever.

How can one experience this deep love of God? David tells us in Psalm 51: by first having one's sins forgiven. Then Habakkuk adds (3:18): by dwelling on God's salvation and enjoying our eternal security in times of great stress when our temporal security is threatened by trouble or persecution.

When we were ministering in Newark, Bill's health was poor; one car was stolen; our second car was totaled (with us in it) as we sat helplessly in a tight traffic jam, watching a seventeen-year-old fail to make a turn and broadside us; our house was robbed twice. How did we feel? Rotten! We did not thank God for our situation, but we did thank God for our salvation.

Bill first began this study of joy under a particularly poignant set of circumstances. In 1977-78 we grew an urban garden, filling it with rose bushes, hydrangea, morning glory, scarlet runner, cosmos, buttons, zinnia, marigold and California poppy. For us the garden was an image of what the city could become again—a microscopic Eden heralding the New Jerusalem.

The garden was bulldozed against our will by those who owned our house to make a parking lot, absentee landlords who simply acted for utilitarian expediency. We took no joy in the destruction of our garden. And yet as Bill worked in his study above the snarl of the bulldozing he was helpless to prevent, he looked within himself—past his fury at this wanton destruction—and found his plateau of peace, that joy that Habakkuk and Peter and Paul knew, the joy that is found only in the favor of the Master Gardener who will re-create Eden.

Drawing on God's Eternal Joy
Properly speaking, then, real joy is the assurance of salvation. It does not depend on our life situation. It is our response to God's unmerited favor toward us. Psalm 34:19-22 tells us, "Many are the afflictions of the righteous, but the Lord delivers that one out of them all. . . . The Lord redeems the life of his servants, none of them who take refuge in him will be condemned!" When Bill first discovered this verse, he took great comfort in its promise that God was going to deliver believers out of all afflictions—until he discovered that the first statement about the many afflictions was temporal, but the second, the deliverance, was eternal—it may not begin till later! This explains why so many of the lives of great believers are so difficult.

McAuley Cremorne Mission, Inc.
434 West 42nd Street
New York, N.Y.
August 25, 1954

Dear Mr. and Mrs. Spencer:

Mr. Joseph Killigrew, superintendent of our McAuley Cremorne Mission, has told me many times of your gifts of paint. Because of these gifts, the men have been able to keep the building in first-class condition.

It is difficult to keep a mission building clean where hundreds of

men come in from the street, and there is nothing better than good
fresh paint, generously applied, to keep the mission clean and attractive.

I am sure that our Lord will greatly bless you for your unselfishness and generosity and that you will be brought up in the prayers
of our men as they meet in their Bible class.

Very sincerely yours,
James E. Bennet
President

"I am sure that our Lord will greatly bless you for your unselfishness
and generosity." What did the young house painter think, two years
after this letter, when calamity rather than blessing again befell him?
Did he think that God had not heard the prayers of the homeless men
in the mission Bible class? Did he think that the mission president's
good wishes were not high enough on the Christian celebrity list to
impress heaven toward a favorable answer? If his church had taught
him anything about the lives of great Christians in the past, he would
have looked elsewhere for the answer to their prayers than to material
blessings.

He would have looked, perhaps, at the life of another city minister,
the exemplary Charles Spurgeon. Spurgeon suffered a great deal of
illness and physical pain during his ministry. Approximately one-third
of the last twenty-two years of his ministry were spent recuperating
from his illnesses. For months at a time, he was laid up with extremely
painful ailments like smallpox and the incredibly painful swelling of
the legs, knees and joints that used to be called gout. On the eve of
his birthday he wrote to his congregation:

On the closing day of my thirty-seventh year, I find myself the
Pastor of a beloved flock, who have borne the test of twelve Sab-
baths of their minister's absence, and the severer test of more than
seventeen years of the same ministry, and are now exhibiting more

love to him than ever.[3]

He wrote once when suffering:

It is a great mercy to be able to change sides when lying in bed. . . . Did you ever lie a week on one side? Did you ever try to turn, and find yourself quite helpless? Did others lift you, and by their kindness only reveal to you the miserable fact that they must lift you back again at once into the old position, for, bad as it was, it was preferable to any other? . . . It is a great mercy to get one hour's sleep at night. . . . Some of us know what it is, night after night, to long for slumber and find it not. O how sweet has an hour's sleep been when it has interposed between long stretches of pain, like a span of heaven's blue between the masses of thunder cloud![4]

Another great Christian, Teresa of Ávila, wrote, "I have been experiencing now for three months such great noise and weakness in my head that I've found it a hardship even to write concerning necessary business matters."[5] St. Teresa has become well known for her classic on prayer, *The Interior Castle.* Raimundo Panikkar writes of Teresa that her relationship to God was so strong that she was not afraid to remonstrate with God about her suffering. Once, he notes, St. Teresa was "complaining to God in prayer about her sufferings and trials. She heard the Lord telling her: 'Teresa, so do I treat My friends!' making her thereby understand the purificatory character of suffering. But Teresa, who knew it already, answered boldly: 'That's why you have so few.' "[6]

Spurgeon too knew when and how to speak to God. "Preaching at the Tabernacle, later in 1871, Spurgeon described how he wrestled in prayer, and prevailed with the Lord, in what proved to be the crisis of that season of suffering:

I have found it a blessed thing, in my own experience, to plead before God that I am His child. When, some months ago, I was racked with pain to an extreme degree, so that I could no longer bear it without crying out, I asked all to go from the room, and leave me alone; and then I had nothing I could say to God but this,

'Thou art my Father, and I am Thy child; and Thou, as a Father, art tender and full of mercy. I could not bear to see my child suffer as Thou makest me suffer; and if I saw him tormented as I am now, I would do what I could to help him and put my arms under him to sustain him. Wilt thou hide Thy face from me, my Father? Wilt Thou still lay on me Thy heavy hand, and not give me a smile from Thy countenance?' I talked to the Lord as Luther would have done, and pleaded His Fatherhood in real earnest. 'Like as a father pitieth his children, so the Lord pitieth them that fear Him.' If He be a Father, let Him show Himself a Father—so I pleaded; and I ventured to say, when they came back who watched me, 'I shall never have such agony again from this moment, for God has heard my prayer.' I bless God that ease came, and the racking pain never returned. Faith mastered it by laying hold upon God in His own revealed character—that character in which, in our darkest hour, we are best able to appreciate Him. I think this is why that prayer, 'Our Father which art in Heaven,' is given to us, because, when we are lowest, we can still say, 'Our Father,' and when it is very dark, and we are very weak, our childlike appeal can go up, 'Father, help me! Father, rescue me!'

"Spurgeon never forgot this experience. Those who are familiar with his writings must have noticed how often he referred to it, and how he urged other tried believers to do as he had done."[7]

When Joseph Scriven lost his fiancée in a drowning accident, he emerged from his heartache singing, "O what peace we often forfeit/ O what needless pain we bear/ All because we do not carry/ Ev'rything to God in prayer!" In his great hymn "What a Friend We Have in Jesus," he was not plastering some superficial makeup on the festering wound of suffering. He was talking about the same poignant counseling with God that Spurgeon did, that Teresa did, that Nicholas Wolterstorff did in his *Lament for a Son,* written when his twenty-five-year-old son Eric was killed while mountain climbing.

Spurgeon, Teresa, Scriven, Wolterstorff knew something that many of us Christians do not seem to know: that the true recourse in suffering is turning to those who care for us, divine and human. And prayer is the great recourse to our divine loving Parent.

Do we think that God was annoyed at Spurgeon and Teresa when they spoke forthrightly out of their pain? Was God angry at Job? Do we remember what God said to Job's friends? "You have not spoken truth like my servant Job" (Job 42:7). God loves the truth. "Your word is truth," says Jesus to his Father in John 17:17.

Further, God loves to hear our prayers. Proverbs 15:8 announces, "The sacrifice of the wicked is an abomination to the LORD; but the prayer of the upright is his delight" (NRSV). Psalm 37:4 exhorts, "Delight yourself also in the Lord; and the Lord shall give you the desires of your heart." Prayer is not simply a duty. It is a gift of love. God delights in us, the Scripture tells us, and we should delight in God. The Hebrew for "delight" used in Proverbs 15:8, *rāṣôn,* means "good will, inclination, pleasure, delight, favor, grace, kindness." The verb *rāṣâh* that accompanies it means "to take pleasure in, to be pleased, to delight, to receive graciously, to love." God loves our prayers! God loves it when we get in touch.

We have talked about taking time to seal oneself off with God and pray. This is what God is waiting for us to do. "O what peace we often forfeit/O what needless pain we bear/All because we do not carry/Ev'rything to God in prayer!" When one's child comes up and says, "Dad [or Mom], I gotta talk to you," does one drop everything and give the child one's full attention? God does. When we say, "God, I've got to talk to you," God is delighted.

In the same way, "Delight yourself in the Lord," reads Psalm 37:4. *'Ānaḡ* in the Hebrew is in the reflexive. The force is for the action to reflect back on oneself. "Enjoy yourself in the Lord," the passage is saying, "take exquisite delight in the Lord." According to the Brown, Driver, Briggs lexicon, the related Arabic equivalent means "to use amorous behavior."[8] The Hebrew too has the implication of the delight that men and women take in each other's company.

After all, why do we have two sexes? So that God can teach us about love of someone different, of oneness in diversity. Prayer communicates the same thing to us: that God loves humans and wants us to love God in return. If you loved somebody but were always too busy to talk to them, what kind of lover would you be? Parents who do not talk to their children when they are young will find their children are not interested in talking to them when those children are older. Couples who do not communicate are headed for misunderstanding and divorce.

When we were researching our book *The Prayer Life of Jesus: Shout of Agony, Revelation of Love,* we were struck with how many times Jesus prayed and how much solace our Lord received through prayer. At every major decision, before every test, each day Jesus sought out his Parent and communicated with God. Jesus and the Father were one, and oneness is what he wanted for his disciples in his prayer in John 17.

People who do not pray, on the other hand, are strangers to God. And God is a stranger to them. Are we Christians expecting to spend eternity with a stranger? We would not marry a complete stranger; would we spend eternity with one? That makes even less sense. God wants to be in touch with us. Pray without ceasing, counsels Paul in 1 Thessalonians 5:17. "Is anyone in trouble?" asks Jesus' brother James. "That one should pray" (Jas 5:13). For most of us this command is fairly easy to obey. Probably more fervent prayers are said in the dentist's office than in the church building.

But when we are not in trouble, we should still delight ourselves in prayer. Prayer is the way we communicate our love to God and feel God's love being communicated back to us. What more joyful sensation can one receive? "If you love me," Jesus said, "you will keep my commandments" (Jn 14:15). One of Jesus' commandments is "Pray, then" (Mt 6:9).

If we develop a full, nourishing prayer life when we are not suffering, then when trouble strikes us, as it will, we will have a Great Friend to whom to turn automatically. God loves us every day. Every day we need to tell God we love God too.

Drawing on God's Temporal Joy

But Scripture does not stop here. It also depicts another type of joy.

Biographer Eric Lax spent two decades studying the enigmatic Woody Allen. Matthew Gilbert, reviewing Lax's findings, observes, "While Lax does not unearth any surprising details about Allen's private life, he does present a man who is cool and standoffish, one who seems to know very little joy. 'Happy is not a word I would ever use in a sentence with Woody Allen,' Lax says." Yet they go on to note, "For a man widely regarded as angst-ridden and hypochondriacal, he has a lot of fun and a set of larky cronies." Woody Allen has become almost archetypal as the modern, troubled psyche. He "seems to know very little joy," we are told, yet "he has a lot of fun."9 At first glance these statements seem antithetical. How can one not be joyful, yet enjoy oneself? However, Scripture agrees with Woody Allen and his biographer.

A joy exists that is temporary, a kind of elation, depending on circumstances, that everyone experiences like the falling of rain or God's general mercy. This joy can be related to enjoying the fruit of one's hard work. We see it depicted in Isaiah 22:13, the joy and gladness that come from eating and drinking in the resignation that tomorrow we die. This is the joy of possessions or earthly relationships. Ecclesiastes 2:10-11 depicts it in the joy of accomplishment, the satisfaction of a job well done. This joy is not without a theological dimension. Psalm 128:1-2 tells us that if we fear the Lord, we shall eat the fruit of the labor of our hands and life will go well for us. Ecclesiastes 3:12-13, 22 enjoin us to enjoy the work that we do.

Of course, when the food we grew is eaten and the good time we are enjoying is finished, this joy itself passes into treasured memory. Even if transitory, it is valuable. This is the biblical doctrine of fun. For those outside the profound sense of God's salvation, this is the only joy that can be experienced. It is dependent on circumstance.

Once, through an error, an airline insisted on giving the authors a first-class trip, secreting us away behind those austere curtains and serving us up a personalized dinner on linen-covered tables with petite crystal saltshakers. We praised God for this passing luxury. As soon as we got off the plane and out in traffic, that was the end of that!

Circumstantial joy is easily removed by day-to-day hassles. Thank God that we have the opportunity, through aligning ourselves with Jesus' death, to be put right with God and to experience what Psalm 4:7 describes: "You have given gladness [joy, rejoicing; also the word for *feast, banquet*] in my heart, more than in the time that others' corn and wine increased." Ultimately this eternal joy is the one that we need, the one that will last.

Jesus Was Happy

But we are creatures living in the now. Do we have to die to be happy? Jesus did not.

Over and over again in Scripture we see Jesus enjoying himself with people, to the point of being called a drunk and the ancient Near East equivalent of a party animal (Mt 11:19; Lk 7:34). A standing joke in Christian circles is that when Jesus and his gang arrived at the wedding at Cana the wine gave out—that's why he had to make more!

A true theology of Jesus might be called "the theology of God's party." Jesus was first revealed to the temple elders at a festival (Lk 2:41-51). His debut miracle was at the wedding at Cana (Jn 2:1-11). He established the sacrament of Communion for the church in his farewell supper feast at the festival of Passover (Mt 26:17-29). We are told that the angels rejoice, that is, celebrate, whenever a sinner repents (Lk 15:3-10). What is the Christian hope? To what are we looking forward? To the marriage supper of the Lamb—God's eternal party (Rev 19:1-9). Those who do not get along with their fellows and think Christianity is a sobering set of disciplining rules at its core are going to be awfully uncomfortable with the eternal levity in heaven.

Jesus' life was one of trouble, of continual rejection, of exhaustion in ministry, of slander by those who should have welcomed him, of ultimate torture and execution. Yet he alleviated this suffering in the two key ways suggested in that comforting letter from the honorable mayor of Plainfield. "Only a deep and abiding faith in God can help," wrote Mayor Crane, and "We are all deeply grieved. . . . Such events are always hard for us to comprehend." Jesus took refuge in the community of the presence of God and the heavenly host (e.g., Mt 4:11) and of people (Lk 10:38-42; 11:5; 12:1-9). Think about that. Jesus, our powerful Lord, drew strength from the loving communal care of others.

The Theology of Communal Joy
Our chief resource for joy, eternal and temporal, is the care of the divine community. Earlier we pointed out that all good theology goes back to the nature of God and of creation. The theology of communal joy is no exception.

The primal confession that Israel was taught about God was curiously plural yet singular. Moses gathers the people of Israel together just before they were to cross the Jordan to conquer the Promised Land, in order to report to them what God had told him on Mount Sinai. To them he gives the first great confession, the primal creedal statement, literally: "Hear, Israel, the Lord [singular], our Godhead [plural], the Lord [singular] is one [singular]" (Deut 6:4).[10] Plurality and singularity are wedded in this definitive revelation of who God is. What explains this oxymoron? What we call "the Trinity" is present in the basic Hebrew creed. Do we think that Christianity is grafted onto Judaism, that it is a development of it? Not at all. It is merely its explanation. Christianity explains the basic tenet of Hebrew faith: who exactly God is.

Therefore, Christians confess God as one God in three Persons. Unity and community in God is the basic confession. True Christianity, then, is in reality the establishing of a set of relationships that began with God.

The one God is three Persons in perfect unity: Parent, Child, Spirit, each totally loving one another. These Persons are so united that God is one God. God is *not* revealed as three gods. God is one God in three Persons. This is the mystery, the holy mysterium of the loving relationship of God that extends to earth in Jesus, who, his disciple John explains, is God "pitching his tent" among us (Jn 1:14).

What Jesus does is reinitiate that practice that God enjoyed in the Garden of Eden, walking in the cool of the evening with God's beloved humanity (Gen 3:8). Jesus takes up residence among humanity, walking with us, laughing with us, suffering with us, extending the loving relationships within the Trinity to humans, networking his gathering of people, his family, his body, as the New Testament calls this divinely initiated community across the earth (1 Cor 12:12-27). Thus, Jesus' prayer in John 17 for his disciples—all his disciples, including his present-day church—is fulfilled. People become one with Jesus, one with God, and one with each other. Therefore, to have a true Christian church we *must* have a loving community related to God and to one another through Christ. Our task is to discover how those relationships, that body, can function as a loving, joyful, healthy, mutually supportive community.

To enjoy all these benefits we must first join the Christian community. No one can experience Christian joy until that one becomes a Christian, of course, through confessing one's sins, humbling oneself before God, asking for the sacrifice of Jesus to be one's own sacrifice for sin, and living one's life under Christ's lordship as a productive, caring part of the Christian family. This last point is very important. If one is not ministering, living and growing, if one is not exercising one's gifts to build up brothers and sisters in Christ, if one is not bearing witness to others about Jesus' great sacrificial act and the joy of living with him, if one is not doing good deeds as Jesus did to help others—fulfilling his "golden rule" (Mt 7:12)—if one is not thinking on things noble, good, beautiful and true, then one is like a plant without water, drooping and wasting away! No one can be happy in that condition. Jesus, "the living bread, the living water," said his food, his sustenance—what made him growing and healthy—was doing the will of God (Jn 4:34).

But suppose you are living a productive life for Christ, or you are determined to do so today. What can you do to increase your daily measure of joy? The first thing you must do is *develop a life of moderation,* in order to function yourself as a member of the Christian community.

Recognizing Our Limitations

Jesus taught us to pray to God as "*our* Father" (Mt 6:9; Lk 11:2). To God we are part of a whole and only responsible to do our part. But many of us are miserable because we take too much guilt and blame on ourselves. We assume too much responsibility. We need to know our limits. In chapter one, we spoke briefly about realizing that we are limited creatures, living in a temporal world. We spoke of sleep as a sacrament, showing our trust in God. God's requirements for people, we note, are simple. They are much less than our requirements often are for ourselves. What does God want from us? Micah 6:8 reveals that God wants us to do justice, to love mercy, to walk humbly with God. Ecclesiastes 2:24 adds to eat, drink and take pleasure in our work. These are simple things. We do not need to build television empires, to get our faces emblazoned on *Time, The London Post, The Daily Gleaner, The Chinese Broadcasting Magazine* for Christ, to paint a huge sign on the moon visible all over the earth: "Repent Now, You Heathens!" We simply need to live out normal lives, exercising the gifts God has given us to enrich the community and help others. We can do this by learning to live in God's rest. Chapter 4 of Hebrews is the great lecture on entering into a life lived in God's rest.

Earlier we noted the creed that Moses gave to the Israelites on the banks of the Jordan. The Israelites had been to the brink of this same Jordan years before. God had ordered them into the land of promise and, out of cowardice, they had refused to go. Their punishment was forty years of suffering. Entering into God's rest works similarly for us. Just as the Israelites, trembling before the "giants" of the land, demanded that God prove that God was authentically with them and was truly more powerful than the Canaanite gods (they even stooped at one point to creating an oversized calf which they could see and touch and carry with them to prove that God was in their presence), so we often tremble before the "giants" confronting us, giving in to fear and creating our own calves of security to rely on rather than casting all our cares on Christ (1 Pet 5:7).

The Sabbath rest in the Old Testament, Jesus explains, was given for the benefit of humans (Mk 2:27). Hebrews 4:9-10 amplifies, "Consequently, there remains a sabbath day's rest for the people of God; for the person entering into his rest also himself rests from his works just as God from God's own works." God worked hard and then God rested. We ought to do the same—work hard and then rest. Resting is a matter of exercising our faith. We are trusting that the one who made the heavens and the earth and even supervised our own births can take care of us when we are not taking care of ourselves.

How should we then use the day we take off? By worshiping God, by enjoying the work we have done and by doing good deeds for others out of appreciation to God. This rest is given so we can appreciate God, walk again, as it were, with God in Eden, and get to know Christ's body on earth, the members of the Christian community.

When we rest in God, what we are saying, essentially, is, "Yes, God, you are sovereign and I as a mortal am limited. I know when I take a day off that you can keep saving the world, that you can provide for my finances when I don't take two jobs during the week and one on the weekends. And I know that I need to take time out to build my relationship with you and with others."

We can trust God to take care of us through our suffering. *God may not prevent trouble from happening to us, but God will care for us through it.* God, after all, knows what we need before we ask (Mt 6:8). The Reverend Nguyen Xuan Tin, one of our Doctor of Ministry students at Gordon-Conwell Theological Seminary, gave us a dramatic example of this truth that God gives us resources before we need them so that we might draw on them when trouble comes.

In December of 1971 a great revival rocked the Nhatrang Biblical and Theological Institute where he was studying for the ministry, spreading out across Vietnam. "God gave us the power to preach the gospel," he said in an interview in *The Alliance Witness* six years later. The reason God poured out the revival, he believes, is that one of the great catastrophes for the church in Vietnam was to occur shortly afterward: a church building collapsed during a bombing, taking the lives of the Christians who had sought refuge there. He adds: "God also was preparing me for the great trial of my life. For it was during the 1972 summer vacation that my fiancée died in Que Son, killed with more than one hundred other Christians in the fighting." The believers strengthened one another, shored up by the extra measure of God's love, and so, "I continued my studies at Nhatrang. Every summer vacation I traveled to many churches in South Viet Nam to give my testimony to the young people. Praise the Lord, God used me to bring the gospel to them. Many repented and believed on Jesus."[11]

One would think that such a catastrophe would end the church. But Christianity is built to deal with suffering. What kills the church is something much more pernicious: refusing to rely on God, refusing to go into God's rest, refusing to enjoy fellowship with God and with one another, refusing to draw on our communal resources and give and receive what we need most for our spiritual and in many cases our physical health: comfort and care from one another.

In our societies we get joy largely from the approval of other people. All of us want to be loved. Over the years Bill has looked at a plethora of books on encouragement, from current classics like Martin Buber's *I and Thou,* Erich Fromm's *The Art of Loving* and Reuel Howe's *The Miracle of Dialogue* to secular popular works like Blanchard and Johnson's *The One Minute Manager* and David Goodman's *Living from Within: The Art of Appreciation in Marriage, Parenthood,*

Work, Growing Up and Growing Older to popular religious books like Alan Loy McGinnis's *The Friendship Factor,* Gene Getz's *Building Up One Another: How Every Member of the Church Can Help Strengthen Other Christians,* Royce Money's *Building Stronger Families* and a multitude of others.

Their message is summarized in the pithy words of David Goodman: "When, in maturity, you review your life's history, you will know that you have lived well if you have loved well, and lived poorly if you loved poorly. This truth is elementary. Too bad, then, that so many of us learn it too late! What dreary lives the non-lovers lead! How rich and full, by contrast, is the life of those who give greatly of themselves in affectionate exchange with spouse, children, family, and friends. Lovers are wise. They give a lot and they get a lot."[12]

How true this statement is. Therefore, how can we love more?

Loving God would seem to be the place to start, of course. But John, the disciple who revealed to us that Jesus was God walking among us, questions that. "If someone may say, 'I love God,' and his brother or sister he may hate, he is a liar," he challenges in 1 John 4:20, "for the one not loving his brother whom he has seen, God, whom he has not seen, he is not able to love." So we must start by loving those nearest us. One way to do this is by helping to ease the load of care on their shoulders.

We mentioned Moses assembling the people of Israel on the banks of the Jordan to give them God's word. Actually, as we study the accounts of Moses, we see that he assembled the people quite frequently for a variety of reasons.

One day when Moses and the Israelites were traveling through Midian, Jethro (or Reuel), Moses' father-in-law, visited him, bringing Moses' wife Zipporah and sons Gershom and Eliezer to join Moses. Jethro, we might remember, was himself a member of the ancient clergy. The text calls him a priest of Midian (Ex 18:1), and his visit turned out to be pastoral as well as familial. Possibly he already worshiped the one living God, or perhaps he began to do so with this visit.

At any rate, seeing God's work among the Israelites, his faith is confirmed, for he exclaims in Exodus 18:11, "Now I know that greater is the Lord than all the gods." And Moses certainly reports with powerful testimony all the great things that the great God did to Pharaoh, turning the Nile to blood, killing the season's fish catch, invading the land with frogs, gnats, flies, pestilence, boils, hail, locusts, plunging it into darkness, and finally slaying the firstborn. Then Moses tells of God's parting the waters of the Red Sea, protecting the Israelites as a shielding cloud, deluging the pursuing Egyptians, and finally delivering Israel through all the subsequent wilderness hardships. Jethro's response, verse 9 tells us, was to rejoice: "for all the good that the Lord had done to Israel, in delivering them from the hand of the Egyptians." And verse 12 tells us he offered a burnt offering and sacrifices to God in gratitude. That evening ended with a big celebratory meal with Moses, Jethro and all the elders of Israel, a perfect night.

The Ancient Art of Burnout
The next day, however, Jethro got a different picture of what was happening in Israel. Remember, he had just spent a night hearing about and celebrating all the great acts God had done for Israel—how Israel had rested in God, relied on God's deliverance and been victorious through every trouble and every battle. Now what did he wake up to see? His son-in-law entangled to the point of gasping in the suffocating coils of ancient-Near-Eastern red tape.

"What is this thing which you are doing with the people?" Jethro demands of Moses in bewilderment. "For what reason are you sitting—you alone—and all the people stand around you from morning until night? This is not good, this thing which you are doing. You will surely be worn out (the Hebrew word is *nāḇal,* wither, decay), both you and this people along with you, because this thing is too heavy for you; what you are doing you cannot do alone" (Ex 18:14-18). Moses had been forced by his position into a trap—the messiah trap, as many call it. The people looked to him exclusively to judge among them and solve their problems.

The trap that Moses had fallen into is one of the most pernicious ones ensnaring active Christians today. The evil one has two ways to annul the ministry of fervent believers: get them to do nothing or get them to do everything. Those who do nothing are no problem for the evil one; they turn into complainers, the never-satisfied whose perfectionistic critique makes them ambassadors of ill will who finally discourage all those trying to minister around them. They are a delight and a great assistance to the designs of hell. The evil one believes every church should have at least one of these (with a couple of stand-ins, by our observation).

The active Christians are more of a problem for the evil one. They are not likely to fall for the temptation of sloth. The strategy, then, is to get the slothful to dump all their burdens on the active, overuse the active to the point of exhaustion—then heap more on and wait for the breakdown. Today we see that breakdown of active Christians occurring everywhere—and nowhere more dramatically than among our clergy.

In April 1991, *Parade Magazine,* the syndicated insert of many national U.S. newspapers, printed a Hank Whittemore survey of "Ministers Under Stress." Whittemore's findings were sobering. He discovered a widespread pattern of long-term stress and burnout. In 1989 the Southern Baptist Convention paid the second largest portion of its $64.2 million paid out to pastors for medical claims to stress-related illnesses (second only to maternity benefits). Roy Oswald, a senior consultant of the Alban Institute, a consulting service serving churches and synagogues nationwide, told him that seventeen percent of the clergy he had counseled, nearly one-fifth, were "suffering from long-term stress or burnout." An increase in sexual misconduct, alcoholism, drug abuse, overeating and other addictions, depression, anxiety, heart attacks, even cancer among clergy was credited to long-term stress.

As William L. Self, pastor of Atlanta's prestigious and powerful Wieuca Road Baptist Church, announced when he resigned: "Unless I quit now my obituary will read, 'Bill Self today sank like a rock— beat up, burned out, angry and depressed, no good to himself, no good to the people he loved.' I did not have a crisis of faith, but of emotion and energy. It's almost impossible for leaders of a congregation to accept that their pastor needs pastoring. So I began to strangle on my anger, finding myself unable to sleep and even losing interest in studies that I love. I was unraveling, collapsing inside and coming to realize that if the church was not going to take care of me, I'd have to start taking care of myself. The church is the only army that shoots its wounded, but I refused to let that happen to me. Instead, I fell on my sword." Ultimately William Self realized it was his responsibility to take care of himself, but before he came to that conclusion he had spun into a destructive spiral.

Episcopal priest the Reverend Richard Busch explained, "I allowed my life to become a work binge of giving, giving, giving, until I gradually became aware of my own pain and loneliness. Over time, I moved from being physically tired to emotionally exhausted and finally wiped out. I was angry with myself and angry at God—just spiritually drained."

In addition to being angry at himself for not observing his human limitations, Busch ought to have been angry at his people who helped force him into that role of "giving, giving, giving" while they were taking, taking, taking. As Father David Brinkmoeller, director of Priestly Life and Ministry at the National Conference of Catholic Bishops, explains, "A priest is expected to be spiritually deep, theologically wise and fiscally clever, while being good at preaching and counseling with young and old. Each person in the congregation expects only a limited something, but the conglomeration can be overwhelming."

Glen Gabbard, director of the C. F. Menninger Memorial Hospital in Topeka, Kansas, which treats many clergy, lays the blame with congregations. "They [the clergy] try to be loving to others in hopes of getting love in return—but often, to their surprise, they're met with a host of problems and become the target of complaints, resentment and disappointment."[13]

In a March 1981 article in *Newsweek,* "Why Pastors Are Fired," Kenneth L. Woodward and Eloise Salholz found the same diagnosis being given by counselor Speed Leas, who studied the reasons for the firing of pastors for the Alban Institute. "Scripture says Christians should love one another, so congregations hate to admit they have emotional conflicts just like families do," he observes. "We live in a culture of fragmentary relationships," amplifies the Reverend John Biersdorf, director of the Institute for Advanced Pastoral Studies in Bloomfield Hills, Michigan.[14] "A new consumer mentality" has arisen, observes the Reverend Luther Kramer, president of the Key Pastoral Counseling Center in Alabama. "Instead of sticking to a church people are shopping around for religious services. Rather than working to resolve issues when they don't get what they want, they go somewhere else. Or they get rid of the pastor—especially if the church isn't gaining members."[15]

California church planter Thang Nguyen quotes a friend as calling this a "chippie generation." We have all heard of the hippies, yuppies, buppies, yippies, he points out. Well, we in the U.S. are the chippies. We believe in everything small—microchips, pocket computers, ear-warmer radios and disc players, hand-held TV sets. We also believe in "chips" of relationships, fragmentary families. And this fragmentation extends to our relationships with others. As a result, we want the pastor to fill in all that our fragmented lives are missing. And when he or she cannot, well, we simply move on, fragmenting that relationship and beginning superficial "chips" of relationships with other people.

"This is not good, this thing which you are doing," Jethro warned Moses. It was not good for Moses, it was not good for the people, it was not good for the community of faith or for bringing in the full reign of God to everyone. "This thing is too heavy for you."

Jethro's solution was to divide Moses' power up among virtuous people (interestingly enough, *'eʿnôš,* the word for ordinary humans, used [Ex 18:21]). "Set such people over them as officers over thousands, hundreds, fifties, and tens. Let them sit as judges for the people at all times; let them bring every important case to you, but decide every minor case themselves. So it will be easier for you, and they will bear the burden with you" (Ex 18:21-22). Jethro threw the overburdening of Moses back on the religious community.

The Moses Trap

When Moses ignored his limitations and the people ignored Moses' limitations, God's plan for the people of God was not accomplished. God had planned for God's people to be "a dominion priestly and also holy" (Ex 19:6). Not just Moses, but the elders as well, had been sent to Pharaoh (Ex 3:18). Deuteronomy 5:24-27 tells us that not just Moses but all the people heard the voice of God on Sinai, and the people confessed to Moses: "The Lord our God has shown us his glory and his majesty, and we have heard his voice from the fire. Today we have seen that a human can live even if God speaks with him." But, terrified, they shifted the responsibility onto Moses, imploring him: "Go near and listen to all that the Lord our God says. Then tell us whatever the Lord our God tells you. We will listen and obey." The people dumped the job on Moses and kept doing so until Moses sat immobilized in the desert. That is the "Moses trap" of the overcommitted.

Paul, who himself knew what it was like to suffer "the daily burden," "anxiety for all the churches" (2 Cor 11:28), calls us to a better way, the way of community, each of us bearing one another's burdens (Gal 6:2). When we do not put his advice into practice, we are forcing our leaders into the sins of stress. Do we think our leaders should all be like Moses—a supposed superleader of God? Moses himself was overstressed and experiencing burnout. Listen to these words recorded in Numbers 11:11-14. "Why," Moses asks God, "did you lay the burden of all this people on me? Did I conceive all this people? Did I give birth to them, that you should say to me, 'Carry them in your bosom, as a nurse carries a nursing child,' to the land that you promised on oath to their ancestors? . . . I am not able to carry all this people alone, for they are too heavy for me." If Moses were a cleric serving today, he would be in counseling. In fact, God sent him Jethro as his pastoral counselor. Jethro did for Moses what God also did in Numbers 11:16-17 when God gave seventy plus two elders to "bear with you the burden of the people." Moses needed seventy-two other people at that point to shoulder the load he had been shouldering alone. How many other people do our pastors and elders and lay leaders need to bear the burden of us?

"Would that all the Lord's people were prophets, and that the Lord would put his Spirit on them!" lamented Moses in Numbers 11:29. Today in the church, now that the veil of the temple has been ripped open and the Spirit of God has rushed out into God's community, every believer, adult and child, has the Spirit of God upon her or him. What Moses wished for has happened: God's anointing Spirit rests on all, God's gifts are given to all, all are under obligation to serve the church—pastors operating today as conveners, as encouragers, as organizers helping the church to serve itself. Every one of us has to shoulder some of the burden so no few people become overburdened. Each of us needs to ask, have I shouldered my share, my maximum burden? Have I allowed others to live within their limitations? Am I looking out for my brothers and sisters in Christ?

These questions are crucial because they are the basis for developing the relationships through which God wants to work to increase our daily joy.

Forgiven, Stand!
   (a song)

Head high with other men,
he stands on his feet again.
Straight, strong,
his whole life changed
from the bed that held him chained,
he's free! Free! By the God of liberty,
freed by the mighty Victor's hand.

Paralyzed in living death,
this world held him oppressed.
Bound by community,
four friends perceived his need—
he's free! Free! By the God of liberty,
freed by a faith that dared to let him rise and stand!

All of his life was his friendships.
All of his hope was their faith,
broken, battered, humbled, shattered—and strong.

Lowered down as in a grave,
he rose in a leap of faith,
rushed out, his mat in hand,
to jump and laugh and embrace his friends.
He's free! Free! By the God of liberty,
Freed by the mighty Victor's hand!
Freed by the mighty Victor's hand.

© *1974 WILLIAM DAVID SPENCER*
based on Mark 2:1-12

9

ENCOURAGING
ONE ANOTHER

*W*here do we get our daily joy? We noted previously that in our societies we largely get joy from the approval of other people. As Christians we cannot expect acceptance, not to mention approval, from the world. Jesus said:

If the world hates all of you, recognize that it has hated me before you. If out of the world you were, the world would love its own, but you are not out of the world, but I have chosen you out of the world. On account of this the world hates you. Remember the saying which I said to you, "A servant is not greater than its master." If they persecuted me, also you they will persecute. (Jn 15:18-20)

None of us servants is greater than our master. In fact, Jesus said, "How horrible when all people might speak well of you" (Lk 6:26). We can expect to be misunderstood by those to whom God's wisdom seems to be foolishness (1 Cor 1:18). That is why God gave us the Christian family on earth, as our chief vehicle of approval and encouragement. Therefore, getting together with our brothers and sisters in Christ is absolutely imperative. It is God's means of increasing our day-to-day joy.

Developing Joyful Relationships with People

Paul gave the quarrelsome Corinthians two crucial pieces of advice for maximizing happier living within the community of Christ. In the lay Bible commentary that we wrote on 2 Corinthians we noted:

2 Corinthians is for us Christians perhaps the most encouraging epistle of all times in the New Testament. We sometimes find ourselves weighed down emotionally when we reflect on the sheer weight of the horrible things we do. Our brightest members fall into gross, publicly mocked sexual sins. We are greedy with our resources and stingy in sharing them with others, often contentious and battling among ourselves, looking more like combatants than community members. We are riddled with horoscopes and other silly superstitions. We are a rebellious lot, starving the true leaders God raises up in our churches and fawning over some glittering fraud with a silver tongue and a shifty eye. All of these sins the Corinthian Christians were guilty of committing. And not only did they commit them, but they also continued to sin after they had been warned by God through Paul to stop. Yet neither God nor his minister Paul abandoned them and closed their church. God persisted in loving these foolish, worldly followers until—most encouraging and delightful of all—God's and Paul's persistence paid off handsomely. . . . The Corinthians mended their ways.[1]

By the time Paul wrote Romans, the formerly stingy Corinthians had made a contribution to the poor in Jerusalem. Forty years later, when

John the disciple was just returning from exile on Patmos, writing down the apocalyptic vision we know as Revelation, the Corinthians were being complimented on their reputation for excellence and firmness of faith, for their sensible and considerate Christian piety, for their hospitality, for their impartiality, for their disciplined young people and blameless women who treated their husbands with affection and for homes run with dignity and discretion! (1 Clement 1:2-3).

What happened? How did they make such a turnaround? What happened is that the advice Paul gave them in 1 Corinthians 12:24-26 was finally heeded. This passage is the blueprint for maximizing joyful Christian living:

> But God arranged the body, having given greater honor to the one who needs it, so that division may not be in the body, but members may be concerned the same about one another. Even if only one member suffers, all the members suffer together. If only one member is being praised, all the members rejoice together. (1 Cor 12:24-26)

These two cardinal pieces of godly advice for creating a joyful Christian community are: suffer with those who suffer, rejoice with those who are praised.

Suffering with Those Who Suffer

Suffer with those who suffer? Isn't this supposed to be a chapter on joy? Why are we talking about suffering again? What does that have to do with joy?

All true joy is experienced in the real world of suffering and pain. Joy is cognizant of the human condition. It looks at the resources within it and beyond it and draws from them what it needs. The Reverend Paul Bricker points out that the apostle Paul was able to minister continually to those initially disappointing Corinthians because his focus was not on their behavior but on the grace that God had given them. "Grace to you and peace from God our Father and Lord Jesus Christ," Paul begins each letter (1 Cor 1:3; 2 Cor 1:2), and

"I thank my God always concerning you upon the grace of God given to you in Christ Jesus" (1 Cor 1:4). God's grace at work in the Corinthians was what Paul focused upon. Eventually, that grace grew within them and flowered into lives of beautiful service to God. The prescription that Paul laid down back in his first letter to them became the means by which the Corinthian community was finally able to become the interconnected body of Christ on earth.

As Paul explained the context of these two principles: "But God arranged the body, having given greater honor to the one who needs it, so that division may not be in the body, but members may be concerned the same about one another" (1 Cor 12:24-25).

When Bill first came down with Crohn's Disease during a taxing and difficult summer city ministry internship, he was unable to return in the fall to his college chaplaincy for a number of months. Lying at home, unable to visit the campus, he reflected on the relationship between this passage and his own condition as an image of it. One day he dictated his thoughts to Aída, who read them that night to the students:

A Message from My Body to Our Body

Dear Friends,

I regret not being able to be here tonight because of rebellion in my personal community.

Like the body of Christ and the body of the Agape Fellowship, each of our own bodies is a microcosmic symbiotic community.

After having been through the complete GI series and numerous related tests, I have discovered that from the top of my head to the tip of my toe I am in excellent condition—with one exception. In my colon I have a deep-seated, uncooperative, rebellious, dissident infection that has seized a small area and is warding off the rest of my cooperative. It lies in wait and when called on to perform its functions shirks its duty and stirs up fever and pain. As a result, my whole community suffers debilitating weight loss, fever, cramping, tension and discouragement.

Many communities have a perfect system except for one individualized, self-motivated, diseased colon who is dedicated not to serve but to be served.

My prayer for myself and each of you is that God will make each of us listening ears and helping hands to one another, that we will have no diseased colons spiritually, and that Agape and each of us will become healthy, serving-others-oriented bodies of Christ.

With love,
Bill

God intends for us to concentrate on each other, so that no divisions, no rebellions occur because a part feels left out, or overburdened, or treated with little honor and low regard. Concern for one another is God's intention.

What is the first way Paul directs us to show concern? Suffer with members who suffer so that all members suffer together. We notice that this piece of advice does not necessarily remove our problems and catastrophes. What it does is gives us comradeship, sympathetic communal concern for our well-being, which mitigates the effects of the occasional disasters and miseries this world of pain forces us to undergo. All of us are forced to suffer at one time or another. How crucial then—and how needed—is this advice to suffer together and not make light of one another's heartaches!

When Bill came down with his chronic illness, nothing galled him more than people telling him his illness "could be worse" or "was not that important" or "would be over soon." All of those were well-intentioned lies. The chronic illness drags on and on—twenty years at this writing. Bill was subjected to all those silly "health" and "opportunity" fads. Some told him it was a gift from God for which he should be thankful—the "thank God I have cancer!" syndrome. If it was such a great gift, Bill did not see why they were not praying for it too. Some people liked to ignore it—the "you never looked so good, so it can't be that bad" approach. "My, how do you stay so thin?" people would gush. Bill would reply, "Oh, just come down with this stuff and you'll be as thin as you want." At one point, frustrated, Bill made up a page entitled "Sense and Nonsense About Illness," composed of all the fatuous things people said to him. He wrote:

I wouldn't want to have a world free of troubles and disease now because:

1. Disease and misfortune make us more spiritual.

2. We learn to pity and have sympathy for others.

3. Seeing others in distress teaches us to be more appreciative of our health and good fortune.

4. Illness and distress make people more dependent on others, which is good for them (being too independent is a sin).

5. In our imperfect state we would be bored if we had a world free of problems (honestly, someone really said this!).

6. It wouldn't be good for us. Hardship, disease and misfortune test and prune us and teach us things we couldn't know in any other way. Therefore, they are to be welcomed as challenges, loving trials, beneficial testings, "opportunities for praise."

That is the list written under the "Nonsense" section. Nothing is listed under the "Sense" section.

Bill, deeply troubled by all the sick perspectives masquerading as Christian about sickness, began to realize that he himself had to take others' pain seriously and not try to sweep it aside. Why, he still wonders, is that so difficult to do? One reason suggests itself: others' burdens are heavy!

Sharing Burdens Is Difficult

Most of us are familiar with the famous insignia of Boys Town: a larger boy carrying a smaller boy through the snow and explaining cheerfully to Father Flanagan, "He ain't heavy, Father, he's my brother!" Neil Diamond popularized that slogan in a song that The Hollies turned into a major hit.

But most of us feel more like exclaiming, "He's heavy!" and complaining with Cain, "Am I my brother's keeper?" (Gen 4:9). We may not murder our brother or our neighbor or our spouse physically, but we certainly boil over at some of the dumb things they do. And while our oldies stations blare "He ain't heavy . . . ," our comedians amuse us with jokes about good-for-nothing brothers-in-law, pushy mothers-in-law, husbands named Fang. A visitor from outer space might conclude that the normal earthly custom is to spend half of our lives embarrassed by, exasperated with or openly despising those we claim we love!

Certainly, sometimes our loved ones do exasperating or even stupid things. So do we. But we may be persecuting them as the innocent Abel was persecuted, as our Lord Jesus was persecuted, because of the inadequacies in *ourselves.*

Did you ever wonder why Cain's sacrifice was rejected? After all, Scripture does tell us to give a portion of the first fruits of our labor back to God. But look what happened when someone did—God was angry. No wonder Cain was furious. But God explains God's rejection and rebuke of him in Genesis 4:6-7:

> And the Lord said to Cain, "Why do you glow with anger and why has your face fallen? Is it not so, if you do good, your face will be lifted up with cheerfulness? And if you do not do good, sin lies in wait at the door, and it longs for you, and you must rule over it."

Obviously, God had given some previous directions specifying what God had wanted. Abel had gotten those directions right. No doubt they presaged the blood sacrifices that Israel would eventually practice to atone for its sins, culminating ultimately in the blood sacrifice of Jesus for us on the cross. Cain, on the other hand, did not follow God's previous directives. And so he interfered with nothing less than a symbolic Christ-type, an image of God's plan of salvation. God takes these symbols in our world very seriously.[2]

Yet God does not damn Cain eternally to this terrible spot of not having measured up and therefore having been rebuked and rejected by the God of the universe. For God inquires: "Why are you angry? If you do well, will you not be accepted?" The Scripture suggests that if even Cain, whose name has come down to us, like Judas's, as synonymous with sin (e.g., "raising Cain"), had done well, God would have accepted him.[3]

How did Cain respond? Did he redouble his efforts to do good? Step over to Abel, with a humble "Gee, Abel, I really screwed up at the sacrifice, do you think you could help me out with a couple of lambs or rams? Artichokes are in season and I can trade you a couple of bushels—and about those figs you wanted . . ." No. He put the blame on his brother and responded with murderous envy. Cain, by laying the burden of death on his brother, laid a corresponding burden of condemnation on himself. How many times do we respond like Cain? Push the burden of our faults on others in classic projection? If we don't share our burdens, we ourselves will give—and receive on ourselves—oppressive burdens ultimately too much to bear. Jesus, our Savior, realized this when he told us to bring our heavy burdens to him and take on a new light burden of salvation (Mt 11:28-30). That new lighter burden is designed to free our shoulders of our former cares so that we can now fulfill Paul's injunction in Galatians 6:2: we can ease one another just as Jesus eased us.

Think of that. The main focus of our ministry is bearing the burdens of our good-for-nothing brothers-in-law, pushy mothers-in-law, husbands, wives, children, that rotten kid who always sits in the pew in front of us. The inverse, Jesus' brother James warns us, produces misery: "What causes wars and what causes fightings among you? Is it not from this very source: out of your passions that are at war in your members? You desire and do not have; so you kill. And you covet and are not able to obtain, so you fight and wage war. You do not have, because you do not ask! You ask and do not receive, because you ask wrongly, in order to spend it on your passions—unfaithful creatures!" (Jas 4:1-4). Looking out for number one in the Christian community, looking out for our own "passions" and appetites, only leads us to disaster.

Looking Out for Number One

The secular world is currently learning this lesson. In a fascinating article in the February 24, 1991, *Boston Globe Magazine,* Nathan Cobb notes that the "Me Generation" seems to be giving way to the "We Generation." Where Robert Ringer's *Looking Out for Number One,* Rhett Butler's "Frankly, my dear, I don't give a damn," and suntanning with one's ears plugged by a Sony Walkman were the props of the past, today Deborah Tannen's *You Just Don't Understand,* John Donne's "No man is an island," and "attending a church supper" after having spoken on one's car phone with call waiting are the marks of the present. As he quotes relationship trainer Julio Olalla of the Newfield Group, which offers courses in human relationships:

> Before, the idea of "relationships" was considered a flaky, California type of idea. People had no time for it. There was this crazy search for the "self," and relating took second place to finding the self. But now, today, the concern about relations has increased. And we're not just talking about romance. Yes, marriage is nothing but relating. But your job is nothing but relating, too. And your friendships are nothing but relating . . . the individual is a social construction.[4]

New relationship-oriented groups are springing up everywhere. One such phenomenon is the men's movement, begun "because boys in our society don't grow up with their fathers around," according to one organizer, Al DeGroot. Interviewer Eric Schwartz, editor of the *Hamilton/Wenham Chronicle* in Massachusetts, explains, "Where once sons learned at their father's knee about everything from work to family relations, there was a void created as dads were called off to work outside the home. As a consequence, the theory goes, men in our culture have gotten out of touch with their own masculinity."⁵

The church was just such a small group organization long before the world rediscovered the cell-group structure. We should be the ones most helping our families, most fostering healthy relationships.

The problem is that instead of "leavening" the world, instead of showing others the right relational way so they will not have to take centuries to rediscover it, we are following the world's way, letting the world's errors conform us to its fragmented image, so that Christian business begins to look as ruthless as secular business, Christian rock stars get divorced like secular rock stars, Christian religious power-mongers glitter and oppress like secular powermongers. Such conforming cannot help but come back upon us and destroy our very relational structure—that which makes the Christian community unique, our source of continuing life, health and joy.

Putting Others First
Instead, the disciple John tells us we should be others-oriented like Jesus. He explains in 1 John 3:16: "In this we have known love, because that one on behalf of us laid down his life; and we ought to lay down lives on behalf of the brothers and sisters." John has just warned his hearers in 3:12 not to be like Cain, who murdered his brother, but instead, "let us not love in word or speech but in deed and truth" (1 Jn 3:18). The apostle John himself built his entire ministry on this precept, once, according to the historian Clement, even charging into the center of a gang of bandits to bring one back to repentance in Christ.⁶

Another strong tradition tells us that when John became very aged he could only with difficulty be carried to church in the arms of his disciples. He could not speak much, but what he used to say over and over was, "Little children, love one another." Exasperated with hearing the same thing over and over, his disciples and the other elders once exclaimed, "Master, why do you always say this?" "It is the Lord's command," replied John, "and if only this be done, it is enough."⁷ John, being borne by others, was still bearing their burdens in his love for them.

Others' burdens are heavy to bear. This is true. But they are surely not as heavy as the burden of sins we once bore. Nor are they as heavy as the burden of loneliness we will bear if we cut ourselves off from the Christian community. This is the burden that ultimately weighed Bill's father down in sorrow to his grave.

What do we look like? Cain, staggering around, complaining, under the weight of guilt of the dead bodies of our brothers and sisters killed in spirit by our hatred, selfish ambition and bitter envy? Or are we like Paul and John, throwing our burden of sin on Jesus, and, light and strong now, able to dash to catch falling family members and help them shoulder their difficulties by sharing that shouldering with them? The premium paid back in the gratitude of those we help and the shining blessing of the Lord's approval is more than recompense for whatever difficulties our assistance causes us. This is the beginning of joyful living, and it is the mark of a true Christian.

Recognize Pain
A key factor in suffering with those who suffer, which is another way to say bearing one another's burdens, is developing the ability to recognize what is pain for someone else. Suffering, after all, is not always as clear-cut as illness. Pain is very individual. What is pain or catastrophe for one person is sometimes nothing more than a minor difficulty for someone else. Hence comes so much needless hurting by callousness. What we all have to do is to develop sensitivity and discernment to recognize hurt in others, even if it is not hurt to us. And then not to make light of it.

For example, as Beth Spring pointed out in her 1987 *Christianity Today* article "When the Dream Child Dies," "the pain of infertility causes much hidden grief in our churches." As one woman lamented, "I could not share this burden with anyone. . . . My peer group so valued children as a reward and so stressed that God will give you the desires of your heart that I could never admit that we, the leaders, were experiencing a barren field." Spring catalogs a list of fatuous responses inflicted on the infertile by the well-meaning that rivals Bill's list of nonsense about illness, responses like "Just relax," "Adopt—then you'll get pregnant" or "Take a long vacation."[8]

Scripture focuses upon three different kinds of pain: *pain innocently suffered* in the world of pain (or inflicted on us by those who share this world with us), *pain from evil* (the absence of God) and *pain for good* (the presence of God).

We have already discussed in detail the pain that comes to us from the fallen world because we are fallen mortals, subjected to death in its many limited and final forms. Psalm 104:27-30 captures the agony of the second category:

[Your creatures] all look to you
to give them their food in due season;
when you give to them, they gather it up;
when you open your hand,
they are filled with good things.
When you hide your face,
they are dismayed;
when you take away their breath,
they die and return to their dust.
When you send forth your spirit,
they are created;
and you renew the face of the ground. (NRSV)

When we disobey God, we experience the pain of punishment, the pain of God's displeasure, of God's absence.

The third category differs from the first two in that it introduces us to *a pain that can be good for us*. To repent is a painful experience. To see who God is and to compare God with what we are is painful. A proper response to that pain of conviction and the full realization of our guilt and uncleanness before God is to regret all the wrong we have done, to throw ourselves on God's mercy and worship God.

Pain in this sense is helpful to us. Those with conditions that leave them with no active nerve endings have no way to be warned if they are being burned. Pain demands attention. It is a sentry calling a loud warning to us.

Bill's father used to warn him not to be like many who sense a physical pain in their body and ignore it, growing used to it over time and compensating mentally for it. "That's how you die," he would warn. "When you finally acknowledge it, it's too late." How sadly ironic that he ignored this good advice himself in his final days when a stomach tumor festered untreated. Pain is God's way of protecting us in the fallen world. It cries out, "I am injured (physically, emotionally, spiritually)—I need attention." When we inflict pain on others we are interrupting the sentry system of God. God will not hold us blameless for that.

Conflict between people produces pain. The discipline of "Conflict Dynamics" is an attempt to channel this pain into something helpful and constructive. If it helps two people or two groups to become more loving or just toward one another, then it has produced positive results. Before Aída went to seminary and was called by God to teach the Bible, she was trained as a social worker. Working as a community organizer in New Jersey, serving underrepresented, underprivileged constituencies, she learned that change is painful but often unavoidable. Sometimes the short-term pain of the swift operation will forestall the long-term pain of illness, injury—or oppression.

However, lest this statement be misunderstood, the goal is to understand and treat each other better, not remove each other from the face of the earth. One has to judge whether the pain of confrontation will be *less* devastating than the cumulative pain of nonconfrontation. If the new pain achieves better conditions for all together, then this pain was worth it.

C. S. Lewis points out that the strongest argument against love is that it might lead to suffering.[9] The difference between love and kindness is this acceptance or avoidance of pain. In kindness one kills a sick dog so it will avoid pain. Love, however, sometimes necessitates helping a loved one go through and not avoid a necessary painful situation. The current debate on euthanasia is argued along these lines. What is true with humans' dealing with one another is also true with God's dealing with us. God's love may cause us pain. Individually and corporately we need to be purified and have our evil removed. From God always emanates a continuous burning fire. Isaiah is touched by a hot coal to purify his lips to speak forth God's truth (Is 6:6-9). Moses experiences God as a burning bush (Ex 3:2-4). The New Jerusalem will have "no need of the sun nor of the moon in order that they might shine on it for the glory of God gives it light, and its lamp is the Lamb" (Rev 21:23). We often speak about burning in hell. We may burn entering heaven! If we want to be like Christ, if we want to approach God, we must be cleansed and our works must be tried by fire (1 Cor 3:12-15). We do not have to welcome pain, as we noted in the "Nonsense" list, yet we recognize its worth.

But pain is not simply a human experience. Nor is it limited to the animal world. Pain is not only a mortal reality but a divine one as well. God can empathize with our pain because God has felt pain too. Genesis 6:6 talks about God's regret: "And the Lord was sorry that he had made people on the earth, and it grieved him to his heart." When God sees evil in God's good creation, God knows pain. When God walked among us, God experienced both human and divine pain. "He was despised and rejected by people," prophesies Isaiah in 53:3, "a man of sufferings, and acquainted with grief; as one from whom people hide their faces he was despised, and we esteemed him not."

As we become more like God, we will share a similar pain when we see people pursue evil, neglect good, act callously toward the suffering of others. When God sees pain, God responds. God declares in Exodus 3:7-8: "I have surely seen the oppression of my people who are in Egypt, and I have heard their cry on account of their taskmasters, because I know their sufferings. And I have come down to deliver them out of the hand of the Egyptians." God's response, of course, was to send a human to alleviate their pain—Moses.

Solomon with his God-given wisdom had a plethora of good advice about taking others' pain seriously. One who sings songs to a heavy heart, Proverbs 25:20 counsels, is like one who pours vinegar on a wound! Instead, Solomon warns, we should be careful what we say. Our words should be healing instead of rash (Prov 12:18), soft (15:1; 25:15), gentle (15:4), slow to anger (15:18; 16:32; 19:11). We should give an apt word in season (25:11-12), ponder how to answer (15:28; 29:20). Our words should be few (14:23; 17:27-28; 21:23; 29:11; Eccles 6:11). Wise people listen before speaking (Prov 18:13). They know that a broken spirit is worse than a sickness (18:14), so they are patient and forgiving (17:9). They do not fight with others (17:14, 19; 20:3; 26:20-21) and they do not meddle in others' lives when they are not invited (26:17). The difference between ministering and meddling is often a thin line, harder to pace than the white line the intoxicated try to walk on New Year's Eve under the glare of the traffic police's searchlight.

The secret here for each of us lies in developing discernment and true caring. By suffering together, we can share and alleviate the pain of catastrophe through empathetic intervening, through expressions and actions of care by our Christian community. That kind of true empathy goes beyond words, or it takes our faltering words and transfigures them.

When the wonderful Joe Bayly, Christian educator, president of David C. Cook Publishing Company, author of classic stories like *The Gospel Blimp* and "I Saw Gooley Fly," died, his obituary recounted all of the suffering he had experienced—losing three sons, a baby to cystic fibrosis, a five-year-old to leukemia, his nineteen-year-old to hemophilia in a sledding accident: "Moments after his 5-year-old died of leukemia, Bayly was in an elevator with a nurse who had cared for the boy. She broke an uneasy silence by saying, 'I wish I could say something that would help ease your pain.' Bayly replied, 'You just did.' "[10]

Rejoicing with Those Who Are Praised

Bill felt somewhat nervous about doing it. He realized that never in his church experience had he heard anybody make an announcement like this. After all, what did this have to do with spiritual things? When we say, "I'd like to announce that Teddy has given his life to Christ!" we are all delighted and in many cases applaud. That is *spiritual!* But this announcement . . .

So Bill kept the trophy hidden until the last minute. And then when the worship leader said, "Are there any announcements?" he jumped up before he could lose his nerve and, waving the trophy, announced, "Yes, I have one. I want to mention that on Tuesday our son Steve won the Northern Massachusetts/Southern New Hampshire Middle School wrestling championship at 68 pounds. I brought his trophy and everybody can see it after the service."

What was the reaction? The entire body cheered and clapped. A week later another father got up and announced his son had won a place in a statewide competition for band. Then someone announced that another member had been given an advancement in his job. Then the father who had commended his son's band achievement was recognized himself for winning a cash bonus at work for the excellence of his on-the-job performance. "Yes," Bill said to himself, "this is what the body of Christ is supposed to look like." Why should we spend our lives seeking to separate the spiritual from the secular? No secular exists for Christians—*all* we do is for the glory of Christ. When we honor Christ in the workplace, in our sportsmanship, by the recognition of our excellence, the body should cheer us on. It should celebrate, because when Christians are honored truly, Christ is honored.

"If only one member is being praised, all the members rejoice together" (1 Cor 12:26). That is Paul's second crucial piece of advice for maximizing joyful Christian living.

What is odd is that sometimes people find Paul's first piece of advice, to suffer with those who are suffering, easier to put into practice than to rejoice with someone else when that person is being praised.

In the very next chapter, 1 Corinthians 13:4, Paul tells us "love is not envious or boastful." That is the negative way to state what our passage is phrasing positively. Love is not envious, so when somebody is being praised, love does not covet the honor. Instead, if only one member is being praised, all the members rejoice together.

Praise in Greek means literally "a word of glory." It is the word which we use as a cognate in English to build our word *doxology,* that glorifying hymn many of us sing each Sunday to honor God. Now we are commanded to recognize and celebrate a word of glory given to each other. Paul reminds us in 1 Corinthians 13:4 that love is also not boastful. Proverbs 25:27 points out that we cannot say a word of glory about ourselves, "It is not good to eat much honey, nor is it glory to search out one's own glory." Instead, we have to receive our human doxology from outside ourselves. 1 Corinthians 12:26 phrases its injunction in the passive tense: "If only one member is being praised."

Therefore, when someone rightly receives glory from a source beyond that person, Paul declares that our proper response is to commend that brother or sister for the honor received. This is not boasting, for another boasts on our behalf!

To counteract a person's being honored by tearing that person down when he or she is praised for accomplishments by others, supposedly so that "they won't get a swelled head," is an odious act of sheer envy thinly disguised as virtue. "What causes wars and fightings among you?" asks James, Jesus' brother. Your passions cause war among your members (Jas 4:1). Such conflict should never be permitted, especially in a Christian community or family.

Remember, as the beginning of our text states, we are supposed to be a body without division. We should take a positive lesson from our own physical bodies, the source of Paul's metaphor. If somebody says to you, "Say, you know, you really have a good mind! Wow, are you smart!" do you not feel warm and delighted all over? You don't say, "Hey, what about my rippling muscles?" or "Yes, but you didn't mention my eyes—like deep, clear pools." No, your body cooperates and everything feels affirmed and rejoices together.

Look at what happens when one runs. The heart pumps faster, the blood carries more food and oxygen to the muscles, the legs move faster in larger strides, the lungs breathe in air faster, the eyes become more watchful. This is cooperation. This is the mutual care that should characterize the body of Christ.

The truly spiritual person is the one who guards against bitter envy and instead expresses supportive approval for others when they are being praised.

The same James who warned that passions cause war and fighting when they are not controlled gives us a picture of what a supportive Christian should look like. Literally he writes:

> Who is wise and learned among you? Prove out of good behavior his works in gentle [that is, humble] wisdom. But if you have bitter jealousy and selfish ambition in your [plural] heart, do not boast and lie against the truth. That is not the wisdom coming down from above, but one that is earthly, unspiritual, demonic. For where envy and selfish ambition are, there are restlessness and all worthless evil deeds. But the wisdom from above is first pure [or holy], then peaceful, gentle, obedient, full of mercy and good fruits, without prejudice [or favoritism], sincere. But fruit of righteousness in peace is sown by the ones who do peace. (Jas 3:13-18)

This is what characterizes a truly wise person, filled with godly wisdom. This kind of Christian brings peace, not disorder, is gentle, not harsh, does not use education or learning as a weapon to slug others but as an aid to assist, is not arrogant or closed-minded, is full of mercy, is not cruel or judgmental, is just [impartial], conducting a life of good action, unadulterated by selfish ambition or envy.

How can we achieve such a life? First, we should control our passions and school ourselves to be glad when others in the Christian community succeed. If we praise them and rejoice with them, our own time will soon come. God never leaves any of us lacking.

Next, we must cut out that biting put-down humor that mars so much of the Christian church. We forbid it in our home. Teasings such as "Hey, ugly!" and "Take my wife, please!" and "Are you on your knees or standing up?" and "Oh, no, are you going to sing? Pass the cotton!" are the cancer of community. They rot it out from the inside until it is ailing and ultimately dies in silent agony.

Instead, we must practice that word "to rejoice together," *synchairō*. One word in Greek, it appears seven times in the New Testament. It means "to congratulate" or "to take part in the joy of another." This is what happened to Elizabeth and Zechariah, the parents of John the Baptist. When neighbors and kinsfolk heard that the Lord had shown great mercy on them by Elizabeth's pregnancy, they rejoiced with her (Lk 1:57-58). This is also what the man who found his lost sheep was requesting, when he called to all, "Rejoice with me, because I found my lost sheep" (Lk 15:6), or the woman with the lost coin, "Rejoice with me, because I found the coin which I lost" (Lk 15:9). This is the kind of joy experienced in heaven when a sinner repents. Jesus told the Pharisees and scribes that the angels have a party (Lk 15:10).

In our own homes and in our churches we can get a head start on heaven, on that great party called the marriage supper of the Lamb to which we are heading. We can start by rejoicing with others here and now. And in doing so we make ourselves more "rejoiceable with," so that when our time comes, then others will want to affirm us. This we can do by continually encouraging one another.

Summary

What have we learned about God's plan for joyful living? Christianity is communal. Through mutual cooperation and support, God brings in God's reign and with it joy to each of us. Over twenty words are used in the Old and New Testaments to describe joy. Ultimately, caring joy comes from our assurance of eternal salvation. When we are distressed, we need to draw on God's eternal joy as a resource. But for day-to-day joy, a temporal enjoyment is also provided to us from the work we do and from eating, drinking, enjoying the good things

God puts in this world for our use.

Further, God is communal in nature. God gives us one another so we can learn about loving others, so that eventually we can love the Great Other. That is why we cannot claim to love God whom we have not seen if we do not love one another whom we continually see. Understanding this, we need to rely on our relationships to bring us joy. First, each of us must become a Christian and in this way get to know God, learning to rely on God, learning to pray to God. We soon learn to relax, recognizing our limitations and avoiding the trap Moses fell into, not taking undue responsibility (that is, doing God's job) and not heaping undue responsibility on other humans. Instead, we should suffer with those of us who suffer and rejoice with those who are being praised. In this way and in other ways we should help to bear one another's burdens. In fact, our every effort should be expended in encouraging one another.

Out of sorrow and disappointment Bill's father neglected the wise opening words of the mayor's letter so many years ago, to draw on *both* an abiding faith in God *and* the concern of the community. He retained the first, but in disappointed sorrow he lost the second. Bill's mother, struggling under the same sorrow, swallowed her pride and held onto both. Through great trial and great grieving she was able to endure, today having another "daughter" given to her, and a grand-child, and a loving church.

Let us all heed the Scriptures, for in them God has given words for a joyful life: "not neglecting to meet together, as is the habit of some, but encouraging, and all the more as you see the day drawing near" (Heb 10:25).

Vapors Gather in the Morning
       (a song)

Vapors gather in the morning,
Grain blows gently in the fields,
We ask the reason why the seasons must be real.
But God's love will still be ours,
Yes, and God's love will still be ours.

Someday the heavens will be broken,
Someday the dust of earth will fade,
Someday the world we know will lie in a silent grave.
But God's love will still be ours.
Yes, and God's love will still be ours.

God's love will live a constancy,
While all else fades.
God's love knows only constancy.
It will remain.

Maybe we will not live forever,
We'll pass as surely as the dawn.
Someday the morning sun will shine to find we are gone.
But God's love will still be ours.
Yes, and God's love will still be ours.
Yes, and God's love will still be ours.

WILLIAM DAVID SPENCER, 1971

10

THE JOY
OF THE MORNING

*F*or four years we lived in downtown Newark, New Jersey. Every time we would walk down to a department store, a fortuneteller would stand on her steps and yell out: "Want your fortune told? Only a dollar today!" We were so tired of hearing her offer that we would sometimes cross the street just to avoid her. But one day Aída had the nerve to reply: "Thank you, but I already know what the future holds for me, and it is wonderful!"

Jesus has taught us to pray: "Thy kingdom come, thy will be done, on earth as it is in heaven." And this is exactly what God will do. God's kingdom will be complete on earth, just as it now is in heaven. The firmament separating earth and heaven will be no more. The question "if God exists and God is good, why does suffering exist in the world?" will no longer be asked. God's favor, the joy of the morning (Ps 30:5), will continue forever. Weeping will appear to be only last night's bad dream. That is the vision which draws us through and gives us hope.

At his father's funeral, Bill announced that his father finally had "gained what he cannot now lose. He has gotten straight what can no longer become crooked on him. He is home. And as a loving and generous father, he is again enjoying the delightful company of his own beloved daughter Carol in that most happy family gathering of his Father and ours."

Why then do any of us ever have to suffer? All suffering is explained by understanding who God is. Because God is just and God is love, pain and suffering exist. We needed the book to explain this premise.

We have observed that we often notice only our own suffering, but suffering is general in what our world has become. Our world did not begin with suffering. All of creation was declared good by God. God intended for people to enjoy food, beauty, wisdom. But God is characterized by grace *and* truth, and God's commands, while not impossible, are real and carry with them real consequences if disobeyed. People were made responsible and able to choose. Individual free will was real in Eden's garden. Confusing the serpent's likeness with God's was an evil choice that bore authentic, far-reaching individual and collective consequences for humans, animals and nature. Death entered and the world was plunged into pain—a world that human sin created under the serpent's dominion, where children like Carol die and painters like Father Spencer are hurt. Life is difficult in this world that sin has cursed, but God has not abandoned humanity. God still comforts and calls for human response. True love must be voluntary, obedience genuine in a mutually honored covenant of love between God and humans.

In response to the entanglements of a world invaded by evil, Christians try to free people from shame, to help people repent from their sins. The Christian task is to stop or lessen others' pain, fighting evil and injustice.

Sometimes the best response is a firm, gentle word. Sometimes it is silence. Sometimes it is action. Death and accident and misunderstanding should be expected in all our lives. Life should be ordered by Christians so that we are ready for death or calamity at any moment. And each day should be enjoyed and lived fully. Those suffering should be allowed to express pain. People in pain are to be treated as full persons, as each of us would want to be treated.

For any person suffering, the means God has given us are both divine and human. God provides us first with the privilege of prayer, through which we can deal with our loneliness, actually entering God's presence and asking for deliverance.

Then sufferers need to recognize their own and others' mortality. Sufferers must remember that for a Christian suffering is not eternal. But neither are we eternal in this mortal state. Some of our suffering comes not from the fallen world but from a false sense of our immortality, expressed in overwork, in living only for long-range goals and in not resting. God has put eternity in our hearts so we might seek God and God's eternal will. God intends for us to eat and drink and enjoy our work, living for our work for God's reign today and redeeming the time we are given. God will gather our work up and preserve what is of eternal significance.

Further, sin is a serious problem, no matter how minor it seems. A favorite children's sermon of Bill's is to ask on a hot Sunday morning if the children are thirsty. "Yes," they all reply. Then from a cooler he pours out a luscious glass of cool, sparkling water. "Who wants it?" "Me!" they all sing out, grabbing for the glass. "Oh, just one more thing," Bill says, producing a small bottle of India ink marked "Poison." He shows it around and then drops one inky drop into the water. "Let's stir it in," he says. "There, it's disappeared mostly. Okay, now who wanted that drink?" Nobody! "You, Jamie?" "No way!" "Chris?" Chris covers his mouth. "Anna?" Anna scrunches her head down and blocks her face with her arms. Well-taught and wise children learn swiftly that the consequences of sin, as of poison, are real and deadly.

Our first response to suffering is that God is punishing us for our sin and we should look inside to see if we need repentance. This is the place to start: seeking repentance, confessing our sins to one another so that we might be healed (Jas 5:16).

Having done this, if we are not relieved, we next need to realize that not all suffering is caused by punishment. Understanding this keeps us from heaping false guilt on those already suffering. In that way we do not add to the burdens they already bear. What both sufferers and those seeking to comfort them need to ask is, "What is my responsibility before God?" We must remind ourselves that God is glorified when people are healed from their suffering, but not disgraced when they are not.

Our Lord Jesus' being crucified was not only an action which God did to bring us cleansed into the divine presence, but it was also an action which instructed us about the very nature of God. When we suffer for righteousness's sake we become more Christlike, suffering vicariously and receiving God's blessing.

Still, the spiritual person lives out in community the life of "Christ crucified." Crucifixion living identifies a person with those who are members of God's family, working hard yet enduring economic difficulties, being slandered, resisting evil for the sake of advancing God's reign among people. It expresses itself in teaching, preaching, interdependent leadership, obeying God's laws, and enduring "weakness"—physical discomfort from the persecution of false believers, from the rigors of traveling to spread the reign of God, from working hard while often not having all the physical necessities required, and from experiencing the mental anguish that comes from passionate concern for others' growth in Christ.

Some may conclude that a very serious kind of testing was involved in Bill's family's difficulties. Just when Bill and his father had been thoroughly active Christians for about the same number of years, some great physical catastrophe struck them. For Bill's father it was accident, for Bill a chronic disease. Bill is convinced that his father's

suffering was simply part of a world of pain and that both their suffering was evil's persecution in an attempt to block their growth and
active lives of service to others.

Carol's situation was entirely different. This "little girl" with "her
sweet testimony" may have been tested and found complete by God
and ready to enter her "Home with Christ," to apply the words of the
Bowery Mission director. Perhaps Bill and his parents, far less complete in their sanctification, needed vastly longer lives to be worked
into the proper attitude for heaven. First Corinthians 5:5 and 11:30
tell us that some people who have blundered into a cul-de-sac of sin
have gotten so far off track that God swiftly calls them home. Other
people, like Enoch, grow so close to God that they simply "are not,"
for they step into God's presence (Gen 5:24). Memories of Carol, who
once while lost in a department store was found propped up on a
counter preaching to the saleswomen, suggest the latter.

Testing is an inward advancement of God's reign. God is a God who
examines and judges humans. God prunes us as a gardener prunes, for
humans are not pure, and God's cleansing activity is necessary. God
is an examining, searching, investigating God who searches for love
demonstrated in action, which itself becomes a means for humans to
identify with the God who suffers for us. God searches to purify,
looking for faith. God's goal is always for us to mature. God, however,
does not tempt us. Our own desires for economic or social superiority,
our selfish ambition, our envy, greed and lust do that, as does our
testing of God.

Christ taught, preached and healed in the midst of the fallen world
to teach humans we need not act in a fallen way. We need to be
reconciled with God and one another, being individually and corporately just. We need to heal people physically, psychically, emotionally
and spiritually to bring all under God's reign.

What the church should do is keep actively in mind its mission to
promote God's reign. The church should be the locus of judging and
healing, whether it does so by enabling its members to repent when

they are spiritually sick, anointing them with oil and praying for them
when they are physically sick, or wrestling with the evil within them
and around them and driving it out when people are oppressed and
possessed. Responding to suffering is a mammoth task, but what did
we expect when we began to follow a Lord who laid down his life for
his friends?

Why do some suffer beyond normal punishment for sin, beyond
evident persecution, beyond the limits of testing, beyond the normal
exigencies of a fallen world of sin? The final category is a repository
called mystery.

By all common sense and by Proverbs's scriptural sense, the righteous ought to be rewarded with temporal blessing. Inversely, the
wicked should suffer temporally for their wickedness. Such is the
understanding of Job's friends. Such is the understanding of the book
of Proverbs. But as true as this often is, it was not true in Job's case,
and his friends' common sense did not provide true statements about
Job. Like the wondering deacons and the whispering funeral attenders
Bill encountered as a boy, Job's friends were deeply disturbed; their
whole sense of the universe was thrown out of balance if Job (and
Bill's father and sister) did not have *some* secret sin somewhere to
explain the severe trouble they had somehow incurred (all of Job's
generous acts and Bill's father's rescue mission work notwithstanding).
But Job is blameless, and he is not being tested so that he will be
purged from evil. To Job his suffering is a complete mystery.

God's response is not to explain, though somewhere afterward the
reason does come to light: that war in heaven has caused God to send
forth Job as champion into a most difficult arena. Instead, God af-
firms right responses to suffering. And God rejects unwise ones, no
matter how right they are in other circumstances or how scriptural
sounding. When Job finally gets his hearing in God's presence, the
entire question of how a righteous person can suffer becomes moot.
Perhaps the reason is that Job confronts a suffering God who should
not be suffering either.

Why a specific righteous person is suffering is a question that has value only to a certain point. That point passes swiftly if each of the other categories is examined unsuccessfully. Beyond that point we need to trust that *God is good even in the midst of our adversity.* Our activity, then, should be invested in seeking alleviation for that suffering.

After all, the healing task is not ours alone—it is a communal task to care for one another. This is the theology of communal love that flows from the nature of God. God has given us overwhelming resources—God's self and one another. Joyful living is attainable despite the troubles of a fallen world, so we need to draw on God's provisions of eternal and temporal joy. We need to develop a joyful relationship with God, drawing our strength through prayer, recognizing our limitations and resting in God, not taking God's place and falling in a "Moses trap" of overwork, but doing our part for God. At the same time we must develop joyful relationships with people, putting communal joy into practice, just as God has done for us.

There is no neat explanation for the two accidental events that blighted Father Spencer's life. He was a newly Christian man living in a world of pain. Some of that pain reached out and seized him when his child died. God was not remote: God's child had also died. The evil that killed Jesus killed little Carol. Like Jesus, Carol, who at eleven years was a radiant Christian with "a sweet testimony," was gathered up into the arms of her heavenly Father, awaiting the resurrection that would give her victory over eternal death. That victory in the covenant was assured her by God's Son Jesus.

Like Job, Father Spencer suffered further calamity at the mysterious will of God, that permission that took Job's first children, his livelihood and his health. Unlike Job, however, he did not have what he lost restored directly to him. Indirectly, Aída became a second Carol; real estate work—working for someone else—replaced his own contracting business. Health was not restored fully. Job's boils apparently ceased, but despite Father Spencer's determined persistence, his left hand and leg were never able to regain full capacity free of pain, and a wound on his heel never healed. Job lived one hundred and forty years after his trials, seeing four generations and blessed with more possessions and wealth than he had at the beginning (Job 42:10-17). Father Spencer lived exactly thirty years after the second of his two great trials. For years afterward he tried various churches and kept doing his evangelistic talks, but he had become estranged from the Christian community from which he should have drawn his greatest comfort—as such he was a man bereft of family. Cutting off the Christian community in time of trouble is cutting off the key resources that God has given us. Prayer and conversation, communion and comfort, personal and intercessory prayer, silent nearness of another's empathetic support in sorrow—these are the keys to survival.

We need to take into account the insidious power of the evil that opposes us. The Christian community should be seen as comrades in arms, one falling after another, each picking up and patching up the fallen comrade, the whole army moving together into thickening battle. Warriors suffer. Warriors die. But warriors win too. Like wounded warriors go the saints of God. Christians limp through the war of this life with heels bruised by the bite of the serpent. Yet these wounds of ours are often signs of our victory as well as our symbols of suffering. Our heels have been bruised, true, but evil's head has been crushed. The contest is not equal. We have joy in the midst of battle, for our opponent's wound is mortal and our victory immortal. Through Christ's triumph, the war is ours. Our victory is greater than our suffering. The night of weeping is yielding even now to an eternal day of joy. The means of this transition is reflected in our loving acts for one another.

The disciples glorified God that they were worthy to suffer in Christ's name. They knew the war was real and did not expect to emerge unscathed. Neither should we.

What we need to concentrate on is extending comfort and helping all experience joy. This joy is the well-being that comes from knowing

we rest and work in the love of God and the Christian community—
and rip this joy, if we have to, from the grasping claw of evil. We
worship a God who suffered and died. All of us can expect to do the
same. But we worship a God who laughed and who loved and who
conquered death in ultimate victory! And we can expect all these
things too.

God has given us God's love and the love of one another. A house
united cannot fall; against the church of Christ united the gates of hell
will not prevail.

Joy is not the other side of suffering, as if joy exists only when
suffering is removed. Joy comes *in the midst* of suffering from our
great spiritual resources: the love of God and of our fellow humans.
That love is what helps sufferers cling to the great virtue that carries
them through: perseverance. That supportive love is what makes the
difference between those who are saved in suffering and those who are
lost. And that love is what will enable us to stand united, victorious,
in the joy of God's eternal morning.

Appendix A: Study Questions

These questions are suggestions for group or individual study, for either discussion or lecture options. They can be used as an eight- to ten-week curriculum. The number of questions used will depend on the time available. Appendix B can be used as a supplementary handout or for further study as a group if there is enough time.

Sessions 1-2: World of Pain; Response to a World of Pain
The introduction begins with a story. Read that story out loud ("A man in a thriving church. . . . His partner looked away"). Ask: How would you analyze this true story biblically? Why do you think this family suffered? Should they have done anything differently? Jot down everyone's response (on a transparency or poster board if available). Do not evaluate the responses at this time. Use them to interest the group in the topic: "That's what we are going to study." At the last session, you may again show people this list of initial comments and ask if any would care to change their responses as a result of the study.

A. Presentation Approach (which can always be combined with one group question)

Briefly summarize the main points of chapter one and the key responses to suffering found in chapter two. Photocopy Appendix B.1 as a handout. Ask participants to give one example in their own lives of someone effectively making one of these responses to suffering.

B. Group Discussion (discussion may be more productive if group members work through the questions on their own in advance)

1. Read Genesis 3:1-6: Why did Eve and Adam eat the fruit?

   Read Genesis 3:7-19: What were the results?

   Were they free *not* to eat the fruit?

   The category "World of Pain" refers to what kind of sufferings? Read Genesis 3:21: What did God do? How is God's action a model for us?

   How are Ecclesiastes 3:10-14 and James 4:13-17 mutually explanatory? How is rest an act of faith?

2. In light of the fact that our life is as fleeting as a vapor, what are you pleased that you are doing as preparation for God's judgment?

   What would you like to change? When will you make that change?

3. Read the satire by fictional minister Gil Gamesh. What are the flaws in his thinking?

4. Optional: open or close the session with a song that deals with suffering from a fallen-world perspective.

C. Self-Study

Read a book of the Bible and jot down the reasons people suffer. (Books especially helpful are Gen, Prov, Lk, Rom and 1 Jn.)

Suffering for Fun and Profit

by the Rev. Gil Gamesh

Lately I have been observing that rash of cheap sensationalistic books that have afflicted the market on a topic of grave importance, suffering, and I think it's high time someone of competence got his two cents out of it (or even more—you never know).

In my case, for a log tibe now I habe bid a subberer ob hay feber. And I want everybody to know that the chaps who write all those books—and me, too—are right! Suffering is a great way to further your career. I think there's nothing better for you than a good backache in the morning—sort of sets the whole day in perspective.

You see, I wholeheartedly subscribe to the view that we ought to thank God for every problem—for problems are opportunities to praise. Why, just last week I had plenty of opportunity to praise. Some half-wit ran into my car, the manse roof sprung a leak and I got a hay fever attack. It was a great week for praisers.

If you look hard enough, there's good scriptural basis for this view. Why, just look at Jesus in the Garden of Gethsemane. How he thanked God for the cross that was coming—"Oh, thank you, Father, that I'm going to suffer. Thank you for this great opportunity!" Hmmm, well, don't look at Jesus, then. He sort of was into thanking God *in* every situation rather than *for* every situation, but it's the same thing really, in a way, I guess.

At any rate, getting beyond Scripture, there is a practical outworking which makes my view worthwhile and shows how it fits with our Judeo-Christian tradition's Protestant work ethic, which certainly must make it right. I am referring to the fact that my hay fever has led me to great things, and that's what counts! Why, out of it have come sermons like my great "Head Colds in the Scriptures: How To Handle Your Sinuses Like the Saints Did." It's all about Luke the physician with a little thrown in about Trophimus. Well, how do we know he *didn't* just have a bad head cold!

Then, of course, my hay fever has led to outstanding academic studies like my monograph "The Sneeze from Ancient Times to the Present with Special Attention to Its Influence on the Art of the Middle Ages." What do you think it was that got Picasso off to his brilliant start one blustery day during a chilly session at the old easel? Those cold attics finally paid off.

Above all, there is my poetry, and particularly we can see the influence in this piece:

There once was a lady named Duffy
Whose nose was incredibly stuffy.
While sneezing in bed,
She blew off her head,
And that, my dear friends,
  is a toughy!

The bard was right: suffering does do its share to produce great art! And you know, and heaven knows, I'm all for anything that pays off—as long as it doesn't hurt too much.

(as told to William David Spencer, 1973)

Session 3: Punishment for Sin

A. Presentation Approach

Briefly summarize the main points of chapter three. Photocopy Appendix B.2 as a handout.

B. Group Discussion

1. Distribute and read the poem that begins chapter three. The words are from three perspectives: a parent's, a child's and God's. Indicate who speaks each

line. What wisdom do you gather from reading all perspectives?

2. Read Luke 20:9-19. Where does this passage describe how God's external infliction of punishment and a human's internal self-infliction of punishment happen concurrently and cooperatively?

God is just *and* merciful. How are these two attributes developed in this passage? How does the parable refer both to a nation and to an individual?

3. Read 1 Peter 4:14-16. Does anyone in the class feel he or she has been punished for sin? What was the situation and how was it resolved? (Optional: Write out answer and keep private.)

4. What types of situations might look like punishment for sin but in reality are something else?

5. What should we do for others who are suffering as a result of punishment for sin?

C. Further Study

Read a book of the Bible and jot down the reasons people suffer. (Books especially helpful include: Lev, Num, Deut, 1 and 2 Kings, 1 and 2 Chron, Is, Ezek, Hos, Joel, Amos, Jon, Mic, Nahum, Hab, Hag, Zech, Mal, Jn, 1 Tim, Tit, Heb, 1 and 2 Pet, 2 and 3 Jn, Jude.)

Session 4: Persecution

A. Presentation Approach

1. Begin class by singing "Hymn of the Comforted."

2. Briefly summarize the main points of chapter four, using either key passages in 1 and 2 Corinthians or Appendix B.3, a thematic overview throughout the Bible.

B. Group Discussion

1. Compare 1 Corinthians 4:8-13 with Luke 6:20-31. (Both passages may be placed on one sheet, side by side.) How does Paul understand Jesus' use of *poor?* Literal? Spiritual? Why be *poor?*

How and why is persecution a part of a Christian life?

Should only apostles lead difficult lives?

Why is it worthwhile being a Christian if one may be persecuted?

What is the difference between "masochism" and rejoicing when one is persecuted? In summary, what is persecution?

2. Have each person divide one sheet of paper into four columns. Write in the first column, "Ways I have been persecuted for resisting evil or promoting God's reign"; in the second column, "Situations that may or may not have been persecution"; in the third column, "Ways I was able to persevere

during these events"; in the fourth column, "Present situations in which I should resist evil more or speak up more on Christ's behalf." Allow time for personal reflection and writing.

Ask people, in the large group or in pairs, to share one item from each column as time allows. If time is limited, columns 1 and 3 may be most helpful to others.

3. Second Corinthians 4:6-12; 6:1-10; 11:16—12:5 also may be used as bases for further study.

C. Further Study

Read a book of the Bible and jot down the reasons people suffer. (Books especially helpful include 1 Sam in comparison to Esther, Ps, Jer, Lam, Dan, Mt, Mk, Acts, 1 and 2 Cor, Gal, Eph, Phil, 1 and 2 Thess, 2 Tim, Rev.) Reading 1 and 2 Corinthians would supplement the chapter discussion.

Session 5: Testing

A. Presentation Approach

Briefly summarize the main points of chapter five, using Appendix B.4 as a handout.

B. Group Discussion

1. Read aloud Exodus 31:18—32:35 by having five persons read the following parts: narrator, Aaron, the Lord, Moses, Joshua, the people (the rest of the class). Compare to the poem (also read aloud) "Baptizing the Graven Image" at the beginning of the chapter. Where does the Exodus passage refer to punishment for sin and where to testing? Bill contrasts the "human" creations with God's creations. Who is "the image shaped by God's knives"?
2. The Bible uses legal, metallurgical and educational images to explain God helping us become mature believers. Read Genesis 22:1-18. Which of these images (testing, purification, training) best explains God's commands and actions in this passage?
   Compare this passage to Luke 3:22; Hebrews 11:17-19 and James 2:21.
   What aspect of Genesis 22 do each emphasize?
   "God wants voluntary active love from us." Do you agree? If yes, how are God's actions a model for our own behavior toward others?
3. Close with a song that uses metaphorical language to describe life as a training ground, such as "Spirit of the Living God," "Teach Me Thy Way, O Lord," or "Teach Me Thy Will, O Lord."

C. Further Study

Read a book of the Bible, such as James, and jot down reasons people suffer.

Hymn of the Comforted

Words and Music by
William David Spencer and
Aída Besançon Spencer

Transcribed by
Tom Morton

Session 6: Promoting God's Reign

A. Presentation Approach

1. Read James 1:17-18 and use as a basis for prayer.
2. Briefly summarize the main points of chapter six. Use Appendix B.6 as a handout.

B. Group Discussion

1. Use one of these passages to discover what God's reign is. Of what actions is God's reign comprised? (Mt 10:7-14; 4:23-25; Lk 9:1-6; Mk 6:6-13).
2. Read James 5:12-20. Why would James command the happy person to sing? Do you think "sing" is literal or an attitude or an action? Why?
   Similarly, why does James command the sick person to call for the elders?
   Has any one here asked elders to pray for them? Was any faith involved?
   Look at note 30. What meanings for "oil" best fit this passage?
   Look at note 32. What meanings for "save" (v. 15) best fit this passage? Why?
   How is confession of sin related to healing? To whom should we confess?
   How is James 1:17-18 related to 5:12-20?
   Has anyone in the group ever asked for anointing with oil by elders? What did you learn?
3. Look at the last note for the chapter. Have different group members read a sampling of these passages. Summarize what you learn from each passage.
   Has anyone in the group ever experienced demon possession or exorcism? In what way was it like or unlike the biblical texts?

C. Further Study

Read a Gospel, jotting down all of Jesus' responses to suffering.

Session 7: Mystery

Preparation: Reading the book of Job would help all students.

A. Presentation Approach

1. Read Psalm 27 and pray that all may "behold the beauty of the Lord."
2. Briefly summarize the main points of chapter seven, either using key passages in Job or using Appendix B.5, a thematic overview throughout the Bible.

B. Group Discussion

1. Can the righteous suffer? According to the text, did Job have some sin that needed to be removed? Read Job 1:1, 8; 2:3; 42:7-8; Ezekiel 14:12-20.
   Read Job 42:5-6. What makes Job stop asking God for a response?
   Read James 5:1-11. How did Job "persevere"? How is he a model to us of

what actions are acceptable to God?

"Either a friend like the friends of Job or death": What can this Jewish popular saying mean? (*Babylonian Talmud* Baba Bathra 16b).

2. Four suggestions are made at the end of this chapter:

Do not reduce all suffering to one cause. Encourage people to dwell on God's nature. Stay in the Christian community. Ask what can be done *now*. What resources does your church have for helping people who are suffering? What can be done to improve these resources? In which of these four suggestions do you have most strength and in which do you need more growth? How can you improve?

C. *Further Study*

Read Job and jot down each reason for suffering as it is mentioned. What is God's perspective in the narrative? Whom does God affirm? Another helpful book to read is Habakkuk.

Sessions 8-9: Joy in the Midst of Suffering; Encouraging One Another

A. *Presentation Approach*

1. Briefly summarize the main points of chapters eight and nine, using Appendix B.5 as a handout.

2. Read Matthew 25:31-40. Compare Jesus' teaching here to the poem at the beginning of chapter eight, "Nursing One Another." Explain in what way they communicate the same message.

B. *Group Discussion*

1. List on a board all the scriptural passages for joy listed under "Scriptural Words for Joy." Have each participant look up the context of at least one passage to answer: What is the source of joy? What is the duration of joy? (Here are some key references: Ezra 6:22; Neh 8:10; Ps 13:5; 16; 51:8, 12; Hab 3:18; 2 Cor 6:10; 8:2; 1 Pet 3:14; Is 22:13; Eccles 2:10-11; 3:12-13, 22; Ps 128:1-2; Ps 4:7.)

Organize the responses among temporary and long-lasting joys.

How can we experience each one of them? Have participants cite examples in their own lives of these different types of joys.

2. Read Exodus 18:1-27 silently.

Read aloud 18:1-12. In what ways did Moses minister to Jethro?

Read aloud 18:13-18. What was Moses' ministering flaw?

Do any of the participants think they too have Moses' flaw? Read 18:19-26. What was Jethro's solution? Would you call his solution "shared ministry"? What experience do you have of "shared ministry"? How is it help-

ful? What dangers need to be avoided? See also Galatians 6:2 and Numbers 11:11-29.
3. Read 1 Corinthians 12:24-26. Have members of the group each share one current reason for "suffering" and one current reason for "rejoicing." Pray (request and praise) for each other.
   After prayer, ask if anyone can offer a specific way to ease another's burdens or to share their joy.

C. Further Study
Read Philemon as a letter of reconciliation and note Paul's techniques to reconcile Philemon, Apphia, Archippus and Onesimus.

Session 10: The Joy of the Morning
A. Presentation Approach
Summarize the four basic types of suffering and give one example of a response to each type. Analyze a current news problem in the light of these guidelines.
B. Group Discussion
1. Look again at the summary of evaluations from session one. Ask if anyone cares to change or to comment on their initial responses.
2. Read the two short stories that follow, or assign them for private reading. Possibly two different class members can read them expressively.
   What is the irony (the clash between appearance and reality) in "Venus in Evening" and in "Celia's Journey"? What does "Venus in Evening" warn are wrong responses to suffering? What is the hope of "Celia's Journey"?
   The stories and poems in this book may inspire some readers to compose their own poems, songs, short stories or drawings, to highlight one or more key teachings of this study. These creative compositions may be shared at this final class session.

Venus in Evening
Brilliantly attired, the silvery sun recessed. Her train cast mother-of-pearl down the aisle of the sky. The boughs applauded. Then the night ushers rolled up the last of her crimson carpet and retired. All was still.

Celia sat in the darkness beneath the bowers watching with the wind till the hosts of heaven began to gather. Venus had come silently long ago, a mere attendant. And now her little sisters filled the hall dashing and dancing as if they would present her, the pendant jewel in a shimmering necklace of lights. Her velvet setting deepened in hue, and she replied through shades of azure into white till at last she blazed forth Queen of the Host, resplendent.

Hushed moments later the retinue of the evening star swept down the vast aerial promenade in every direction, reclining at last in silent state on the edge of the horizon.

And Celia sighed.

The morning star, Venus, had known her in another season—the season of Celia's birth. With the babe in her arms her mother had watched in weary victory as the star gently visited her travail: Venus, strangely warm, majestic, aloof yet so full of promise, gazing down upon her and her child, reflecting.

And now the seasons themselves fled Celia's sight. Her own night approached like those shadows on her horizon, moving against her, against her wishes like the night itself. They were on the pathway, now beside the bower. And now they were upon her.

"Here's another one. Who is it? Mrs. Griggs! My, my, we're a bad girl tonight. Now we know we aren't supposed to stay out after nightfall. Come on now—no, take her arm further up above the elbow, so you don't hurt her. Come on now. Up we go! She can walk—let her lean on you. We don't want to miss our television tonight!"

Celia let them take her. How could she stop the night? No one could—until One did! Venus was the evening star now, but in a little while she would become the morning star. That was the season her night was passing to—forever.

"Watch our step! You see what happens when we remain out in the night?"

They stepped through the garden gate, and as they did, she saw the star still blaze above them. Celia suddenly stopped, disengaged her arm, and with the dignity of her years strode back to the bower.

Yes, she was remaining, but it was through the night!

William David Spencer, 1980

Celia's Journey

It appeared to be about midmorning when she arrived at the edge of a lovely green sward. By now the rough rocky land fell away and the going became infinitely easier. For she was old, so very very old, and as she had reflected just a year ago, now she stumbled rather than walked. But on the soft grass at last her way became much easier. Strange how much stronger she felt now than when she had set out. She had been near fainting then. No, she must have fainted. She had felt her head spin, but then she had kept on walking.

There was a small lovely rise before her, one she had evidently been watching for some time. She had been wondering how she would get over it.

"Now I can never get across such an obstacle without a hand or at least a stick. And where is my walker? Why, I'm not even in it—not using it at all!"

Suddenly over the rise shattering her reverie came a head on broad shoulders and a large muscled chest and there was a handsome young man, swinging along in a broad gait—one step on the hill, another carrying him over the crest and down toward her.

She stopped, shielding her eyes. Perhaps this young man might help her. "Son," she called out as best she could. But the effort was wasted, for indeed he was coming directly toward her. Unnerved and a tiny bit frightened, she stayed waiting, too old to run or even to resist.

He was before her now. "My Beautiful One." His voice was rich and deep.

Thunderstruck, she looked up, and he took her in his arms. "The city is just ahead."

"James!" She finally gasped. "Jimmy?"

"Of course, Celia."

And then her tears flowed.

Together they went over the hill, and with each step rather than wearier she felt refreshed.

At last she saw the city. The Bridal City. She had never seen a city gate before this and vaguely wondered how they would enter. But the gate was not bound.

As they approached it a figure stepped out—one who had been obviously waiting—a magnificent crowned Sovereign, great and mighty.

"Lord, my dear wife, Celia," said James.

"Welcome, My Radiant Daughter," said the sovereign.

And the tall lovely princess stepped forward and embraced them, smiling.

William David Spencer, 1976

Appendix B: Biblical Passages That Support Each Reason for Suffering

1: World of Pain (chaps. 1—2)
A. Basis for a World of Pain
   Gen 1—3
B. Meaning of a World of Pain
   Mt 13:28-29; 1 Jn 5:19; Eph 2:2; 6:11-12; Rom 5:12-14; 8:18-23
C. Response to a World of Pain
   1. Free from Shame and Lessen Pain
      Gen 3:21; Ps 103:6; Prov 15:13; 17:22; Heb 13:17
   2. Be Present
      Prov 10:19
   3. Allow Expression of Pain
      Prov 14:10; 25:20; Rom 12:15
   4. Treat Person as a Full Person
      Prov 16:24; 17:17
   5. Draw on Spiritual Resources
      Gen 2:18; 2 Kings 6:17; Mt 6:6; 14:13, 23; Mk 1:35; 6:30-32; Lk 4:42; 5:16; 9:10; 22:41; Acts 17:28; Heb 10:25; Jas 5:16; 1 Jn 4:4
   6. Recognize Mortality
      Eccles 3:11-14; Ps 34:19; 127:1-2; Lk 12:33; 1 Cor 15:19, 32; Eph 5:16; Heb 4:9-10; Jas 4:15; Rev 21:4

2: Punishment for Sin (chap. 3)
A. Misunderstanding of Concept
   Lk 13:1-9; Jn 9:1-4

B. Covenantal Aspect
   Gen 2:16-17; 3:16-17; 6:18; 9:8-17; Ex 19:4-6; 23:23-33; Lev 26:3-45; Deut 7:6-26; 11:13-29; 28; Prov 2:20-22; 1 Kings 11:38; Jer 7:5-7; Mal 3:7
C. Externally Inflicted
   Deut 9:4-5; Ex 34:6-7; 1 Sam 2:12-36; 3:10-14; 4:11-22; 2 Kings 17:13; 22:16-17; Ps 103:10-13; Prov 11:20-22; 15:29; Eccles 12:14; Jer 40:2-6; Ezek 33:11; Amos 3:2; Mic 1:5-7; Mt 13:41-42; 23:37-39; 27:19; Lk 13:34-35; Acts 5:1-11; 1 Cor 5:13; 2 Thess 1:5-10; Heb 9:27-28; 2 Pet 3:8-10
D. Internally Inflicted
   Prov 1:11-33; 2:11-12; 6:6-15, 27-33; 7:22-23; 10:4; 11:17; 12:9-11; 14:15-16, 23; 15:19; 27:12; Jer 2:14-19; Rom 1:18-24; 1 Cor 11:28-32; Jas 5:1-3
E. Communal Repercussions
   Num 14:33; Deut 24:16; 2 Kings 14:5-6; 2 Chron 25:4; Jer 43:4-7; Ezek 9:4; 18:4, 20
F. Response
   Prov 17:5; 24:17-18; Ezek 25; Mt 1:21-23; 1 Pet 4:12-19

3: Advancement of God's Reign: Persecution (chap. 4)
A. General Persecution (Resistance from Unbelief)
   Ps 9:13; Jer 20:2; Dan 3:8-18; Mt 17:12; 24:9; Mk 8:31; Lk 6:20-29; 8:13; 9:22-23, 43-62; 14:25-33; 22:28; 24:26; Jn 17:14; 16:33; Acts 17:5-9; 21:28-29; 1 Cor 1:17-2:8; 2 Cor 4; 6; 11—12; Gal 2:19—3:1; 5:11; 6:12-17; Col 4:3; 1 Thess 1:5-6; 2:1-6, 14; 3:1-7; 2 Thess 1:4-7; 2 Tim 1:8-12; 2:3-10; 3:10-12; Heb 2:18; Jas 1:2-11; 5:1-11
B. Identification with the Messiah
   1. Model of Jesus
      Jn 15:18-21; 1 Pet 2:21-25
   2. Blessing or Privilege
      Acts 5:41; Rom 8:17; 1 Cor 4:10-21; Phil 1:29; 3:8-21; 1 Pet 4:12-14
   3. Vicarious
      Is 53:4-10; Acts 5:40-41; 1 Cor 12:25-26; 2 Cor 1:4-9; 11:28-29; Gal 4:19; Eph 3:1, 13; 5:1-2; Phil 2:4-8, 17, 30; Col 1:24-29
C. Response
   Mt 26:36-38; Phil 4:10-19; Col 4:18; 1 Thess 3:2-3; 2 Tim 1:8; 2:3; 4:9-14

4: Advancement of God's Reign: Testing (chap. 5)
A. God Examines and Searches for Love
   Gen 22:1-14; Deut 13:1-5; 1 Kings 8:39; Prov 20:27; Job 1:9-12; Lk 16:15;

Acts 1:24; 15:8; Rom 8:27-28; 1 Cor 2:10-11; 2 Cor 8:8; 1 Thess 2:4;
1 Pet 4:12; 1 Jn 3:20; 4:8
B. God Purifies
Lev 11:44-45; Ps 11:5; 66:10-12; Prov 17:3; Is 28:16; Jer 1:10; Mt 13:41;
1 Cor 3:10-15; 11:28-32; 1 Thess 1:5; 2:4; 5:21; 1 Tim 3:10; 2 Tim 2:23-26;
Gal 6:4; Jas 1:2-4; 12; 1 Pet 1:7; 1 Jn 4:1
C. God Trains
Deut 8:2-20; Prov 3:11-12; 6:23; 9:7-9; 12:1; 13:24; 1 Cor 4:14-15;
Gal 3:23-4:7; 2 Tim 3:16; Tit 2:11-12; Heb 5:8; 12:6; Rev 3:19
D. God Does Not Tempt
Mt 4:1-11; 18:7; 26:41; Lk 4:13; 20:18; Rom 14:13; 16:17; 1 Cor 1:23; 7:5;
10:6-13; Gal 5:11; 6:1; 1 Thess 3:5; 1 Tim 6:9; Heb 3:8-9; Jas 1:13-14;
2 Pet 2:9; 1 Jn 2:10; Rev 2:14; 3:10

5: Responding to Suffering by Promoting God's Reign (chap. 6)
A. God's Reign Is an Important Biblical Theme
Judg 8:23; 1 Sam 8:7, 20; 2 Kings 18:19—19:7; Ps 47:2, 8; 55:19; 74:12; 93;
95:3; 97:1; 99:1-5; 118:9; 146:3; Is 30:2; Jer 2:18; Hos 13:10; 14:3; Mt 3:2;
4:23; 9:35; Lk 9:2; 11:2; Acts 1:3; 19:8; 20:25; 28:23
B. Teaching Is a Way to Promote God's Reign
Lev 26; Deut 11; 1 Kings 9:6-9; 2 Chron 17:7-10; Mt 4:23; 5—7; Mk 1:39;
2:15-17, 23-28; 3:14; 4:1, 33-34; 6:7; 8:31; 12:41; 13:10; 14:1-9; Lk 6:6;
7:36-50; 10:1; 12:12; Jn 6:60-69; 9:30-34
C. Proclaiming Is a Way to Promote God's Reign
Is 52:7; Dan 3:4; Mt 4:17; 10:7; Mk 1:15; Lk 4:18-19; Rom 10:14-15;
1 Cor 1:23; Rev 5:2
D. Healing Is a Way to Promote God's Reign
   1. Healing Is Part of God's Reign
      Mt 4:23; 10:7-8; Lk 9:1-2, 11
   2. Curing Illness Is Different from Casting Out Demons
      Mk 6:13; Lk 13:32; Acts 19:12
   3. Healing Has Always Been Part of God's Work
      1 Kings 17:17-24; 2 Kings 5; Lk 4:40-41; 5:15; 6:17-19; 8:42-55; 18:35-43
   4. Healing Can Be a Spiritual Gift: Miracle Worker
      Mt 11:20; 13:54; Lk 6:17-19; 19:37; Jn 4:47-54; Acts 2:22; 6:8; 8:6-7;
      10:38; 19:11-12; 1 Cor 12:10, 28-29; 2 Cor 12:12
   5. People Who Heal May Also Be Persecuted
      Acts 3; 4; 5:12-18; 6:8, 12; 8:13; 9:1-2

6. Healing Has Counterfeits
   Mt 7:21-23; Acts 8:9-13; 2 Thess 2:9
7. Healing Can Be a Spiritual Gift: Healings
   Jer 30:17; 1 Cor 12:9, 28, 30; 1 Tim 5:23
8. Healing Has Different Techniques
   2 Kings 2:21; 4:5, 16, 33-35, 43; 5:13; 6:17; Mk 1:41; 2:11; 5:28-29, 41;
   6:56; 7:33; 8:22-25; 9:27, 29; Lk 4:40; 5:13, 17; 6:10, 19; 13:13; 14:4;
   22:51; Jn 4:50; 5:8-15; 9:3, 6; 11:43; Acts 3:6-7; 4:30; 9:12, 17, 34, 41;
   14:3, 10; 16:18; 19:11-12; 28:8
9. Healing Can Be Part of the Gift of Faith
   Mk 2:5; 11:21-25; 1 Cor 12:9; 13:2; Jas 5:15, 17
10. Healing Is Offered to All Believers
    2 Kings 20:2-6; Is 38:2-6; 1 Cor 12:29-30; 1 Jn 5:14
11. Healing Is a Gift Given to Elders
    Deut 19:15; Mk 6:12-13; Jas 5:13-18
12. Exorcism Is One Aspect of Healing
    Mt 8:16; Mk 6:13; 9:19-23; Lk 9:1
13. The Bible Describes Exorcism
    Mt 8:28; 9:32; 12:22, 44-45; 17:18; Mk 1:24-26; 5:3-9; 9:18-26; Lk 11:19;
    Acts 8:7; 16:18; 19:13-16; Jas 2:19

6: Mystery (chap. 7)
2 Sam 6:11; Job 35:10-14; 36:26; 37:19; 38:2, 41; 42:1-6; Ps 17:15; 51:11;
Hab 3:17-19; 1 Cor 13:9-12; 2 Cor 12:7-9
Response
Job 2:11-13; 13:8-9; Lk 18:1-8; Gal 6:2; Jas 5:11

7: Joy in the Midst of Suffering (chap. 8)
A. Scriptural Words for Joy
   Ezra 3:12 (śimḥâh); 6:22; Neh 8:10 (hedwâh); Job 8:19 (māśôś); Eccles
   9:9 (re'ēh ḥayyîm); Ps 5:11 ('ālaṣ); 13:5; 16:11; 27:6 (terû'âh); 30:5
   (rinnâh); 34:19-22; 43:4 (gîl); 51:8, 12 (śāśôn); 66:1 (rûa'); 98:8 (rānan);
   149:5 ('ālaz); Is 32:14; 35:2; 52:9 (pāṣaḥ); 65:14 (ṭûb); 65:19 (śûś);
   Hab 3:18; Mt 2:10; Lk 1:44 (agalliasis); 6:23 (skirtaō); Acts 2:28
   (euphrosynēs); Rom 5:11 (kauchaomai); 2 Cor 6:10; 8:2; 1 Thess 3:9
   (chara, chairō); Philem 7, 20 (oninamai); 1 Pet 3:14
B. Drawing on God's Eternal Joy
   Prov 15:8 (rāṣôn, rāṣâh); Ps 37:4 ('ānaḡ); Mt 6:9; Jn 14:15; 17;

1 Thess 5:17; Jas 5:13
C. Drawing on God's Temporal Joy
  Ps 4:7; 128:1-2; Eccles 2:10-11; 3:12-13, 22; Is 22:13; Mt 11:19; 26:17-29;
  Lk 2:41-51; 7:34; 10:38-42; 11:5; 15:3-10; Jn 2:1-11; Rev 19:1-9
D. Theology of Communal Love
  Gen 3:8; Deut 6:4; Lk 11:2; Jn 1:1; 4:24; 17; 1 Cor 12:12-27
E. Recognizing Limitations
  Ex 3:18; 18; 19:6; Num 11:11-29; Deut 5:24-27; Eccles 2:24; Mic 6:8;
  Mt 6:8; Mk 2:27; 2 Cor 11:28; Gal 6:2; Heb 4; 1 Pet 5:7; 1 Jn 4:20

8: Encouraging One Another (chap. 9)
  1. Suffering with Those Who Suffer
     Gen 4:6-9; 6:6; Ex 3:2-8; Ps 104:27-30; Prov 12:18; 14:23; 15:1, 4, 18, 28;
     16:32; 17:9, 14, 19, 27-28; 18:13-14; 19:11; 20:3; 21:23; 25:11-12, 15, 20;
     26:17, 20-21; 29:11, 20; Eccles 6:11; Is 6:6-9; 53:3; 63:10; Mt 11:28-30;
     Mk 3:4-5; Rom 12:15; 1 Cor 1:3-4; 3:12-15; 12:24-26; 2 Cor 1:2; Gal 6:2;
     Eph 4:30; Heb 2:18; 1 Jn 3:12-18; Rev 21:23
  2. Rejoicing with Those Who Are Praised
     Prov 25:27; Lk 1:57-58 *(synchairō);* 15:6-10; 1 Cor 13:4; Jas 3:13—4:1

Notes

Preface
[1]"Baptist Missionary Cites 'Beating,' Sues Convention," *Charisma* 8 (June 1983): 79.

Chapter 1: World of Pain
[1]All stories cited from the *Plainfield Courier News* (Plainfield, New Jersey), Final City Edition, August 27, 1956, pp. 1-2. "African American" is now a more appropriate term than "Negro."
[2]The sixth- or seventh-century Roman Missal sings: "O fortunate crime which merited to have such and so great a redeemer." See also John Hick, *Evil and the God of Love* (New York: Harper & Row, 1966).
[3]J. B. Phillips, *God Our Contemporary* (New York: Macmillan, 1960), p. 89.

Chapter 2: Response to a World of Pain
[1]This is the premise of an earlier book. Readers who would like to read more may consult A. B. Spencer, *Beyond the Curse: Women Called to Ministry* (Peabody, Mass.: Hendrickson, 1985).
[2]Those wishing to discover more exciting examples from mystery literature featuring clergy should consult W. D. Spencer, *Mysterium and Mystery: The Clerical Crime Novel* (Carbondale, Ill.: Southern Illinois University Press, 1989).
[3]Charles Merrill Smith, *Reverend Randollph and the Avenging Angel* (New York: Putnam, 1977).
[4]Margaret and Glenn Arnold, "Jim Johnson's Tale: Pastor Founded Wheaton Media Program," *Wheaton Daily Journal,* 1987, p. 4.
[5]William A. Blake, "Beliefs of the Rastafari Cult," thesis, Jamaica Theological Seminary, 1961, pp. 4-10.

[6]Neil Spencer, "The Toughest Peter Tosh: The Selection 1978-1987" (Hollywood: Capital Records/EMI, Inc. 1988), liner notes.

[7]Sarah Francis, "Clergy Fight for Separation of Church and Weekend Sports," *Boston Globe,* April 25, 1991, pp. 25, 31. Shortly after this chapter was written the problem ironically came home to us when our son Steve, the 1990 middle-school Big East Regional Wrestling Champion in his weight class and silver medalist in 1991, was faced with the same dilemma. The 1992 championships began with weigh-ins Sunday morning and matches during church time. Steve, at thirteen, coming to real personal faith, elected not to go to the tournament, though he had been undefeated and unscored upon in his weight class during the season. "God is more important," he explained. At least for high school our town has a ban on Sunday wrestling tournaments and matches.

[8]Jesus' teachings on prayer and example in prayer are elaborated in *The Prayer Life of Jesus: Shout of Agony, Revelation of Love, A Commentary* by W. D. Spencer and A. B. Spencer (Lanham, Md.: University Press of America, 1990). See also Brother Lawrence, *The Practice of the Presence of God* (Old Tappan, N.J.: Revell, 1958).

[9]Joni Mitchell, "Woodstock" (Siquomb Music, 1970).

[10]G. K. Chesterton, *The Father Brown Omnibus* (New York: Dodd, Mead, 1951), p. 112.

[11]George MacDonald, "The Girl That Lost Things," in *The Gifts of the Child Christ,* ed. G. E. Sadler (Grand Rapids, Mich.: Eerdmans, 1973), 2:6-8. The poem concludes:

> So, girls that cannot keep things,
> Be patient till to-morrow;
> And mind you don't beweep things
> That are not worth such sorrow.
>
> For the Father great of fathers,
> Of mothers, girls, and boys,
> In his arms his children gathers,
> And sees to all their toys.

Chapter 3: Punishment for Sin

[1]Abram is told that his descendants will not return to the land of Canaan for four generations because "the iniquity of the Amorites is not yet complete" (Gen 15:16). See also Deut 12:31; 18:10-14; 20:17-18; Lev 18:24-28; 20—23; Num 33:56; 1 Kings 16:3; 21:2; 2 Chron 33:2.

[2]See also Jer 1:16; 2:8, 13, 20-21, 34; 3:2-3, 20; 5:7-8, 19, 28; 6:13; 7:5-9, 18, 30-31; 9:13; 10; 14:15; 16:11; 17:3, 21; 19:4; 22:3; 32:23, 34; 34:11; 36:31.

[3]The NIV and NRSV read, "we must . . . sent me," whereas the KJV reads, "I must work . . . sent me." The differences depend on which Greek manuscripts the editors chose. The earliest Greek manuscripts support "we must . . . sent us."

[4]Gen 6:5-13, 18-22; 9:8-17.

[5]See, for example, Ex 5:3; 15:25-26; 23:24; 32:35; Num 21:5-6.

[6]See also Is 5:2-7; 27:2-6.

[7]Ezek 18:4, 20; 9:4; 16; Jer 31:30; 2 Chron 25:4 and 2 Kings 14:5-6 (quoting Deut 24:16).
[8]Prov 17:5 NRSV. See also Prov 24:17-18; Ezek 25.

Chapter 4: Advancement of God's Reign: Persecution
[1]Eusebius, *The History of the Church from Christ to Constantine,* trans. G. A. Williamson (Minneapolis: Augsburg, 1965), 5.1. This is a delightful work from the early 300s by the bishop of Caesarea, full of stories about Jesus and the early church. See also A. B. Spencer, "Early Church Heroines: Rulers, Prophets, and Martyrs," *Christian History* 7, no. 17: 12-16.
[2]See also our discussion of 1 Corinthians 2:6-16 in *Conflict and Context: Hermeneutics in the Americas,* eds. Mark Lau Branson and C. René Padilla (Grand Rapids, Mich.: Eerdmans, 1986), pp. 242-56.
[3]See also W. D. Spencer, "The Power in Paul's Teaching (1 Cor 4:9-20)," *Journal of the Evangelical Theological Society* 32 (Mar. 1989): 51-62.
[4]2 Cor 10:1; 2:17; 4:2-5; 10:12, 15, 18; 11:5-21; 12:1, 11, 14. See also A. B. Spencer and W. D. Spencer, *2 Corinthians,* Bible Study Commentary (Grand Rapids, Mich.: Zondervan, 1989), chap. 5.
[5]George MacDonald, *At the Back of the North Wind* (Ann Arbor, Mich.: University Microfilms, 1966), p. 69.

Chapter 5: Advancement of God's Reign: Testing
[1]Walter Bauer, William F. Arndt and F. Wilbur Gingrich, *A Greek-English Lexicon of the New Testament* (Cambridge, U.K.: Cambridge University Press, 1957), p. 405. Peter is the person who uses the term.
[2]Francis Brown, S. R. Driver and Charles A. Briggs, *A Hebrew and English Lexicon of the Old Testament,* trans. E. Robinson (Oxford, U.K.: Clarendon, 1907), p. 748-49. Karl Feyerabend, *Langenscheidt Pocket Hebrew Dictionary to the Old Testament* (New York: McGraw-Hill, 1969), p. 248.
[3]For example, in Gal 3:24—4:7 Paul uses as synonyms "son" *(hyios)* and "heir" *(klēronomos).* The "son" if an "infant" is a potential "heir." Now even females are "sons," because they too are heirs. For more information see A. B. Spencer, *Beyond the Curse,* pp. 65-71.
[4]Alan D. Levy, "Silver," in *Collier's Encyclopedia* (1963), 21:31-34; B. Smith Hopkins, "Gold," in *Collier's Encyclopedia* (1963), 11:197-98; Paul E. Desautels, *The Mineral Kingdom* (New York: Ridge, 1968), pp. 199-200.
[5]See also Frederick C. Grant, *The Economic Background of the Gospels* (New York: Russell & Russell, 1926), pp. 66-71; Donald Guthrie, *New Testament Introduction,* 3rd ed. (Downers Grove, Ill.: InterVarsity Press, 1970), p. 746; Josephus *Antiquities* 20.8.8.
[6]Eusebius *The History of the Church* 2.14-16.
[7]Jas 2:4; 3:14; 4:1-4; 5; 1 Cor 10:13; 7:5; Ps 95:7; Heb 38:9; Lk 4:13; 1 Tim 6:9.
[8]Henry George Liddell and Robert Scott, *A Greek-English Lexicon,* 9th edition, ed. H. S. Jones and R. McKenzie (Oxford, U.K.: Clarendon, 1940), p. 1604.
[9]George MacDonald, *The Princess and Curdie* (New York: E P. Dutton, 1949), pp. 64-68

Chapter 6: Responding to Suffering by Promoting God's Reign

[1]For example, God as "king": Ps 47:2, 8; 55:19; 74:12; 93; 95:3; 97:1; 99:1-5; God as more reliable than foreign allies: Ps 118:9; 146:3; Hos 13:10; 14:3; Is 30:2; Jer 2:18; 2 Kings 18:19-19:7.

[2]For example, Mt 3:2; 4:23; 9:35; Lk 9:2; Acts 1:3; 19:8; 20:25; 28:23.

[3]See Bruce M. Metzger, *Lexical Aids for Students of New Testament Greek* (Princeton, N.J.: Theological Book Agency, 1969), pp. 7-10.

[4]Lev 26; Deut 11; 1 Kings 9:6-9; 11:9-12; 14:15-16.

[5]2 Kings 14:25; 15:29; Nahum 3:19; Hos 10:14; Ezek 23:10, 25.

[6]Jn 11:25; Acts 4:2; 1 Cor 15.

[7]For example, synagogues: Mt 4:23; Mk 1:39; Lk 6:6; 13:10; temple: Mk 12:41; dinners: Mk 2:15-17; 14:1-9; Lk 7:36-50; beside the sea: Mk 4:1; in the fields: Mk 2:23-28.

[8]Liddell and Scott, *A Greek-English Lexicon*, pp. 371, 421.

[9]Joseph Henry Thayer, *Thayer's Greek-English Lexicon of the New Testament* (Marshallton, Del.: National Foundation for Christian Education, 1889), p. 346; see also Dan 3:4.

[10]Mt 4:17; 10:7; Mk 1:15.

[11]Francis MacNutt, *The Power to Heal* (Notre Dame, Ind.: Ave Maria Press, 1977), pp. 134-35.

[12]For example, Lk 4:40-42; 5:15; 6:17-19; 8:42-43: 9:11-14, 37; 12:1; 14:25; 18:35-37.

[13]Mt 13:54; Lk 6:17-19; 19:37; Jn 4:47-54; Acts 2:22; 10:38.

[14]In Acts 3 Peter and John heal the man lame from birth. In Acts 4 they are arrested. In Acts 5:12-16 the apostles do many signs and wonders. In Acts 5:17-18 they are arrested. In Acts 6:8 Stephen does "great wonders and signs." In Acts 6:12 he is arrested and then killed. Philip does "signs and great miracles," while Saul persecutes the Christians (Acts 8:13; 9:1-2).

[15]Liddell and Scott, *A Greek-English Lexicon*, p. 815; Thayer, *Greek-English Lexicon*, p. 295; see also Eccles 10:4; Jer 30:17.

[16]Col 4:14; Gal 4:13-15. See also A. B. Spencer and W. D. Spencer, *2 Corinthians*, pp. 130-31.

[17]For example, Lk 4:40; 5:17; 6:19; 14:4; 22:51; Mk 1:41; 2:11; 5:28-29; 6:56; 7:33; 8:22-25; Jn 4:50; 5:8-15; 9:6; 11:43. See also Bernard Martin, *The Healing Ministry in the Church* (Richmond, Va.: John Knox, 1960), part one, for a listing of data about the healing ministries of Jesus and the disciples.

[18]Mk 9:29; Acts 3:6; 9:17, 34; 14:10; 16:18; 19:11-12; 28:8. Also in the Old Testament healing, even by the same person, was done sometimes by command (2 Kings 2:21; 4:5, 16, 43; 5:13) and sometimes through prayer (2 Kings 4:33; 6:17).

[19]Thayer, *Greek-English Lexicon*, pp. 663-67.

[20]The negative interrogative particle *me* expects a negative answer. Bauer, Arndt and Gingrich, *Greek-English Lexicon*, p. 519; A. T. Robertson, *A Grammar of the Greek New Testament in the Light of Historical Research* (Nashville: Broadman, 1934), pp. 1168, 1175.

[21]See Spencer and Spencer, *Prayer Life of Jesus*, pp. 87-91.

[22]The definition of "elders" *(presbyteros)* is never clearly defined. It is a plural term referring to people associated with a gathering of people *(ekklēsia)*. Jethro recom-

mends that Moses find able, trustworthy people who can sit as judges so that Moses will not have to bear the burden of judging all the people (Ex 18:13-27). Moses still feels overburdened and asks God for help. God tells him to choose seventy among all the elders of Israel to receive the Holy Spirit (Num 11:16-30), but two more also receive the Spirit. Elders are assumed in the New Testament to be a part of the early church (Acts 20:17). Elders are synonymous with "overseers" or "bishops" (Acts 20:17, 28; Tit 1:5, 7; 1 Tim 3:1; 5:17). From these references we can learn that elders do some kind of oversight and teaching. (See also 1 Pet 5:1-4.) When Paul describes "overseers," he mainly develops the type of person who should be an overseer, not their responsibilities (1 Tim 3:2-7; Tit 1:5-9; 2:2-5).

23Liddell and Scott, *Greek-English Lexicon,* pp. 715, 810; Thayer, *Greek-English Lexicon,* p. 258.

24Thayer, ibid., p. 675; Liddell and Scott, ibid., p. 2018.

25Spencer and Spencer, *Prayer Life of Jesus,* p. 131. See chap. 5 on "Jesus' Words for Prayer."

26Jn 4:46; 5:3, 5; Mt 8:14-17; Lk 13:11-12; Acts 4:9; Phil 2:26-27; Gal 4:13-15; 1 Tim 5:23. These references refer both to the verb, *astheneō,* and to the noun, *astheneia.*

27Josephus *Antiquities* 8.11.1 [266, 273]; Wis 4:16; 15:9; 4 Macc 3:8; 7:13. See also Hippocrates *Diseases* 3.16 [148]; Liddell and Scott, *Greek-English Lexicon,* pp. 872-73.

28A. T. Robertson explains that in the positive imperative "the distinction between the punctiliar (aorist) and the durative (present) is quite marked" (*Grammar,* p. 855). Nevertheless, Francis MacNutt recommends periodic prayer, but focused on the succeeding specific healing need, as diagnosed by a physician (*Power to Heal,* pp. 37, 53).

29Liddell and Scott, *Greek-English Lexicon,* p. 2007. See, for example, Ex 29:7, 21; 2 Kings 9:1-3.

30Dr. Madhukar N. Shah of Shah Medical Associates in Beverly, Mass., gastroenterologist and head nutritionist of Beverly Hospital, mentioned in an interview with Bill on May 26, 1993, that olive oil is high in Vitamin E and in fatty acids. Like any fat-soluble plant oil, if it is rubbed into the skin these nutrients will enter the body through osmosis. Vitamin E is good for skin cells and is generally therapeutic. Oil also helps to prevent evaporation of water from the skin during strenuous exercise or in very dry weather.

   In the fourth-century B.C. play "Farmer" *(Georgos)* by Menander, Myrrhina's son kept on "anointing" *(aleiphō)* Cleanetus, his employer, after he "had laid open his leg with a deep cut while hoeing, 'rubbing him down' *(ektribō),* washing the wound, bringing him food to eat, comforting him where he is suffering, and by his care restored and brought him through alive again" (45, 60). In the ancient archetype of our contemporary Merck medical manual, Hippocrates (also fourth century B.C.) lists many different types of remedies. He mentions fat and warm substances as helpful to promote the growth of tissue, but not good for inflamed and unclean wounds (*Affections* 38). Olive oil strengthened and promoted phlegm (*Affections* 55). Warm olive oil and wine were considered externally helpful when people could not wash (*Affections* 42 *[aleiphō, elaion]),* to reduce swelling (with grain, *Diseases* 2.30), to wash ears after pus had come out of them *(Diseases* 3.2), and to heal in some cases of tetanus (*Internal Affections* 52 *[aleiphō]*). The crisis from pleurisy could be eased by moist vapor baths and anointing *(hypaleiphō)* with olive oil (*Diseases* 3.16). One enema was made from soda, honey, sweet wine and olive oil (*Internal Affections* 20). Drinking olive oil helped against constipation (*Regimen in Acute Diseases* 51). For the eyes, he recommended a dry ointment made of paste moistened with oil of bitter unripe olives (*Regimen* 65).

Oil as a staple of ancient society: Rev 6:6; Deut 7:13; 8:8; 11:14; 28:51; 1 Kings 5:11; 17:12; 2 Kings 18:32; 2 Chron 2:10; 31:5; 32:28; Neh 5:11; 10:39; Prov 21:17; Hos 2:5, 8, 22; Jer 40:10; 41:8; Ezek 16:13, 19; Lk 16:6; oil used in and on food: Ex 29:2, 40; Lev 2:4-7; 7:12; 8:26; Num 6:15; 7:13, 19; 8:8; 11:8; 18:12; Deut 32:13; Ezek 46:14; 2 Chron 11:11; oil to light lamps: Mt 25:3-8; Ex 27:20; 35:14, 28; Lev 24:2; Num 4:9, 16; oil after a bath or before exercise: Deut 28:40; 2 Sam 14:2 *(aleiphō);* 2 Kings 4:2 *(aleiphō* LXX); Mic 6:15 *(aleiphō);* Esther 2:12 *(aleiphō);* Josephus *War* 2.8.3; Liddell and Scott, *Greek-English Lexicon,* pp. 527-28; oil as a symbol of holiness or dedication of a priest: Ex 29:7, 21; 30:30; Lev 8:2, 10-12, 30; 10:7; 14:15-18; 21:10-12; Num 35:25; oil as a symbol of dedication of a ruler: 1 Sam 10:1; 16:1, 13; 2 Sam 1:21; 1 Kings 1:39; 2 Kings 9:1-3; Ps 89:20; oil poured over stones, tent of meeting, ark of covenant, altar, and grain offerings: Gen 28:18; 35:14; Ex 29:23, 40; 30:23-26; 31:11; 40:9; Lev 2:1-2, 6, 15-16; 6:15, 21; 7:10; 9:4; 14:10, 12, 21, 24, 26-29; 23:13; Num 15:4, 6, 9; 28:5, 9, 20; Ezek 45:24; oil not used over sin offerings or in offerings of jealousy which had to do with sin: Lev 5:11; Num 5:15; oil used in healing: Isa 1:6; Ezek 16:9; Lk 10:34; Mk 6:13 *(aleiphō);* Jas 5:14; oil used in celebration: Ps 23:5; 104:15; 141:5; Eccles 9:8; Lk 7:46 *(aleiphō);* possibly Ps 45:7; Heb 1:19; Deut 33:24. The rabbis also mention the healing benefits of oil, *Babylonian Talmud* Yoma 77b; *Mishnah Shabbath* 14:3-4.

[31]Thayer, *Greek-English Lexicon,* pp. 75, 565. The ancient Jews would pray and lay hands on the sick (e.g., *Genesis Apocryphon* 20.22, 29; Mk 5:23; Lk 4:40).

[32]Salvation from illness: Mt 9:21-22; Mk 3:4; 5:23; Lk 8:50; Jn 11:12; Acts 4:9; 14:9; salvation from demonic possession: Lk 8:36; salvation from sins: Mt 1:21; Acts 2:40; salvation from natural disasters: Mt 8:25; 24:22; Acts 16:30?; 27:20,31; 1 Cor 3:15; Gen 19:17; salvation from eternal death: Mt 10:22; 16:25; 19:25; Lk 8:12; 13:23; 19:10; Jn 3:17; 5:34; 10:9; 12:47; Acts 2:21, 47; 4:12; 11:14; 15:1; 16:31; Rom 5:9; 8:24; 9:27; 10:9, 13; 11:26; 1 Cor 1:18, 21; 1 Cor 5:5; 7:16; 9:22; 15:2; Eph 2:5, 8; 1 Thess 2:16; 2 Thess 2:10; 1 Tim 1:15; 2:4, 15?; 4:16; 2 Tim 1:9; 4:18; Tit 3:5; Heb 5:7?; 7:25; Jas 1:21; 2:14; 4:12; 5:20; 1 Pet 3:21; 4:18; Jude 23; salvation from death: Mt 27:40, 49; Jn 12:27; Gen 19:20; 32:8, 30; 47:25; Deut 33:29; Josh 8:22; 10:40; 1 Sam 19:11-12; 27:1; 30:17; salvation from political oppression: Jude 5; Judg 2:16, 18; 3:9, 31; 6:14-15, 36-37; 7:2, 7; 8:22; 10:1, 12-14; 12:2-3; 13:5; 1 Sam 4:3; 7:8; 9:16; 10:1, 27; 11:3; 14:6, 23, 39, 47; 17:47; acting on someone's/something's behalf: Judg 6:31 idol; 1 Sam 23:2, 5 city; 1 Sam 25:26, 31, 33 oneself (exhaustive in New Testament and Gen—1 Sam). See footnote 51 for references to demons.

[33]Robertson, *Grammar,* pp. 925, 1004, 1016.

[34]F. Blass and A. DeBrunner, *A Greek Grammar of the New Testament and Other Early Christian Literature,* trans. and ed. R. W. Funk (Chicago: University of Chicago Press, 1961), pp. 234-35.

³⁵The aorist imperative would be ingressive; in other words, emphasis is laid on the beginning of the action, or constative, which treats the act as a single whole entirely irrespective of the parts or time involved. Robertson, *Grammar,* pp. 831-35.

³⁶Gal 4:13-15; 2 Cor 12:7-9; 1 Tim 5:23; 2 Tim 4:20.

³⁷Paul uses the same technique in 1 Tim 2:11. He uses the plural for "women" in 2:9-10 but the singular in 2:11-15. Both James and Paul switch to the singular one sentence *before* the illustration begins.

³⁸*Calvin's Commentaries: Ephesians-Jude* (Wilmington, Del.: Associated Press, n.d.), p. 2586. See also John Calvin *Institutes of the Christian Religion* 4.18-21 and Thomas Manton, *James,* Geneva Series Commentary (London: Banner of Truth, 1693), p. 449. James Hardy Ropes sees the gifts of healing as psychosomatic. See *A Critical and Exegetical Commentary on the Epistle of St. James,* International Critical Commentary (Edinburgh: T & T Clark, 1916), pp. 305-7 for an overview study of anointing in the church.

³⁹A study of the church in the first through third centuries shows that the gifts of the Spirit continued after the apostolic period. For reasons for a change of practice see W. D. Spencer, "The Chaining of the Church," *Christian History* 7, no. 17: 25; and R. Kydd, *Charismatic Gifts in the Early Church* (Peabody, Mass.: Hendrickson, 1984).

⁴⁰For example, Francis MacNutt, *The Power to Heal; Healing* (Notre Dame, Ind.: Ave Maria Press, 1974); *Praying for Healing in the Family* (Notre Dame, Ind.: Ave Maria Press, 1981); Emily Gardiner Neal, *A Reporter Finds God Through Spiritual Healing* (New York: Morehouse-Barlow, 1956); Claude A. Frazier, ed., *Faith Healing: Finger of God? Or Scientific Curiosity?* (New York: Thomas Nelson, 1975); Ruth Carter Stapleton, *The Gift of Inner Healing* (New York: Bantam, 1976).

⁴¹MacNutt, *The Power to Heal,* p. 27.

⁴²Spencer and Spencer, *Prayer Life of Jesus,* p. 102. "And fasting" is not in the best-quality ancient manuscripts. See also MacNutt, *The Power to Heal,* pp. 41-45. He found out that if some healing started to take place, further prayer would usually lead to still more healing.

⁴³MacNutt, *Healing,* pp. 266-69; MacNutt, *Power to Heal,* p. 53.

⁴⁴Mt 8:16; Mk 6:13; Lk 9:1; Acts 19:12.

⁴⁵Rudolf Bultmann, *Jesus Christ and Mythology* (New York: Scribner's, 1958), p. 15.

⁴⁶William Peter Blatty, *The Exorcist* (New York: Harper & Row, 1971), pp. 173-74, 223-24.

⁴⁷Kurt E. Koch, *Christian Counseling and Occultism,* trans. A. Petter (Grand Rapids, Mich.: Kregel, 1965), pp. 22-23.

⁴⁸Ibid., p. 53.

⁴⁹Ibid., pp. 209-10.

⁵⁰Ibid., p. 212.

⁵¹Mt 8:28; Mk 1:24; 5:3-4; 9:18, 26; Acts 19:16. Demonic possession results in self-destruction (Mk 5:5), sometimes loud crying (Mk 1:26; 5:5; 9:26; Acts 8:7), sometimes silence (Mt 9:32; 12:22). Demons may have names (Mk 5:9). They fear God (Jas 2:19). Jesus would rebuke demons (Mt 17:18): "Come out unclean spirit, out of the human" (Mk 5:8), "Be silent and come out of him" (Mk 1:25), "You spirit that keeps this boy

from speaking and hearing, I command you, come out of him, and no longer enter him" (Mk 9:25). The Jews had exorcists themselves (Lk 11:19). Josephus says exorcism began with Solomon. He mentions a contemporary Eleazar who would cure a demon-possessed person by putting to his nose "a ring which had under its seal one of the roots prescribed by Solomon, and then, as the man smelled it, drew out the demon through his nostrils, and, when the man at once fell down, adjured the demon never to come back into him, speaking Solomon's name and reciting the incantations which he had composed" (Josephus *Antiquities* 8.2.5 [45-48]). The Bible, of course, records no such remedies by Solomon. The difference with Jesus was the methodology, not the intent itself.

Chapter 7: Mystery
[1]These quotations from Job are from the NRSV.
[2]Some ancient rabbis ascribed the lifetime of Job to the days of Moses, Joshua, Jacob or the time of the judges (*b. Talmud* Baba Bathra 14b-15b). Job lived more than 140 and perhaps up to 240 years, around the same length as some of Noah's descendants (e.g., Gen 11:18-24; Job 42:16 LXX). Like Noah and Abraham, he offered burnt offerings without assistance of a priest (Job 1:5; Gen 8:20; 22:2). Unlike the patriarchs, but like Noah, Job was a monogamist (Job 31:9-12; Gen 7:7). The land of Uz seems to take its name from Uz, one of Noah's descendants (Gen 10:23), or, less likely, Uz, one of Esau's descendants (Gen 36:28). The money mentioned in Job 42:11 is also mentioned in Gen 33:19 and Josh 24:32. An endnote in the Septuagint translation of the Old Testament identifies Job with Jobab, King of Edom (Gen 36:33) (R. K. Harrison, *Introduction to the Old Testament* [Grand Rapids, Mich.: Eerdmans, 1969], p. 1040). In addition, Eliphaz may possibly refer to the flood in Job 22:16.
[3]Gen 39:1-4, 21-23; 41:37-45.
[4]Job 13:4-5;16:2. See also 19:2.
[5]Elihu is a possible narrator for the book. Only his speeches are not evaluated at the end. He modestly introduces himself only at the beginning of his speech. Some critics think that Elihu's speeches are a later addition to the text (e.g., E. Dhorme, *A Commentary on the Book of Job,* trans. H. Knight [London: Nelson, 1967], pp. xcviii-cx). The same reasons can be used to support Elihu as the contemporary collector of all the speeches. Elihu reviews the whole previous debate. His style is more pompous and stilted, unlike the concise, vigorous and unaffected style of the elders. R. Jamieson, A. Fausset and D. Brown propose that Job wrote the book but they mention that Lightfoot attributes it to Elihu (*A Commentary, Critical and Explanatory on the Old and New Testament* [New York: Revell, 1978], p. 309).
[6]Job 39:20, 28; 40:18; 41:13.
[7]The Jews had a popular saying: "Either a friend like the friends of Job or death" (*b. Talmud* Baba Bathra 16b).
[8]We cannot be sure exactly how far they traveled since we cannot be sure of the location of the land of Uz nor of the land of the friends. Uz is most likely Edom (Lam 4:21). The two most likely locations are the region between Edom and northern Arabia and Hauran, south of Damascus. Josephus explains that Uz lies between Palestine and Celosyria (*Antiquities* 1.6, 4). See also R. K. Harrison, *Introduction to the Old Tes-*

tament (Grand Rapids, Mich.: Eerdmans, 1969), pp. 1027, 1039.
9See also W. D. Spencer and A. B. Spencer, *The Prayer Life of Jesus: Shout of Agony, Revelation of Love, A Commentary* (Lanham, Md.: University Press of America, 1990), pp. 40-63.
10See ibid., appendix C.
11See Spencer and Spencer, *2 Corinthians,* pp. 130-31.

Chapter 8: Joy in the Midst of Suffering
1Eleanor H. Porter, *Pollyanna: The Glad Book* (Boston: Page, 1913), pp. 217-23.
2C. S. Lewis, *Letters to Malcolm: Chiefly on Prayer* (New York: Harcourt, Brace and World, 1964), p. 93.
3Susannah Spurgeon and Joseph Harold, *C. H. Spurgeon Autobiography, 2: The Full Harvest, 1860-1892* (Edinburgh: Banner of Truth Trust, 1973), pp. 194-95.
4Ibid., p. 196.
5Teresa of Ávila, *The Interior Castle,* trans. Kieron Kavanaugh and Otilio Rodriquez (New York: Paulist, 1979), p. 33.
6Teresa, *The Interior Castle,* p. xvii.
7Spurgeon and Harold, *Full Harvest,* p. 197.
8Brown, Driver and Briggs, *Hebrew and English Lexicon,* p. 772.
9Matthew Gilbert, "Getting Close to Woody Allen," *The Boston Sunday Globe,* June 16, 1991, pp. A39, A50.
10E. Kautzsch and A. E. Cowley, eds., *Gesenius' Hebrew Grammar,* 2nd ed. (Oxford, U.K.: Clarendon, 1910), pp. 398-99.
11"God Leads His Dear Children: An Interview with Nguyen Xuan Tin," *The Alliance Witness: A Journal of Christian Life and Witness* 112 (Sept. 21, 1977): 19-20. See also a full account of the revival in Orrel N. Steinkamp, *The Holy Spirit in Viet Nam* (Carol Stream, Ill.: Creation House, 1973). Steinkamp was a professor of Old Testament and Hebrew at Nha Trang Bible Institute at the time of the revival.
12David Goodman, *Living from Within: The Art of Appreciation in Marriage, Parenthood, Work, Growing Up and Growing Older* (Kansas City, Mo.: Hallmark, 1968), pp. 20-21.
13Hank Whittemore, "Ministers Under Stress," *Parade Magazine,* April 14, 1991, pp. 4-5. Stephen Locke and Douglas Colligan cite clinical studies linking the acquiring of infectious diseases with attitude (*The Healer Within* [New York: Dutton, 1986], pp. 124-28). See also Herbert Benson, *The Relaxation Response* (New York: Avon, 1975), especially "Victims of Stress," pp. 16-27.
14Kenneth L. Woodward with Eloise Salholz, "Why Pastors Are Fired," *Newsweek,* March 23, 1981, p. 80.
15Whittemore, "Ministers Under Stress," p. 5.

Chapter 9: Encouraging One Another
1Spencer and Spencer, *2 Corinthians,* pp. 7-8.
2See A. B. Spencer, "God as a Symbolizing God: A Symbolic Hermeneutic," *Journal of the Evangelical Theological Society* 24 (Dec. 1981): 323-32.
3John Calvin believed the same of Judas, that he could have avoided destroying Jesus,

arguing, "But it would be a most unfounded argument, if anyone were to infer from this, that the revolt of Judas ought to be ascribed to God rather than to himself, because the prediction laid him under a necessity" (John Calvin, *Calvin's Commentaries: John-Acts* [Wilmington, Del.: Associated Publishers and Authors, n.d.]), pp. 879-80.

4Nathan Cobb, "Goodbye, Me. Hello, We," *Boston Globe Magazine,* February 24, 1991, p. 19.

5Eric Schwartz, "Men's Group Leader Looks to Growth of New Male Consciousness," *Hamilton/Wenham Chronicle,* July 31, 1991, p. 1, cols. 1-5. See also "Men's Movement Could Do Some Good," p. 4, cols. 1-2. An analysis of the theology of the current men's movement will be found in Bill's chapter on male deities in Aída's forthcoming book analyzing god and goddess worship (Baker).

6Eusebius *The History of the Church from Christ to Constantine* 3.23.

7Jerome (in Gal 6:10) quoted by F. W. Farrar, *The Early Days of Christianity* (New York: Funk & Wagnalls, 1883), p. 402.

8Beth Spring, "When the Dream Child Dies," *Christianity Today* 31 (August 7, 1987): 27, 29.

9C. S. Lewis, *The Four Loves* (New York: Harcourt, Brace and World, 1960), p. 168.

10"Joe Bayly: Editor, Author, Humorist, Dies at 66," *Christianity Today* 30 (Sept. 5, 1986): 47.

Appendix A: Study Questions
1First published in *Daughters of Sarah* 7 (July/August 1981): 14-15.

References for Further Study

In addition to sources cited in the notes, we recommend the following useful books:

Atkinson, Celia. *The Gospel of Suffering.* London: A. R. Mowbray, 1930.

Bingham, Rowland V. *The Bible and the Body: Healing in the Scriptures.* 4th ed. Toronto: Evangelical Publishers, 1952.

Bufford, Rodger K. *Counseling and the Demonic.* Resources for Christian Counseling 17. Dallas, Tex.: Word, 1988.

Carmichael, Amy. *Rose from Brier.* Fort Washington, Pa.: Christian Literature Crusade, 1933.

Claypool, John. *Tracks of a Fellow Struggler: How to Handle Grief.* Waco, Tex.: Word, 1974.

Cone, James H. *The Spirituals and the Blues: An Interpretation.* New York: Seabury, 1972.

Fretheim, Terence E. *The Suffering of God: An Old Testament Perspective.* Overtures to Biblical Theology. Philadelphia: Fortress, 1984.

Gordon, Ernest. *The Fact of Miracle.* Francestown, N.H.: Marshall Jones, 1955.

Green, Michael. *I Believe in Satan's Downfall.* Grand Rapids, Mich.: Eerdmans, 1981.

Howard, David M. *How Come, God? Reflections from Job About God and Puzzled Man.* Philadelphia: A. J. Holman, 1972.

James, Edgar C. *God, Man, and Disaster.* Chicago: Moody, 1981.

Jones, D. Caradog. *Spiritual Healing: An Objective Study of a Perennial Grace.* London: Longmans, 1955.

Jones, E. Stanley. *Christ and Human Suffering.* New York: Abingdon, 1933.

Kaiser, Walter C. *A Biblical Approach to Personal Suffering.* Chicago: Moody, 1982.

Keller, Timothy J. *Ministeries of Mercy: The Call of the Jericho Road.* Grand Rapids, Mich.: Zondervan, 1989.

Kitamori, Kazoh. *Theology of the Pain of God.* Richmond, Va.: John Knox, 1958.

Koch, Kurt E. *Christian Counseling and Occultism.* Trans. A. Petter. Grand Rapids,

Mich.: Kregel, 1965.

Lewis, C. S. *A Grief Observed*. London: Faber & Faber, 1961.

Lloyd-Jones, D. Martyn. *Why Does God Allow War? A General Justification of the Ways of God.* London: Hodder & Stoughton, 1939.

McNeill, Donald P., Douglas A. Morrison and Henri J. M. Nouwen. *Compassion: A Reflection on the Christian Life.* Garden City, N.J.: Doubleday, 1982.

McWilliams, Warren. *The Passion of God: Divine Suffering in Contemporary Protestant Theology.* Macon, Ga.: Mercer University, 1985.

Maston, T. B. *Suffering: A Personal Perspective.* Nashville: Broadman, 1967.

Moberly, Elizabeth R. *Suffering, Innocent and Guilty.* London: SPCK, 1978.

Money, Royce. *Building Stronger Families.* Wheaton, Ill.: Victor, 1988.

Morrice, William. *Joy in the New Testament.* Grand Rapids, Mich.: Eerdmans, 1984.

Neal, Emily Gardiner. *The Healing Power of Christ.* New York: Hawthorn, 1972.

Nevius, John L. *Demon Possession and Allied Themes: Being an Inductive Study of Phenomena of Our Own Times.* New York: Revell, 1894.

Oates, Wayne E. *The Revelation of God in Human Suffering.* Philadelphia: Westminster, 1959.

Ohlrich, Charles. *The Suffering God: Hope and Comfort for Those Who Hurt.* Downers Grove, Ill.: InterVarsity Press, 1982.

Peterman, Mary E. *Healing: A Spiritual Adventure.* Philadelphia: Fortress, 1974.

Peterson, Michael. *Evil and the Christian God.* Grand Rapids, Mich.: Baker, 1982.

Price, Eugenia. *Getting Through the Night: Finding Your Way After the Loss of a Loved One.* New York: Dial, 1982.

Proudfoot, Merrill. *Suffering: A Christian Understanding.* Philadelphia: Westminster, 1945.

Simon, Ulrich. *A Theology of Auschwitz: The Christian Faith and the Problem of Evil.* Atlanta: John Knox, 1967.

Sutcliffe, Edmund F. *Providence and Suffering in the Old and New Testaments.* New York: Thomas Nelson, 1953.

Tengbom, Mildred. *Help for Bereaved Parents.* St. Louis: Concordia, 1981.

Vetter, Robert J. *Beyond the Exit Door.* Elgin, Ill.: David C. Cook, 1974.

Watson, David. *Fear No Evil: One Man Deals with Terminal Illness.* Wheaton, Ill.: Harold Shaw, 1984.

Wendland, Johannes. *Miracles and Christianity.* Trans. H. R. Mackintosh. New York: Hodder & Stoughton, 1911.

Wenham, John W. *The Goodness of God.* Downers Grove, Ill.: InterVarsity Press, 1974.

Westberg, Granger E. *Good Grief: A Constructive Approach to the Problem of Loss.* Philadelphia: Fortress, 1971.

White, John. *Magnificent Obsession.* Downers Grove, Ill.: InterVarsity Press, 1990.

Willimon, William H. *Sighing for Eden: Sin, Evil and the Christian Faith.* Nashville: Abingdon, 1985.

Wise, Robert L. *When There Is No Miracle: Finding Hope in Pain and Suffering.* Glendale, Calif.: Regal, 1977.

Wood, Nathan Robinson. *The Witness of Sin: A Theodicy.* New York: Revell, 1905.

Subject Index

Scripture Index